THE MACHINERY OF GOVERNMENT
IN CANADA

LIBRARY OF
D.K.C.
DAVID T. COLVER

THE MACHINERY OF GOVERNMENT IN CANADA

Audrey D. Doerr

Ⓝ METHUEN

Toronto New York London Sydney Auckland

Copyright © 1981 by Methuen Publications
A division of the Carswell Company Limited

All rights reserved. No part of this publication may be
reproduced, stored in a retrieval system or
transmitted in any form or by any means, electronic,
mechanical, photocopying, recording or otherwise,
without the prior written permission of Methuen
Publications, 2330 Midland Avenue, Agincourt,
Ontario, Canada.

Canadian Cataloguing in Publication Data

Doerr, Audrey D.
    The machinery of government in Canada

ISBN 0-458-94660-5 pa.

1. Public administration—Canada. 2. Canada—
Politics and government. I. Title.

JL108.D63   354.7101   C80-094774-6

Printed and bound in Canada

2 3 4 5   81   85 84 83 82

To the "Doctors' Shop"

Contents

Preface ix

1 / Introduction 1

2 / The Constitutional and Political Context 12

3 / The Administrative Setting 42

4 / Public-Service Managers
and Their Departments 77

5 / The "Private" Public Sector:
Nondepartmental Bodies 106

6 / Mechanisms for Coordination,
Consultation and Consensus Building 136

7 / Perspectives on Responsive Government:
The Federal-Provincial Interface 165

8 / Conclusions 190

Bibliography 205

Index 219

Preface

This book is concerned with the practice of public administration in the government of Canada. It attempts to provide a general overview of the essential elements of the machinery of government and the processes of management and policy making from 1968 to 1979. The book is organized around the central principles of ministerial responsibility as they pertain to administration in the public service. The first chapter provides background to the period under review and sets out the organization of the rest of the text. Chapters 2-5 focus on organization and structure, including cabinet, central agencies, departments and nondepartmental bodies. Chapters 6 and 7 examine the processes of consultation and collaboration within the public service, between the executive and other institutions and interests as well as between federal and provincial governments. The final chapter considers the recurring issues of accountability and control of and in the public service.

In writing a general text, one benefits from the work of others in the field. In the area of public administration, the contributions of academics and practitioners provide a bountiful base of information and analysis. The work of academics—especially former mentors and colleagues—has been most helpful to the author, as the notations and references in the text will testify. A major debt is also owed to the practitioners. Numerous federal government officials have directly and indirectly assisted the author in developing an appreciation and understanding of the internal workings of government. In particular, I wish to thank Gordon Smith for the tutelage and the challenges he provided for me. A special note of appreciation is extended to Nicholas d'Ombrain, a former colleague, for his encouragement of this endeavour.

AUDREY D. DOERR

THE MACHINERY OF GOVERNMENT IN CANADA

1
Introduction

Within the last two decades, the federal public service has been subject to dramatic changes in its structure and management. In a historical perspective the changes have quantitatively surpassed those of any other period since Confederation. Their impetus can in large part be attributed to a coincidence of forces and pressures within the political system and within the public service itself.[1] In the process of expanding state activity and state intervention, the federal public service has been both an instrument and an object of change. As an instrument of change, it has been used as an active agent in initiating and effecting reform. As an object of change, it has been required to reflect and accommodate changing political priorities and management concerns.

The purpose of this book is to examine the executive machinery of government, that is, the cabinet and the supporting public-service organizations of the federal government, with particular emphasis on the period 1968 to 1979. The main theme is the operational implications of the principles of ministerial responsibility and accountability for management and policy making in the federal public service. A major aspect of the discussion focuses on the complexity of the processes that evolved over this period of expansion in government activities and that have resulted in new problems of public-service administration. As adjustments and changes have been made, the integrity of the system has sometimes been challenged. This chapter traces briefly the background to the contemporary period of government and outlines the framework of discussion in following chapters.

Until the 1960s, one might argue that growth and innovation in the federal public service had been accommodated within traditional departmental structures and by traditional management systems.[2] The organization of the public service had by and large evolved gradually from Confederation, experiencing growth and occasionally decline in terms of numbers.[3] Periods of war and postwar reconstruction prompted rapid expansion of government activities. Although these periods were occasionally followed by a reduction in the size of the public service, it was always at a higher level than before the expansion occurred. A growing population and the development of a welfare-state system in Canada after World War II ensured a steady increase in the size of public sector administration.

The 1960s, however, opened a new era for public-service activities. A qualitative as well as quantitative shift in government administration took place. A changing public agenda at the political level and a major reorientation of public-service management accompanied by a highly accelerated pace of government activities contributed to a quiet and sometimes not so quiet revolution in public policy making and administration in the federal public service. New structures and new techniques were employed in response to changing and growing demands both within and outside the public service.

The period was one of affluence and optimism. It was believed that governments could, with the appropriate application of technology and deployment of resources, overcome economic and social maladies.[4] The influence of Keynesian economic philosophy—which had been woven into the policy fabric of senior economic departments such as Finance—provided the basis for active state intervention.[5] The emphasis on central coordination implicit in Keynesian economics combined with a political commitment to reduce regional disparities through the use of a wide range of fiscal levers—that is, spending and taxing powers—resulted in the federal government's asserting a strong centralist orientation in its policies and programs.[6] The state of federal-provincial relations in Canada evolved accordingly. The process was largely extraconstitutional in that adaptations were achieved through shared-cost programs and the dominant economic influence of the federal government was demonstrated by the use of its spending power.[7] The budgetary surpluses at the federal level allowed the federal government to proceed almost without obstruction into areas of provincial jurisdiction in the interests of correcting the regional fiscal imbalances and of establishing minimum levels of services across the nation as a whole.[8]

These developments did not take place without opposition from the provinces as governments clashed over priorities and program objectives.[9] Since provincial cooperation in some form was essential to the effective implementation of national programs initiated by the federal government, extensive consultation and coordination between the two levels of government were required. "Executive federalism" served to support a high degree of provincial participation in national policy processes.[10]

For their part, the provinces began to enhance their own capacities to develop strategies, design programs and deliver services within their own territories. Province building accompanied federal efforts at nation building, although at an uneven pace. The result was the promotion of a higher degree of interdependence and integration between the two levels of government than in the past.[11]

While the federal government adjusted its political agenda and moved on the one plane to expand and to enhance its role and functions in Canadian society, considerable attention was also focused on the organization and management in the public service. Within the machinery of government itself, pressures for reform and indeed "modernization" were strong. The Royal Commission on Government Organization established in 1960 conducted a comprehensive review of organization and management in the public service. Its terms of reference were to recommend changes that would "best promote efficiency, economy and improved service in the despatch of public business." To that end, the five-volume report provided the basis for extensive restructuring of the central financial- and personnel-management systems as well as for several departmental reorganizations. The work of the Royal Commission on Bilingualism and Biculturalism established in 1963 provided the background to the 1966 Policy Statement on the introduction of a program of institutional bilingualism for the public service. The Preparatory Committee on Collective Bargaining in the Public Service of Canada, also established in 1963, recommended a complete revamping of the system of employer-employee relations in the government of Canada. The introduction of Planning, Programming and Budgeting Systems resulted in a major reorientation of budgeting and financial-management practices. In an effort to improve the responsiveness of the federal public service and to provide political and administrative leadership in certain management and employment practices, the federal government launched the public service into a period of rapid and radical internal reform.

While these changes in governmental administration were desirable and even necessary, considerable strains were placed on the public service as a result of the compact time frames in which the changes were introduced.[12] Within the space of a few years, several major pieces of legislation or amendments to existing statutes were passed to effect these changes.[13] By the time the first Trudeau administration took office in 1968, the government machinery was already undergoing a major metamorphosis in policy, program and management operations.

The new administration not only supported but also extended the scope and nature of the reforms, particularly at the political level of management, the cabinet. A major contribution of the first Trudeau administration was to attempt to more clearly identify government priorities and objectives as well as to rationalize the structures and processes of government to better achieve them. The style of the administration emphasized rational planning processes and in this sense marked an important juncture in the evolution of policy making in the federal public service.[14] The restructuring of the cabinet committee system and the changes in the Prime Minister's Office, the Privy Council Office and the Treasury Board Secretariat were integral parts of an attempt to develop a central planning and coordinating capability.[15]

The response to these reforms by the departments and agencies was mainly to construct complementary structures. For example, the reorganization of the cabinet committee system and the creation of planning divisions in the Privy Council Office and the Treasury Board Secretariat led to the gradual but steady emergence of departmental planning, policy and/or evaluation units. Senior interdepartmental committees flourished as key mechanisms for interdepartmental policy coordination.

By the early 1970s, the executive machinery of government represented a highly sophisticated and complex network of organizations and processes. The focus on policy development and coordination created a new breed of professional public servants—the policy analysts and policy coordinators. These individuals enjoyed a high profile in central agency and departmental activities and were often promoted rather quickly to senior-executive positions. The focus on policy development and coordination had a particular impact at the deputy-minister level. The importance attached to providing policy advice considerably enhanced the role and responsibilities of the deputy, adding pressures to an already demanding position.

Increasing recognition of the value of nondepartmental bodies as policy instruments—crown corporations, regulatory commissions, advisory councils—was also apparent. Attempts to coordinate the activities of departments and nondepartmental agencies were undertaken, adding another level of complexity to the integration of structures and functions in the public service as a whole. Analytic distinctions which were made among policy, program and administrative functions within and between these departmental and nondepartmental organizations were often blurred in actual operations.

Although the emphasis on rational planning and the rate of innovation and change subsided after 1972,[16] the basic structure and process of the systems, however imperfectly implemented, were in place and continued to evolve in response to political needs. Political and economic circumstances were changing rapidly: by the mid-1970s a whole new environment emerged that demanded new goals and approaches, new techniques to deal with the problems. The age of affluence was quickly being replaced by an age of scarcity.[17] Adjustments in the nature and scope of government activity were required.

In response to high rates of inflation, slowed economic growth and high rates of unemployment, the federal government implemented a restraint program in 1975 designed primarily to fight inflation through wage and price controls along with reduced government spending and employment.[18] That the emphasis was placed on reducing the *rate* of growth reflected a certain pessimism about the ability of the government to reduce absolute levels of spending and public-sector employment.[19] But the continuation of high rates of inflation and unemployment increased the pressure on the federal government for ameliorative action and extended government activity.

Although the implementation of the controls program represented dramatic coercive action by the government to deal with economic problems, it lacked credibility and, indeed, commitment and support from all affected parties during the eighteen-month period it was in effect.

Shortly after the program was underway, attention was turned to developing measures that would make it possible to end the controls.[20] In October 1976, one year after the policy statement on the program, the government issued a working paper entitled "The Way Ahead," which reiterated its general commitment to limit government spending and to control public-service wage increases.[21] The document entertained a discussion of the role of government in society and recommended a "middle road" for state intervention in the ensuing years.[22] However vague and ambivalent, the Galbraithian arguments put forward in the paper endorsed a mixed economy that would seek to serve the interests and foster the cooperation of government, business and labour and proposed a tripartite approach for determining how economic and social benefits should be distributed. Essentially the role of government would be one that recognized the need for and supported an increase in the reliance on the market system on the one hand and that fully supported and served the social goals and aspirations of Canadians on the other. Social responsibilities of government nevertheless had to be weighed against the need for fiscal restraint.[23] By 1978, the federal government was introducing direct cutbacks in government programs to slow the continuing increases in government spending.

It was also at this time that cracks began to appear in the management systems within the public service. In the mid-1970s the Auditor General[24] mounted a major offensive against abuses and deficiencies in financial-management practices, which he found to be "significantly below acceptable standards of quality and effectiveness."[25] His criticisms were sufficiently severe to prompt the government to take corrective action on a number of fronts. One element of the response was the establishment in 1976 of a Royal Commission on Financial Management and Accountability. While the scope of its terms of reference were not as broad as those of the Royal Commission on Government Organization, the Lambert Commission conducted the first major external review of financial practices and accountability systems in government since the Glassco Commission study some fourteen years earlier.[26] Its final report, released during the federal election campaign of 1979, was highly critical of the state of affairs in public-service management and recommended extensive reforms throughout the public service and in Parliament with a view to strengthening accountability and control systems. The reform and innovation of the previous decade now required a period of consolidation and control in public-service management.

By the end of the decade, the cycle of growth and innovation begun in the 1960s had come full circle. The 1960s had been a period of expansion, marked by an abundance of resources and large doses of optimism and faith in the ability of "systems" techniques to solve societal problems. There was a strong political commitment to the pursuit of broad economic and welfare goals in government policies and programs. The structures and processes created and refined from 1968 into the early 1970s concentrated on the development of comprehensive policies and programs. The approach contributed in no small way to expanding the conceptual horizons of what government's functions were and how they could be performed, but the integration of policy proposals, program designs and effective delivery systems was weak. The system seemed to be overreaching itself, in that the objectives desired, the methods employed and the time frames identified were less than realistic. The stress placed on the public service contributed to a weakening of accountability and control.

By the mid-1970s the changing external environment of government created further complications. The need for a redefinition of the federal government's role was emerging on two planes. At the level of federal-provincial relations, the election of a separatist government in Québec in 1976 and the sabre rattling of resource-rich Western provinces created pressures for change in the centralist orientation of federal policies and programs. A renewed effort at constitutional reform begun in 1975 and the establishment of a Task Force on Canadian Unity in 1977 did little to ease the tensions. On the second plane, the deteriorating economic situation forced the federal government, for its own part, to take increasingly stringent measures to restrain government expenditures. As popular sentiment shifted away from support for "big" government, new strategies involving greater participation of the private sector were sought. But a new consensus was not forthcoming and the general election of May 1979 resulted in the formation of a minority Progressive Conservative government committed to a modified approach in the workings of the Canadian federal system and a smaller role for government in society. However, this administration was shortlived. In less than seven months, the Government was defeated in the House of Commons and a general election called. A majority Liberal Government under Mr. Trudeau was returned in February 1980. The Progressive Conservative interregnum provided a transition period in which the direction of federal public policy and administration was examined and questioned. The period from 1968 to 1979 had been one of active government and, by the end of the 1970's, a reassessment of needs and resources in many areas of administration was already underway.

Within a changing political and economic environment, however, it is the role of the public service to provide for continuity as well as adaptability and change. The operating principles of government in a cabinet-parliamentary system and the essential needs and concerns of administration in the public sector remain constant. The cycle of expansion, restraint and consolidation over the last two decades has been accommodated within the basic institutional framework. While the nature of public-service activities has undergone dramatic change, the rules governing those activities have not changed and continue to provide the basis for accountability and control of government action.

In assembling the essential parts of the executive machinery of government, Chapter 2 begins with a consideration of cabinet in the parliamentary setting. The composition and complexion of this committee reflects the representation of interests of the elected members of the party in power and of the different regions of the country. The responsibility of the executive—individually and collectively—to the legislature provides the basis on which its supporting structures in the public service are made to operate. The prime minister's role as head of this collective executive is instrumental in promoting collegiality and consensus decision making. He sets the style of political management and provides for the overall direction and coordination of government policies and programs.

Chapter 3 focuses on the role of central management. While the collective design and development of government policy is coordinated by cabinet, one of its committees, the Treasury Board, provides for the central management of the public service. The needs of central management support the collective responsibility of ministers, in that all administrative matters that pertain to the public service as a whole are coordinated through a central body. The Treasury Board and its Secretariat provide this coordination in the main through the determination of the allocation of resources, and the setting of management standards and the initiating and monitoring of management policies and practices for the public service. As the scope of its responsibilities has expanded, the Board has played an increasingly influential role in management processes. The needs of central management have become an all-pervasive force in effecting change and providing administrative leadership in the public service.

What the central policy and management agencies provide in terms of support for the collective responsibilities of ministers, the departments provide in support of ministers' individual responsibilities. Chapter 4 considers the role of deputy ministers and the departmental side of policy and management in the public service. As senior policy advisers and agency managers who report directly to ministers, deputies play a key role in ensuring that political decisions are translated into government action. They must nevertheless work in concert with the central agencies in the performance of their policy and administrative functions. Their responsibilities are therefore conditioned by both individual and collective interests of ministers.

The links of ministerial responsibility become more difficult to trace as one moves outside the circle of agencies that report directly to ministers. Chapter 5 examines the heterogeneous satellite system of non-departmental bodies that reflects neither a consistent nor coherent scheme of responsibilities and functions. In terms of numbers, these agencies represent the largest portion of public sector administration. The range of functions they perform is very broad. The extent to which they directly serve the policy interests of government or are subject to administrative control and, more importantly, accountability to the executive and Parliament varies widely.

While the principles of ministerial responsibility—collective and individual—form the essential parameters of public-policy making and administration, the techniques and processes employed to coordinate policy and program activities inside and outside the public service add another vital element to the operations of the machinery of government. These techniques and processes are set out in Chapter 6. In developing policy and mobilizing support for it, accommodations must be made for the various affected interests. Interdepartmental committees and integrated portfolio designs have been used within the public service; varying kinds of committee structures have evolved to provide liaison with affected groups outside the public service. These processes have created series of relationships between and among different organizations inside and outside the public service. In turn, the machinery of government has been shaped around the interactions of the different sets of actors included in a particular policy or program structure.

Chapter 7 deals with federal-provincial relations and considers how the development of collaborative mechanisms has served to complicate and even frustrate the operations of government. The strain on policy and management functions within the federal public service created by the expansion of government activities during the 1960s and 1970s has been compounded by the competitive interaction between federal and provincial governments. As each level of government has expanded its horizons, the constitutional division of powers has been displaced as an effective means of providing jurisdictional parameters for government activities at each level. The elaborate network of intergovernmental collaborative devices which have emerged have further endangered the effective accountability of governments for their actions. Solutions to these problems are difficult to determine in the highly constrained decision-making environment created by these developments. New perspectives on the nature of the problems are needed.

The final chapter reexamines the issue of accountability and control from three perspectives. First, the exercise of political control is aided by the structures and techniques that support cabinet decision-making. Second, internal management systems provide means whereby accountability and control may be strengthened. Third, the role of Parliament is critical in maintaining responsibility and responsiveness of government.

In the final analysis, the operation of the machinery of government seeks to achieve efficient administration on the one hand; a responsive and responsible public service on the other. These values can compete with one another and create tensions in a Cabinet-parliamentary system that is continually seeking a balance between collective and individual ministerial interests and operating within a federal state. Maintaining accountability in an organizational structure that is as complex and as large as the public service is often a complicated process. The constitutional and political framework within which it must operate will be our starting point.

Notes

1. See J.E. Hodgetts, *The Canadian Public Service: A Physiology of Government, 1867-1970* (Toronto: University of Toronto Press, 1973), ch. 1. On p. 5, the author notes: ". . . the public service is not organized, nor does it operate, in a social vacuum: it is shaped not only by the particular nature of the purpose for which it has been created but also by the physical, social and institutional features of the community it serves. In a quite literal sense it is a part of all that it has met. Moreover, the public service is also shaped by the need to adapt to certain internal pressures stemming from the competitive struggle between each of the organizational components to survive or expand, as well as by the compulsion to redefine its own role in relation to changing goals."

2. For a discussion of the structural development of the federal public service, see Hodgetts, ibid., ch. 5, 6 and 7.

3. In 1914, the federal public service numbered approximately 25,000. As a result of the war effort, this number doubled by 1920 but fell to slightly less than 40,000 in 1924. In 1931, the number had risen to 46,000. In 1946, following World War II, approximately 117,000 people were reported to have been employed in departments and noncommercial agencies. In 1960, the Glassco Commission reported that 132,000 civil servants were employed under the *Civil Service Act*. This number had risen to 199,700 by 1969 and 283,000 by 1977. See "Senior Personnel in the Public Service of Canada: Deputy Ministers," in *Submissions to the Royal Commission on Financial Management and Accountability* (Ottawa: Privy Council Office, 1979), pp. 3-19 and 3-20.

4. See Richard Simeon, "The 'Overload Thesis' and Canadian Government," *Canadian Public Policy* (Autumn 1976), pp. 541-51. Note especially pages 541 and 542.

5. The influence of Keynesian philosophy on government policy found its first major expression in the 1945 White Paper on Employment and Income and its theme of high levels of employment and price stability. These economic goals have been reiterated and refined in subsequent policy papers and studies into the 1970s. For a discussion of the document and its development, see W.A. Mackintosh, "The White Paper on Employment and Income in the 1945 Setting," in S.F. Kaliski (ed.), *Canadian Economic Policy Since the War* (Canadian Trade Committee, 1965), pp. 9-21.

6. See Thomas A. Hockin, *Government in Canada* (Toronto: McGraw-Hill Ryerson, 1976), pp. 60-61.

7. See A.G.S. Careless, *Initiative and Response, the Adaptation of Canadian Federalism to Regional Economic Development* (Montreal: McGill-Queen's University Press, 1977), pp. 1-8.

8. The primary areas in which federal payments to provinces have been made, in addition to unconditional grants such as equalization payments, include: health and welfare, post-secondary education and economic development. See *National Finances* (Toronto: Canadian Tax Foundation) for the years 1960 on for tables of payments.

9. For example, J.S. Dupré, D.M. Cameron et al., *Federalism and Policy Development: The Case of Adult Occupational Training in Ontario* (Toronto: University of Toronto Press, 1973), demonstrate well the problems of differing priorities and objectives of the two levels of government in a single policy area.

10. See Richard Simeon, *Federal-Provincial Diplomacy: The Making of Recent Policy in Canada* (Toronto: University of Toronto Press, 1972), and, for more recent analyses, D.V. Smiley, *Canada in Question: Federalism in the Seventies*, 2nd ed. (Toronto: McGraw-Hill Ryerson, 1976), and R. Simeon (ed.), *Confrontation and Collaboration—Intergovernmental Relations in Canada Today* (Toronto: Institute of Public Administration, 1979).

11. Hockin, *op. cit.*, chs. 1 and 2.

12. See H.L. Laframboise, "Administrative Reform in the Federal Public Service: Signs of a Saturation Psychosis," *Canadian Public Administration* (Fall 1971), vol. 14, no. 3, pp. 303-25. In commenting on the implementation of the Glassco reforms, of collective bargaining and of language policy, he notes on p. 309: "Taken one at a time the merits of these decisions are defensible or at least arguable. Taken in their totality, and considering the changes consequent upon them, they have resulted in such an increase in the internal administrative work-load that only huge increases in staff numbers and unprecedented demands on available managerial work-time have made their imperfect implementation possible."

13. Changes in financial- and personnel-management systems, including the introduction of collective bargaining, were legislated in 1967 and affected the Financial Administration Act, the Public Service Employment Act and the Public Service Staff Relations Act (new). Government Organization Acts were passed in 1966, 1969 and 1970. The Official Languages Act was passed in 1969.

14. Bruce Doern has written extensively on this subject. In particular see "The Development of Policy Organizations in the Executive Arena", in G.B. Doern and P. Aucoin (eds.), *The Structures of Policy Making in Canada* (Toronto: Macmillan of Canada, 1971), pp. 10-39; and "Recent Changes in the Philosophy of Policy Making in Canada," in *Canadian Journal of Political Science* (June 1971), vol. 4, no. 2, pp. 243-64; and R.W. Phidd and G.B. Doern, *The Politics and Management of Canadian Economic Policy* (Toronto: Macmillan of Canada, 1978), chs. 3 and 4.

15. In particular, see R.G. Robertson, "The Canadian Parliament and Cabinet in the Face of Modern Demands," *Canadian Public Administration* (Fall 1968), vol. 11, no. 3, pp. 272-79; and "The Changing Role of the Privy Council Office," *Canadian Public Administration* (Winter 1971), vol. 14, no. 4, pp. 487-508; M. Lalonde, "The Changing Role of the Prime Minister's Office," *Canadian Public Administration* (Winter 1971), vol. 14, no. 4, pp. 509-37; and A.W. Johnson, "The Treasury Board of Canada and the Machinery of Government of the 1970s," *Canadian Journal of Political Science* (1971), vol. IV, no. 3, pp. 346-66.

16. The general election in October 1972 resulted in the return of a minority Liberal government and a relative shift to a more incremental, ad hoc approach to government decision making. The return of a majority Liberal government in 1974 was not accompanied by any sustained reform efforts as the government was quickly caught up in serious economic difficulties.

17. The event that demonstrated most dramatically the dawn of the new era was the Arab oil embargo of 1973 and the subsequent quadrupling of world oil prices. The ensuing energy crisis highlighted the need for an approach in the affairs of government which emphasized conservation and restraint.

18. See Government of Canada, "Attack on Inflation" (Ottawa: Information Canada, 1975). The White Paper was tabled in Parliament on Monday, October 15, 1975.

19. The scope of the dilemma was reflected in an address to the Vancouver Club made by the then Minister of Finance, Mr. Chrétien, on Monday December 12, 1977. He noted at that time: "Governments have made progress in restraining their expenditures. The rate of increase in public spending two years ago was more than 20 per cent. Last year, it was about 13 per cent. This year it will be 10 per cent or a little less. Our goal is both to hold expenditures within the rate of growth of the economy as a whole, and to deliver government services and government support more efficiently." Notes for Address, mimeo., p. 4.

20. See P.M. Pitfield, "Toward a Post Control Economy," a paper presented to the Annual Conference of the Institute of Public Administration of Canada (Halifax: September 9, 1976).

21. Government of Canada, "The Way Ahead: A Framework for Discussion," A Working Paper (Ottawa: 1976).

22. Ibid. pp. 22-23.

23. See Phidd and Doern, op. cit., pp. 550-55, for a discussion of the policy content of this document.

24. The Auditor General is a unique position in the machinery of government, in that he is an independent officer of Parliament and hence not part of the executive. His main responsibilities are to examine the manner in which public money is expended and accounted for and to report to Parliament on the same. His annual report is considered by the Public Accounts Committee in the House of Commons.

25. Canada, Office of the Auditor General, Report for the fiscal year ending March 31, 1975, p. 4.

26. The terms of reference of the Lambert Commission focused on the financial management and control systems in the public service and the accountability of deputy ministers and heads of crown agencies. They also included a consideration of the interdepartmental structure, organization and process related to these issues—in particular the types of policies, procedures, guidelines and regulations needed to improve financial management and to ensure effective accountability. See Canada, Royal Commission on Financial Management and Accountability, Progress Report (November 1977), p. vi.

2
The Constitutional and Political Context

Government in Canada is the responsible exercise of power.[1] The
institutions and processes that provide the framework within which that
power is exercised and controlled are both traditional and contemporary
in their forms. The constitutional and legal principles that determine their
activities and operations are fundamental to the types of governing
relations any government may seek to establish, to maintain and/or to
modify over time.[2]

In Canada, the British parliamentary system has been made to operate
within a federal state. There are thus two sovereign sources of law—the
federal Parliament and the provincial legislatures—each within their own
spheres of jurisdiction.[3] As each level of government has extended its
activities, however, the lines of jurisdiction between federal and provincial
governments have become blurred. It would not be far-fetched to say
that, in many areas of government activity, a horizontal rather than
vertical division of responsibilities has emerged. In other words, in those
areas of jurisdiction in which both levels of government are active, the
federal government has assumed responsibility for issues of national
concern, while the provinces have exercised their authority over regional
or local issues.[4]

Although Parliament constitutes the ultimate source of law at the
federal level, it is the executive that plays the dominant role in governing.
The initiation, development and implementation of policies and programs
are executive responsibilities that have been delegated to it by Parliament
and that are carried out through the management, direction and supervision of the public service.[5] The key role of Parliament and more
particularly of the House of Commons is to scrutinize and where possible
to influence executive action.[6] This influence, however, is more demon-
strably exercised during periods of minority, rather than majority,
government.

The executive in the government of Canada has several notable
features. It is a collective body headed by the prime minister who plays a
preeminent role in its collective decision-making activities. Cabinet ministers, while appointed as advisers to the crown, are by convention normally
required to be elected members who represent the political party with the
majority of seats in the House of Commons.[7] The fusion of the executive
and the legislative branches has important implications for the exercise
and control of power as well as for the representation of interests in the
cabinet. Our system of responsible government requires that ministers,
who direct the public service, be held accountable in the House of

12

Commons and through Parliament to the Canadian public. The representative nature of Parliament ensures that at any one time a reasonable cross-section of members represents different regions and interests in Canada in the cabinet. The principles and practices underlying this system will therefore be our starting point.

The Ground Rules

The fountainhead of government in Canada rests with the crown in Parliament.[8] While Sections 9-16 of the British North America Act set out the executive authority as being vested in the crown, custom and conventional practice pertaining to the constitution has securely placed the control of the executive in Parliament. By custom, the power of the crown is exercised by cabinet. The principle that executive power flows from the crown but is held accountable by Parliament is the foundation of the system and provides the basis for the individual and collective responsibilities of ministers.[9]

The cabinet is above all a collective executive. It is a committee that must speak with one voice on matters of government policy and management. Each member of the committee nevertheless functions in an individual as well as collective capacity. Hence, the concepts of individual and collective responsibility are central to the operation of our system of government.[10]

The individual responsibility of ministers is based in the constitution; its legal expression is in statutory enactment. Since the pre-Confederation period, for example, the departmental authority of ministers has had a legislative base.[11] Furthermore, constitutionally all initiatives for the raising or spending of money must come from a minister of the crown.[12] In these respects, the lines of accountability of individual ministers to the House are quite clear.

The collective responsibility of ministers is based on custom and convention. Collectively, ministers are sworn to advise the Governor General in the fulfillment of the crown's responsibility to exercise the executive powers. The collective exercise of powers requires solidarity in cabinet ranks. Collegiality and consensus decision making are therefore the underpinning of cabinet operation. Collective leadership is the result of a process of individual initiatives and collective coordination.

Each minister is expected to represent particular interests as a result of holding office. In the "dignified" constitution, ministers are Privy Councillors, appointed advisers to the crown in whom the executive power is vested. In actual practice, ministers are appointed to their offices by the prime minister. They exercise their individual responsibilities in concert with the responsibilities of their colleagues through the convention of collective responsibility. In the exercise of their individual responsibilities, therefore, they must support the actions of their colleagues. The result is a system of overlapping responsibilities. Professor Kroeker has offered this assessment:

> Some ministers have collective functions, such as the President of the Treasury Board, who exercises his responsibilities on behalf of all ministers regarding the development of an Expenditure Budget and the determination of the priority of requests for resources. Other ministers have coordinating functions, such as those of the Minister of Finance, who, in addition to the responsibilities falling directly under his mandate, is concerned primarily with ensuring that the economic policies of the government are coherent, even if specific responsibilities are those of another minister. The majority of ministers have specific mandates—for example, defence. While their primary responsibilities are for their particular or specific mandates, they exercise a collective responsibility for each other's actions. They are also expected to represent regional points of view on subjects outside their own portfolios.[13]

These independent yet overlapping centres of authority, as Professor Kroeker describes them, serve to ensure the resolution of conflict in the collective executive and the united support of all ministers for all government action.[14] The different lines of accountability that derive from the individual and collective responsibilities ensure that power is exercised under certain constraints. The vertical lines of accountability (individual responsibility) intermesh with the horizontal lines of accountability (collective responsibility) and are reinforced through the individual, collective and coordinating responsibilities of particular ministers.

The precepts of individual and collective responsibility of ministers constitute the fulcrum on which the entire system of government revolves. Responsibility is maintained by a system of personal rather than institutional accountability,[15] whether between ministers and Parliament, among ministers or between ministers and their officials. In practice, the accountability of ministers to Parliament is obtained, not through their resignation, but through their answerability to the House of Commons and its committees.[16] General elections rather than motions of nonconfidence, however, are more effective means of checking the "irresponsible" actions of a government. The accountability of public servants is maintained through the ministers they serve. In this way, ministerial responsibility supports the convention of public service anonymity and political neutrality, for in principle it is the minister who must accept responsibility for the actions of his officials.[17]

The role of the prime minister is paramount in ensuring the effective exercise of ministerial responsibility. He is the chief engineer of cabinet solidarity, the prerequisite for the collective exercise of power. It is he who must shape the consensus among ministers for united policy and administration. His instruments for maintaining effective coordination are derived from the prerogative powers.[18] It is the prime minister who appoints and removes ministers and senior personnel in the public service and government agencies. It is the prime minister who initiates the creation or reorganization of departments and agencies and who is responsible for allocating or reallocating ministerial responsibilities accordingly. As chairman of the cabinet, he must act as chief policy coordinator and, in conjunction with his Minister of Finance and President of the Treasury Board, provide for the overall management of government activities. The organization of cabinet and its operation are therefore of primary importance.

The Political Framework

The ministerial nature of our system of government and the federal nature of the cabinet[19] have important implications for the public service as the composition and organization of cabinet responsibilities affect its structure and operations. The requirements of interest representation have contributed to large federal cabinets. Since Confederation, the size of the cabinet has more than doubled. In 1867, there were thirteen portfolios; an all-time high was reached in 1977 when the number of cabinet ministers rose to thirty-four. As the size of the political executive has increased, changes have also occurred in the design and structure of ministerial portfolios as well as in the means of ensuring that effective political leadership is exercised.

Representation of Political Interests

To begin, at any one time a wide range of interests is represented in the federal cabinet. The representation "formula" applied to cabinet making has evolved over the years and reflects both established conventions and changing circumstances.[20] The formula recognizes at minimum: French and English community and language interests, provincial interests, regional interests, "constituency" interests (business and other occupational groups, ethnic groups, women's groups), political-party service and religion. The latter interest has become less important in recent years but was, during the early years after Confederation, a primary consideration in cabinet selection.

Traditionally, certain portfolios have been assigned to ministers from particular areas or who represent particular interests.[21] For example, a Minister of Fisheries will normally be an East or West Coast Member of Parliament; a Minister of Finance will normally be a member who has an established reputation in the business community. Traditions evolve, however, and interest representation can change as the needs of elite accommodation in society shift. The appointment of Jean Chrétien as

President of the Treasury Board, then as Minister of Industry, Trade and Commerce and then as Minister of Finance is an example of a break with tradition. Until his appointment as Minister of Finance in 1977, no French Canadian had ever occupied that portfolio, ostensibly because French Canadian members did not, in their education or experience, represent business interests. Only one other French Canadian, Jean-Luc Pépin, had occupied the Industry, Trade and Commerce portfolio. No other French Canadian has been President of the Treasury Board.

Special recruitment needs may draw ministers from non-elected circles. The appointment of Pierre Juneau, Chairman of the then Canadian Radio and Television Commission, as Minister of Communications in August 1975 represented an attempt to recruit an individual conversant with policy issues in that field. Mr. Juneau was unsuccessful in a bid for election to the House of Commons in October 1975, however, and was required to resign from his cabinet post. He then became an advisor to the Prime Minister and, subsequently, Undersecretary in the Department of State.[22]

A major constraint for any prime minister forming a cabinet is the limited resources on which he can draw. If the electorate in any particular region or province does not see fit to elect members of the party that ultimately forms the government in the House of Commons, that province or region may go unrepresented in the Cabinet. For example, the Pearson administration in the 1960s had difficulty in obtaining representation from the Prairie provinces in the cabinet. A dramatic demonstration of this type of problem followed the 1979 general election and the formation of a minority Progressive Conservative government which had only two out of a total of seventy-five elected members from the province of Quebec. The results guaranteed these two members cabinet posts, but it created serious problems for Prime Minister Clark in seeking additional cabinet members from that province. In this case, two senators from Quebec were appointed as a stopgap measure to increase the number of ministers from two to four, but this still represented a wide discrepancy from the usual ten to twelve seats accorded the province of Quebec in the cabinets of previous years.

The small size of the resource pool can therefore cause frustration for a prime minister who is striving to select competent members while trying to maintain a balance of interests in the cabinet. With the exception of the Diefenbaker government from 1958 to 1962, prime ministers in recent decades have had to select their twenty-five to thirty ministers from about one hundred and twenty to one hundred and forty members. The practice of appointing senators to increase the size of the resource pool has not been widely employed in recent years because of the importance attached to upholding the principle of ministerial responsibility; that is, to be responsible to the House of Commons, a minister must be an elected Member. However, constitutional practice and exceptional circumstances can permit these things to happen. For example, in addition to the two senatorial appointments from Quebec, the Clark cabinet included a third senator from Ontario. The fact that the individual in question, Robert de Cotret, was a freshly defeated candidate in the May 22 election and was appointed a senior financial minister in the cabinet before his formal appointment as a senator did not pass without criticism. However, his expertise and experience were considered ample qualification and justification for his appointment.

The main implication of this process of selection of cabinet ministers is that their primary qualification for appointment is a function by and large of their ability to get elected and the interests—regional, political, personal—they represent. Personal competence, while ideally of equal importance, may in reality become a secondary criterion. From 1968 to 1979, the representation formula was meticulously applied.[23] Despite the frequent changes in ministers, to be discussed below, the cabinet reflected the federal nature of the country and, indeed, the party in power. The balance of interests was important in providing a basis for concerted action by the national government. Combined with particular portfolio interests, however, the representation of political interests often resulted in a complex assortment of government goals and objectives.

Cabinet Shuffling

A key means by which a prime minister exercises authority as head of a collective executive is through the appointment of cabinet ministers. The initial appointment, as noted earlier, is based by and large on the need to represent particular interests in cabinet. While this criterion remains primary in any changes or "shuffles" in ministerial portfolios, which may subsequently be made during the period of any administration, other factors may be brought to bear in the reassignment of ministerial positions. A regular rotation of offices can serve to strengthen the collegial nature of the cabinet and to enhance the political leadership of the prime minister. It may be less than beneficial, however, in its effect on the public service.

Traditionally, cabinet ministers were shifted in portfolios or removed from cabinet only on rare occasions. If a minister did resign, it often reflected a major disagreement of possible crisis proportions within the cabinet. Cabinet making and remaking under the Trudeau administrations marked a shift away from tradition, in that there was a high frequency of resignations from the cabinet for a wide variety of reasons and there were, on the whole, frequent reassignments of portfolio responsibilities among ministers.

A resignation will prompt a minor shuffle under normal circumstances, but conscious efforts to adopt a regular rotational system based in part on assessments of ministerial performance resulted in annual shuffles of major importance in the Trudeau administration of 1974-79. In the first instance, it is interesting to note in Table 2-1 that thirty-two ministers left cabinet ranks during the period 1968-79.

Table 2-1
Cabinet Turnover, 1968-79

	Resignation	Election defeat	Appointment to other office
1968-72	5	4	5
1972-74	3	1	1
1974-79	10	1	2

Sources: Derived from Colin Campbell, *Canadian Political Facts, 1945-76* (Toronto: Methuen, 1976), and press releases from the Prime Minister's office for the period 1968-78.

Of those individuals who resigned from 1968 to 1972, two did so for reasons of disagreement on major policy questions and three retired. Four ministers were defeated in the October 1972 election. The five individuals appointed to other office were mainly ministers who had stayed on from the previous Pearson administration. In the 1972-74 period, two resigned on their own initiative; the third was not invited back into the cabinet. Two were given Governor-in-Council appointments. Between 1974 and 1979 two ministers resigned from the cabinet purportedly over policy differences. Eight others resigned for a variety of personal reasons. Given that the government caucus numbered only 131 to 134 members during this latter period, it is indeed remarkable that cabinet ranks continued to be filled, appropriate representation maintained and the size of the cabinet continued to increase!

Frequent resignations of ministers requiring replacements and the regular rotation of ministers created a fairly high rate of turnover of ministers in charge of departments, as Table 2-2 demonstrates. On the average, there were 5.3 ministers per portfolio during the period 1968-79—or roughly a change of ministers per portfolio every two years.

It could be argued that the processes of collegial decision making can be facilitated by a regular rotation of ministerial responsibilities. The development of common expertise, general administrative ability and diverse policy experience are made possible in this way. Moreover, the regular rotation of ministers can ensure that particular regional, economic or cultural interests, for example, are represented through a broad range of portfolios over time.

Conversely, a high rate of turnover can lead to a lack of continuity in policy direction in a department or at least give the appearance of a lack of continuity. If frequent changes in ministers are accompanied by frequent

Table 2-2
Cabinet Turnover by Department, 1968-79

Portfolio	Number of ministers, 1968-79
Agriculture	3
Communications	7
Consumer and Corporate Affairs	8
Defence	8
Employment and Immigration	6
Energy, Mines and Resources	4
Environment	6
External Affairs	3
Finance	5
Indian Affairs and Northern Development	5
Industry, Trade and Commerce	6
Justice	6
Labour	5
National Health and Welfare	4
National Revenue	9
Postmaster General	7
President of the Privy Council	4
Public Works	6
Regional Economic Expansion	4
Science and Technology	6
Secretary of State	4
Solicitor General	6
Supply and Services	4
Transport	5
President of the Treasury Board	5
Urban Affairs	4
Veterans Affairs	4

Sources: Same as Table 2-1. Portfolio changes end at November 24, 1978, the date of the last major cabinet shuffle during this period.

changes in deputy ministers,[24] a department or agency could be subject to a series of management-succession crises, resulting in very low productivity or performance for the organization.

Three cases stand out. It took seven years for a Competition Act to be brought forward by a Minister of Consumer and Corporate Affairs. Accepting that strong business interests were at work in lobbying, the fact remains that each change in minister brought another delay and, often, reorientation of the bill.[25] Second, the Post Office Department continues to suffer from serious labour-management and management problems. There have been three nationwide postal strikes in the last ten years. There has also been a high turnover in both ministerial and deputy-ministerial officeholders. Finally, the Department of Indian Affairs and Northern Development, since the end of a remarkable six-year term by one minister,[26] has had a high rate of turnover of ministers since 1975. Indian claims processes have slowed down considerably and general clientele disgruntlement is visible once again at a level that reflects a lack of trust and respect for frequently changing ministers.

A change of minister during the life of an administration will not, of course, be as disruptive for a department as a change of minister resulting from a change of government. In the former case, the government policy stays the same although the priorities and implementation may be modified. In the latter case, the policy may be changed entirely. In both cases, however, the public service endeavours to serve the needs of the minister, whatever the needs may be.

Cabinet shuffling is a key function of political management. It is as important as initial cabinet formation. While endeavouring to maintain a proper balance in the representation of political interests, a prime minister must also ensure that ministerial portfolios are headed to the extent possible by able and experienced ministers. The rotation of office provides one means of developing ministerial expertise. It also serves to reinforce the collective process of cabinet over time as ministers develop an appreciation of the problems and policies of different portfolios. Although too frequent rotation can be disruptive for policy and programs within the departments and agencies, it is not always possible to regulate the rate of turnover of ministers. Elections and resignations can be more important factors. Finally, cabinet shuffling is important to a prime minister in strengthening his political leadership by putting a "new face" on his administration, particularly before an election.

As ministers left the Trudeau cabinet, particularly from 1972 on, their replacements were individuals who for the most part might be said to have owed their election to the personal popularity of the Prime Minister. For example, in July 1968, nine members of the cabinet had been ministers in previous Pearson cabinets. In November 1978, there were only two ministers who had held posts under Prime Minister Pearson. Of the twenty-seven ministers who held departmental portfolios in the cabinet in November 1978, eight had been elected to the House of Commons in 1968; six had been elected in 1972.[27]

Ministerial Portfolios

As the size of the cabinet and the scope of ministerial responsibilities have increased, there have also been significant transformations in the design and structure of ministerial portfolios. Historically, the federal government adopted the departmental structure as the administrative means to allocate responsibilities to be undertaken by the public service.[28] A department has been defined as "an administrative unit comprising one or more organizational components over which a minister has direct management and control."[29] The titles of ministerial portfolios traditionally reflected the powers of the federal government as set out in the constitution and/or the general purpose of the department or agency.[30] As new programs were created, they were accommodated within the traditional line departments and common service agencies. As government activities expanded, there was an accompanying proliferation of non-departmental bodies such as crown corporations, regulatory commissions and advisory boards.[31] Although ministerial responsibility for these agencies was indirect, the portfolio responsibilities of ministers included departments as well as other kinds of agencies.[32]

The need to rationalize the composition of ministerial portfolios and to group organizational activities in a fashion that would reflect the policy priorities as well as traditional responsibilities of government became a matter of concern in the early 1960s. The public service had undergone a period of rapid expansion during World War II and had continued to expand in the decades that followed as the scope of government activities increased. For government to play an active role, responsive organizational supports were required.

Two main forces contributed to the restructuring of the government machinery. The first impetus came from the political level. A Liberal party conference, the Kingston Conference on National Problems held in 1960, produced a new political manifesto in the social-policy field.[33] The proposed design for the reorientation of government policies was focused in the areas of regional disparities, manpower policies and social services.

The second main impetus could be said to have come from the work of the Royal Commission on Government Organization, which reported in 1962. While the reorganization proposals in the Report focused on changes in the central-management structures, the basis was also laid for departmental changes as reflected in the Government Organization Act of 1966.[34] A commitment to a further rationalization of the organizational design of government departments combined with a number of innovative forms found expression in two subsequent Government Organization Acts in 1969[35] and 1970[36] and other singular department acts.

Hence, the changing public-policy agenda was translated into a structural response by the federal government. New areas of policy activity emerged: Communications (1969), Consumer and Corporate Affairs (1969), Energy, Mines and Resources (1966 and 1969), Environment (1970), Industry, Trade and Commerce (1969), Manpower and Immigration (1966), Regional Economic Expansion (1969), Science and Technology (1971) and Urban Affairs (1971). In other areas, traditional functions were given a higher profile: the Solicitor General's Department was established as a separate entity from the Department of Justice (1966), the Treasury Board Secretariat was constituted as a separate agency from the Department of Finance (1966), the Indian Affairs Branch was transferred from the Secretary of State's department and joined with northern-development programs into a new department of Indian Affairs and Northern Development (1966) and a new department, Supply and Services, a common-service agency, was created (1969). A major feature of these changes was that the new departments were created from existing structures in the first instance. Thus, reorganizations involved reshuffling existing units and building on them. While this served to provide a basis for development, it often required strong political and administrative leadership to integrate the several parts of the new departments and provide a new focus for them.[37]

An innovative feature of the 1970 Government Organization Act was the provision for the creation of two types of Minister of State portfolios. The first type of Minister of State involved a new organizational design—a coordinative policy agency headed by a Secretary of the Ministry of State (deputy minister) who would report to the Minister of State. Initially, two ministries were established. The Ministries of State for Science and Technology and for Urban Affairs were novel experiments in government machinery, in that they were to be policy agencies devoid of any program responsibilities. Their mandates were to provide leadership in policy development and coordination in these areas across government departments and intergovernmentally. Their design rested on the premise that knowledge was power.[38] Experience demonstrated, however, that some form of program influence was crucial to their effectiveness and, indeed, to their continued survival. The Ministry of State for Urban Affairs was disbanded on March 31, 1979. The Ministry of State for Science and Technology has continued and has evolved as a main monitoring agency for all science-related activities in the federal government.

Two other ministries of state of this type have been created in recent years. For example, in November 1978, a new ministerial post, Chairman of the Board of Economic Development, and a new cabinet committee on Economic Development were created. The minister was initially supported by a small secretariat of officials on loan from the Departments of Finance and Industry, Trade and Commerce. The secretariat was formally constituted as the Ministry of State for Economic Development in February 1979.[39] Second, the Clark administration established a Ministry of State for Social Development upon taking office in June 1979.

The second type of minister of state provided for in the 1970 Act was that of junior minister to assist senior ministers. The position of these ministers has occasionally been misunderstood.[40] According to the Act, they have no independent departmental or program authority and are required to report to and through the senior minister whom they assist. The provision for their appointment thus added a political cosmetic for the representation of special interests and policy areas in cabinet without the requirement to set up a supporting bureaucracy. Ministers of State to assist were appointed during the Trudeau administrations in such areas as: multiculturalism, fisheries, environment, fitness and amateur sport, small businesses and federal-provincial relations. This practice was continued by the Clark administration. In addition to junior ministers for multiculturalism, fitness and amateur sport, small business and industry, and federal-provincial relations, Ministers of State for the Canadian International Development Agency, Treasury Board, Transport, Social Programmes and International Trade were also appointed.

After the Government Organization Act of 1970, no major comprehensive organizational changes were made in the machinery of government for the duration of the Trudeau administrations.[41] The Department of Manpower and Immigration emerged as the Department of Employment and Immigration in 1977.[42] This change represented a new emphasis on policy concerns in this area and provided for an integrated management structure between the department and the Unemployment Insurance Commission. The creation of the Board of Economic Development in 1978-79 was noted earlier. The Government Organization Act of 1979 was essentially of a housekeeping nature.[43] It undid one aspect of the 1970 Act, however, in that the Department of Environment was formally divided into a Department of Environment and a Department of Fisheries and Oceans. In the latter case, the constituency interests[44] and emerging concerns about ocean management with the establishment of the two-hundred-mile economic-management zone off Canadian coasts proved to be the motivating forces for organizational reform.

Nearly fifteen years of organizational reform thus placed a new complexion on cabinet composition. In addition to the traditional cabinet positions such as Finance, Justice, External Affairs, Public Works, National Revenue and so on, a host of new policy-focused portfolios emerged. The changes and the nature of their evolution demonstrate the importance of the cabinet as the symbolic as well as the practical embodiment of political priorities that provides the substantive framework within which the public service organizations will be aligned and focus their respective activities. New types of ministerial portfolios such as the ministries of state represented an increased emphasis on the coordination of policy activities across the public service as a whole. Junior ministerial portfolios such as ministers of state to assist provided managerial flexibility in ensuring the representation of special interests and concerns that arise occasionally or temporarily. A major effect of the reorganizations during the 1960s and 1970s was nevertheless the requirement for new means of coordinating ministerial activities. At the cabinet level, a revamped committee system was to serve that purpose.

Cabinet Coordination

The increased differentiation of functions and sharpened focus on policy issues as reflected in ministerial portfolios was accompanied by an emphasis on the effective exercise of collective responsibility during the Trudeau administrations. It has already been noted that some ministerial portfolios may be said to have collective functions, while others that have specific functional mandates are nevertheless required to coordinate their activities with other departments and agencies. In addition, some portfolios, such as ministries of state, have a coordinative policy function. The distinction that Professor Doern has made between "horizontal" and "vertical" portfolios provides a useful conceptual basis for considering the types of coordination that occur between and among ministerial portfolios.[45]

Traditionally, the central coordinators have been the prime minister, the ministers of Finance, Justice, External Affairs and, more recently, the President of the Treasury Board and the Minister of State for Economic Development. Ministers in charge of common-service portfolios oversaw the provision of standard services for all departments and acted as coordinators in a narrower, administrative sense.[46] Prior to the 1960s, ministers, especially strong ministers, in charge of departments representing essentially clientele or constituency interests ("vertical" line departments) often managed them as private preserves even from the prime minister.[47] Interministerial relations were handled on an individual-to-individual basis. Cabinet committees, with a few exceptions such as the Treasury Board (which has had a statutory basis since 1869), were mainly *ad hoc* ventures established to deal with particular problems that arose from time to time and that required consultation and coordination. During the Pearson administrations, committees were used fairly extensively to deal with major issues as well as routine procedures, but no formalized system emerged.

The changes introduced during the first Trudeau administration and refined in subsequent years placed a high premium on coordination and hence collegiality in cabinet and departmental operations. The organization of the cabinet committee system in 1968 was, and evolved as, a central coordinating structure for government activities. The five initial "operating" committees of cabinet—economic policy; government operations; science, culture and information; social policy; external affairs and defence—grouped the activities of the government into several "policy sectors" that provided the foci for ministerial consideration of policy and program proposals. The coordinating committees—priorities and planning; legislation and house planning; federal-provincial relations; Treasury Board—provided for the examination of proposed government action from a broad "horizontal' as opposed to functional perspective.[48] In addition, there were special committees such as Security and Intelligence, the

Special Committee of Council, Public Service and others such as labour relations or other current problems.

A key innovation of the 1968 committee structure was the establishment of the Cabinet Committee on Priorities and Planning as a first step in attempting to better organize the consideration of government policies and to identify priority government issues.[49] Unlike the other committees, it had an "initiating" rather than a reactive role, in that it sought to establish government priorities and to develop an overall planning approach for government undertakings. The priority-setting and planning process began with an informal meeting of all ministers each fall at Meach Lake.[50] The ideas and views generated by ministers at this meeting would then be compiled and reviewed in subsequent meetings of the Cabinet Committee on Priorities and Planning. The final iteration of the priorities would be considered and endorsed by cabinet.

As this process evolved, more efforts were made to link the priority-setting process with the Treasury Board's exercise of establishing expenditure guidelines; by the mid-1970s, considerable progress had been made in that regard.[51] The Cabinet Committee also considered departmental proposals which were of a priority nature. Consideration by this committee was not undertaken to preempt the role of the operating committees, but rather to give due emphasis to matters of priority concern. As has been stated elsewhere,[52] the committee was not, nor did it operate as, an "inner cabinet" in the sense that it did not make decisions on behalf of cabinet. Its recommendations, like those of other committees, were subject to ratification by full cabinet.

A major objective of the cabinet committee system of the Trudeau administrations was to reduce the workload of full cabinet by delegating initial consideration of proposals and problems to committees. Full cabinet nevertheless gave formal approval to all matters considered by committees. (See Figure 2-1.) In some cases this would involve a reconsideration of the matter; in others, it would simply be a formal endorsement of the committee report. For its part, full cabinet focused its own agenda on critical government issues and, when requested, the contentious issues arising from committee deliberations.[53]

The operation of the committee system, however, was not totally successful in this respect. While it served to provide an organized process for the consideration of diverse governmental and departmental matters and to reduce the workload of full cabinet, it did not reduce the workload of ministers. Each committee had a membership of approximately ten to twelve ministers; most ministers would serve on an average of three committees. Because full cabinet and many of the committees met weekly, ministers had a heavy meeting schedule. As a result, committee attendance in many instances was very low. Moreover, as committee assignments were rotated fairly regularly (usually in conjunction with a cabinet

Figure 2-1
Cabinet Committee System, 1978 (Trudeau Administration)

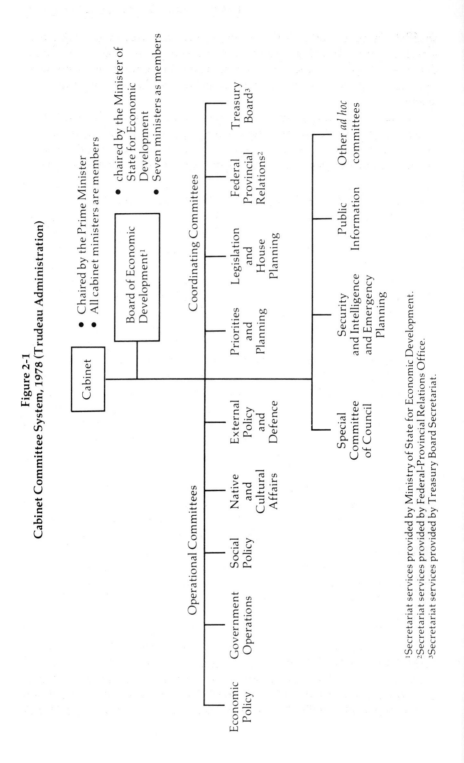

[1]Secretariat services provided by Ministry of State for Economic Development.
[2]Secretariat services provided by Federal-Provincial Relations Office.
[3]Secretariat services provided by Treasury Board Secretariat.

shuffle), there was often little continuity of committee membership over a period of time. In addition to these circumstances, the volume of cabinet documentation prepared for consideration in committee often went unread except by the minister responsible and keenly interested colleagues.

In actual operation, some committees functioned less effectively than others in reaching decisions. When decisions were not reached in committee, full cabinet would be required to reexamine the issue. In 1976, several of the committees were "twinned" in an effort to cut down the number of committee meetings and to attempt to overcome the problem of poor attendance. The less active committees gradually became dormant.

A second main objective of the committee system was to strengthen the political control over the bureaucracy. The emphasis on structured collegial decision making ensured that no single minister or, rather, his officials could exercise inordinate influence in a particular policy or program area and provided an opportunity for ministers collectively to shape government policy. As Professor French has observed in commenting on the exercise of collective responsibility in the Trudeau cabinets, this approach was "due also to the Prime Minister's often expressed conviction that cabinet is less easily captured by the bureaucracy than are ministers operating independently, and of the fact that issues increasingly spill untidily over the confines of any single portfolio, thus necessitating joint consideration."[54] However, it also allowed Prime Minister Trudeau to exercise a strong influence on cabinet and committee proceedings. The search for consensus in the deliberations of ministers would be sensitive ultimately and even initially to views the Prime Minister might express.

The type of formal process that developed around the committee system in effect bureaucratized it. The processing of documents required the formalization of procedures by which ministers would submit cabinet memoranda and supporting papers.[55] The secretariats in the Privy Council Office served as the main clearinghouse and facilitators in organizing the distribution of material and in coordinating the submissions of the different ministers. For their part, ministers and their officials were required to comply with central-agency procedures, thus reducing the scope of ministerial and departmental control over matters of concern to them. Collegiality often meant waiting one's turn on cabinet committee schedules.

In general terms, the efforts to restyle ministerial portfolios and to provide a cabinet committee system that would coordinate ministerial activities and promote collegial decision making resulted in a complex and elaborate system of cabinet operations. These processes of collective decision making nevertheless strengthened the control of the Prime Minister over his committee and in many ways restricted strong individual

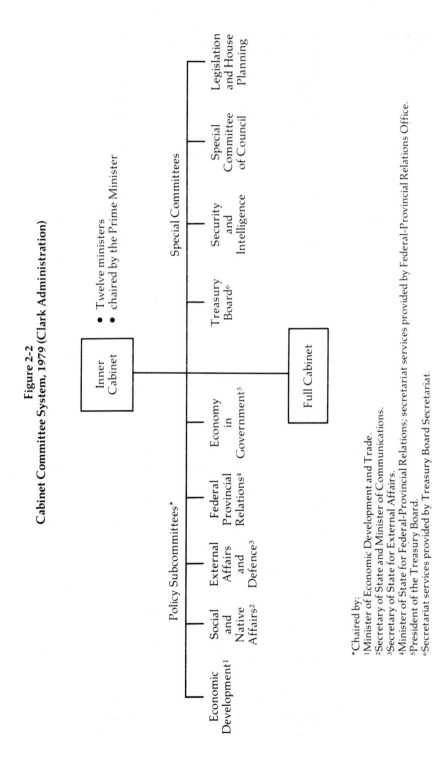

Figure 2-2
Cabinet Committee System, 1979 (Clark Administration)

Inner Cabinet

- Twelve ministers
- chaired by the Prime Minister

Policy Subcommittees*

Economic Development[1]

Social and Native Affairs[2]

External Affairs and Defence[3]

Federal Provincial Relations[4]

Economy in Government[5]

Full Cabinet

Special Committees

Treasury Board[°]

Security and Intelligence

Special Committee of Council

Legislation and House Planning

*Chaired by:
[1]Minister of Economic Development and Trade.
[2]Secretary of State and Minister of Communications.
[3]Secretary of State for External Affairs.
[4]Minister of State for Federal-Provincial Relations; secretariat services provided by Federal-Provincial Relations Office.
[5]President of the Treasury Board.
[°]Secretariat services provided by Treasury Board Secretariat.

ministerial initiatives. While collegiality and consensus are important aspects of cabinet operation, cabinet solidarity should not displace the effective exercise of individual ministerial responsibilities. However, the problem of coordinating the activities of an executive committee, which for political reasons must be large, is no easy task. The more sophisticated and more formalized the process of coordination becomes, the greater the danger of displacing initial objectives.

It is interesting to examine, by way of contrast, the changes in the cabinet and cabinet committee system made by Prime Minister Clark upon taking office in June 1979. Essentially his objectives were the same as Prime Minister Trudeau's in 1968: to streamline cabinet operations and to establish political control over decision making. The essential features of the new system were: a twelve-member inner cabinet with final decision-making authority that would "be responsible for establishing overall priorities of government and for major policy decisions flowing from those priorities";[56] five policy subcommittees, including Economic Development, Social and Native Affairs, External Affairs and Defence, Federal-Provincial Relations and Economy in Government; and four special committees of cabinet—the Treasury Board, the Special Committee of Council, Legislation and House Planning and Security and Intelligence.[57]

The major change in the new structure was that the inner cabinet replaced the full cabinet as the final decision-making body. The inner cabinet seemed to be an extended version of the Cabinet Committee on Priorities and Planning. Linkage was maintained between the inner cabinet and the subcommittees through the subcommittee chairmen, each of whom was a member of the inner cabinet. (See Figure 2-2.) Cabinet subcommittees were to have full decision-making authority, subject to initial direction from the inner cabinet. Full cabinet was to meet regularly, but it was intended to be a forum of discussion, not decision.

While this type of structure served to streamline decision making, in that a smaller group of ministers was to make the final decisions on priority matters and to coordinate the activities of the several subcommittees, it did exclude for the first time a large number of ministers from the final and perhaps—from the point of view of collective decision making— most vital decision-making stage. The emphasis under the Trudeau administrations was on collegial decision making; the elaborate committee process ensured ministers ample opportunity to examine and to express their views on matters coming before cabinet or its committees.[58] The process of conflict resolution was highly complex but served to reinforce cabinet solidarity and consensual decision making. The Clark model seemed to attempt to resolve issues at the subcommittee level, but in actual operations one could foresee considerable difficulty in maintaining effective coordination. The realignment of relationships between and among ministers would be a significant factor in determining whether and how the system would work to overcome some of the problems encountered in the previous system and to improve the process of collective decision making.

Central Capability

The prime minister's preeminent role in the cabinet requires specialized support services. Unlike his colleagues, he has no departmental or portfolio responsibilities *per se*; rather, he serves as the political head and manager of a collective executive. The cabinet is his committee and its affairs are among his primary responsibilities.[59] The central agencies that most directly support the Prime Minister in the discharge of his responsibilities are the Privy Council Office and the Federal-Provincial Relations Office. In addition, he has a personal office staff, the Prime Minister's Office. The agencies constitute the central core of coordinating mechanisms that support the political executive; for this reason, they have a fairly high profile among the departments and agencies of the public service. The Prime Minister's Office is not a part of the public service; rather, it is an office of appointed political aides who serve the prime minister in a personal and political fashion. Its functions, however, are related and complementary to the central public-service agencies that provide the prime minister and cabinet with official advice.

In supporting the prime minister, the structure and organization of these agencies will be designed to support his particular needs. The expansion and refinement of the Privy Council Office and the Prime Minister's Office during the Trudeau administrations were a distinguishing feature of the style of government. Their internal structure was designed to help in the planning and coordinating of the activities of government and in supporting the processes of collective decision making.

The Privy Council Office

In the first instance, the Privy Council Office serves as the central policy-coordinating agency. The senior officer has a dual title, Clerk of the Privy Council and Secretary to the Cabinet. As the senior public servant responsible to the prime minister, he provides leadership to his peers in the public service in addition to his role as chief advisor to the prime minister and cabinet.

The organization of the Privy Council Office has in part been influenced by the cabinet committee system. During the Trudeau administrations, there were three main divisions in the Office until 1975: Plans, Operations and Federal-Provincial Relations; and two thereafter: Plans and Operations. Each Division was headed by a Deputy Secretary to the Cabinet.

The Operations Division housed the secretariats for the functional committees of cabinet: External Policy and Defence; Economic Policy; Government Operations; Social Policy; and Natives and Cultural Affairs. The committee secretariats were small, headed by an Assistant Secretary to the Cabinet, and comprised six to eight officers each. The Secretariat officials set agendas and prepared briefings for the chairmen of the committees and the prime minister. These individuals acted as the facilitators, assisting departments by ensuring that appropriate consultation had taken place and, to the extent possible, that contentious issues had been resolved before a memorandum was brought to a committee. To this end, officials in these secretariats played an active role in the work of interdepartmental committees. Above all, the secretariats had to ensure that any policy or program proposals brought forward by a particular minister were compatible or consistent with existing government policy.[60]

The Plans Division housed the secretariats for the two key coordinating cabinet committees: Priorities and Planning and Legislation and House Planning. The secretariat to the committee on Priorities and Planning was responsible, during the 1968-72 period, for initiating cabinet planning studies and, subsequently, cabinet evaluation studies in conjunction with the priority-setting exercises. But the review capability of the unit was not that pronounced in the first instance and declined in any event after the 1972 election, when short-term political exigencies shifted the focus of government away from long-term planning.[61] The secretariat to the Cabinet Committee on Legislation and House Planning was involved in ensuring that full and proper consultations among all affected parties had taken place in the drafting of new bills or amended legislation and that conflicting interests, which arose in the scheduling of bills for House consideration, were effectively resolved. Its work was focused on the coordination and planning of the legislative timetable for each session of Parliament.[62]

Secretariat services were also provided for other cabinet committees such as Security and Intelligence, Emergency Planning, Public Information and the Public Service. Their role, like that of other secretariats, was to ensure that committee chairmen and the Prime Minister were properly briefed on all matters coming before the committees and that proper liaison was maintained with relevant departments and agencies.

The Plans Division also provided special support services to the Prime Minister himself. The Machinery of Government Directorate served the Prime Minister in support of his prerogatives to allocate responsibilities among ministers and to make senior appointments. It had, therefore, two main divisions—Organization and Senior Personnel.[63]

The Organization Division of the Directorate handled jurisdictional problems between and among ministers and departments; provided ongoing review, analysis and advice on the operation of the cabinet committee system as well as on matters generally relating to cabinet; provided liaison with Government House; and conducted special undertakings.[64] The allocation of responsibilities among ministers became an increasingly important function as a result of the regular rotation of ministers, particularly for the period 1974-79. Because staff work for the creation or reorganization of ministerial responsibilities was done in this unit, it was normally actively involved with the organizational implications of ministerial changes, although the designation of the ministers themselves was done by Prime Minister Trudeau in consultation with his political aides.

The Senior Personnel Secretariat, set up in 1971, was incorporated into the Machinery of Government Directorate in September 1976.[65] It was charged with the responsibility of managing the Governor-in-Council positions and developing senior-personnel policy. It was a small, largely operational unit that provided staff work for the Committee of Senior Officials—Executive Personnel and the Advisory Committee on Executive Compensation in the Public Service in addition to its support to the appointments process *per se*.

Organization and senior appointments were considered key levers of central coordination and influence. These areas of responsibility became more specialized and differentiated over the years. As responsibilities were added, the role and capability of the Directorate might be said to have in some ways approximated that of a central review staff.

The Privy Council Office also provided specialized and often temporary services. For example, the appointment of a special economic adviser in 1976 created a specialized position which reported directly to the Prime Minister. In other instances, special units were created to handle particular issues. These units were either disbanded or transferred elsewhere once the particular issue had been defined and set on course. Examples include the Science Secretariat, the International Women's Year Secretariat and the Office of the Co-ordinator of the Status of Women. In still other instances, units were retained within the agency but reoriented in terms of functions. An example of this shift in responsibility or orientation was the Briefing Team. This section was established during the first Trudeau administration. Its initial focus of activity was the development of policy models and futures studies and research. As the emphasis on these kinds of activities declined, the section was transformed into a Special Projects, then Planning Projects, unit. As the name implied, it handled special projects which other units in the Privy Council Office could not handle.

Federal-Provincial Relations Office

The Office of the Secretary to the Cabinet for Federal-Provincial Relations was formally created by an Act of Parliament in December 1974.[66] The

Secretary became responsible for the former Federal-Provincial Relations Division of the Privy Council Office. In September 1977, a Minister of State for Federal-Provincial Relations was appointed, to whom the Secretary reported. It is interesting to note that the legislation in 1974 created a position of Secretary to the Cabinet for Federal-Provincial Relations but did not in fact create a separate Federal-Provincial Relations Office as such. For all intents and purposes, however, it operated as a separate agency, particularly after the appointment of a special minister.

From 1976, there were two deputy secretaries in the Office. The Deputy Secretary for Federal-Provincial Relations was responsible for three sections: the Secretariat that served the Cabinet Committee on Federal-Provincial Relations and a Regional Analysis Unit; a Policy and Program Review Section; and a Studies and Research Section. The activities of these units were interrelated. The Regional Analysis Section monitored information and reports. The Policy and Review Section maintained "policy desks"; its officials provided liaison with federal departments and provincial governments on policy and related matters of federal-provincial concern. The Studies and Research Section was expanded in 1976 to include an Assessment and Analysis Group, which focused its activities on assessing current relations between the federal government and the provinces. Collectively, and in particular through the Committee Secretariat, the Office served the Cabinet Committee on Federal-Provincial Relations.

A second position—Deputy Secretary (Co-ordination)—was established following the Québec election in 1976. The Co-ordination Unit was small but played an instrumental role in coordinating activities and information across government departments for the federal government's relations with the province of Québec and for providing strategic advice in the constitutional-review process that had been initiated in 1975.

The Office also included a Constitutional Adviser who reported to the Secretary. This person had a key role in developing the federal government's proposal for constitutional reform released in June 1978. A planned internal reorganization for the spring of 1979 was intended to highlight the activities of the Office with respect to the constitutional changes the government had intended to initiate. However, the outcome of the election prevented these changes from being fully implemented at that time, since the priorities of the new government did not place as high a premium on this issue.[67]

In sum, the main functions of the Office were to provide the Prime Minister and the cabinet with assistance in examining federal-provincial issues of current and long-term concern and to promote and facilitate intergovernmental consultation and liaison. It performed much the same kinds of functions as the Privy Council Office in these respects, albeit

within the framework of federal-provincial concerns. The Office coordinated federal participation for all first ministers' conferences and normally
had a representative in the federal delegation of other federal-provincial
ministerial and senior-official conferences. Its officials also participated in
the work of interdepartmental committees within the federal government.

The Prime Minister's Office

The Prime Minister's Office also provides support to the Prime Minister.[68]
It is headed by a Principal Secretary or chief of staff who is the senior
political adviser to the prime minister. The support services of this Office
are political in nature, however, and while liaison is maintained between
this Office and the Privy Council Office, an understanding exists between
the Offices of the different nature of their roles and responsibilities.

The organization of the Prime Minister's Office underwent significant evolution during the Trudeau administrations. In 1968, it was
enlarged and reorganized to include policy advisory sections and five
regional desks for the purpose of liaison and coordination.[69] The desks
disappeared after the 1972 election, having proved to be irritants to
regional cabinet ministers and relatively ineffective in improving communications between the Office and ministerial and constituency offices.
The advisory sections were gradually reduced and official titles dropped as
personnel were changed or shifted.

The Office, largely because of public criticism directed at its size and
operations, continued to be streamlined. From 1975, it was maintained at
ninety positions; half of these were designated to the correspondence
unit. Basically, it served to provide four essential services: political policy
advice; legislative liaison; speech writing and public and press relations;
and correspondence services.

In general, the activities of these Offices received a considerable
amount of attention during the decade under discussion.[70] Their operations were perceived by some to support the emergence of prime-
ministerial government in Canada. While it is evident that the agencies
reporting directly to the Prime Minister maintained a high profile in
government activities during this period, their superordinate influence on
the outcome of cabinet decision making remains a moot point. Their
operations mostly reflected the increasing complexity of political decision
making. Formal structures and procedures are necessary to make complex
processes work. However, while process can affect the substantive issues
and displace substance if allowed, it cannot remove the responsibility for
decision making from those who have constitutional authority to exercise
it.

Summary

Individual and collective ministerial responsibility are the underpinning principles of cabinet operation. The application of these principles to an executive committee as large and diverse (in representation and function) as the Canadian cabinet resulted in a complex network of relationships between and among ministers. For his part, Prime Minister Trudeau placed a premium on strong political leadership during his period in office and to that end emphasized the collegial nature of cabinet operation; hence, he stressed collective responsibility in the exercise of power. The need for coordination in these circumstances led to the development of practices that created a highly formalized system of cabinet committees and supporting administrative structures.

On the one hand, it could be argued that these highly complex and elaborate developments in and around the cabinet represented a necessary response to the scope and complexity of the issues with which government had to deal during the period. On the other hand, it could be argued that the emphasis on coordination in these areas was carried too far and was formalized beyond what was required. On balance, both arguments have a certain validity, in that the responsible exercise of power in an age of big government requires techniques to ensure that responsible and responsive action can be taken. The extent to which the process can be refined and formalized to a high degree, functioning as it does in a dynamic and constantly changing political environment, is nevertheless a major issue.

The Clark administration came to office in June 1979; it attempted to demonstrate that a more streamlined approach could be taken in structuring cabinet decision making. A two-tiered cabinet committee system was intended to increase efficiency as well as maintain the representation of interests. Above all, political control of public-service activities was to be enhanced.

Although the style of prime ministerial management affects the priorities and activities within central agencies that support cabinet decision making processes, the functions they perform are essentially coordinative in nature. Agencies at the centre command an overview of activities across departments and agencies and thus assist the processes of decision making through coordination of policy and planning activities. In this way, the prime minister is aided in the exercise of collective leadership in government.

Notes

1. See "Responsibility in the Constitution. Part I: Departmental Structures," in *Submissions to the Royal Commission on Financial Management and Accountability* (Ottawa: Privy Council Office, 1979), pp. 1-1 to 1-68, for a comprehensive discussion of the nature of responsible government. As stated on page 1-4: "The need to control the exercise of power by the state is basic. The means we have chosen are also basic: the vesting of constitutional responsibility in ministers."

2. See Sir Geoffrey Vickers, *The Art of Judgment: A Study of Policy Making* (New York: Basic Books, 1965), especially ch. 1.

3. The classic definition of federalism is perhaps best represented by K.C. Wheare's statement: "By the federal principle I mean the method of dividing powers so that the general and regional governments are each, within a sphere, co-ordinate and independent." Wheare, *Federal Government*, 4th ed. (London: Oxford University Press, 1963), p. 10.

4. See Chapter 7 below for discussion of this matter.

5. See "Responsibility in the Constitution. Part I," pp. 1-1 to 1-3.

6. As A.H. Birch states on p. 203 of his book, *The British System of Government* (London: George Allen and Unwin, 1968): "It is a basic principle of the British Constitution that the function of Parliament is not to govern the country, but to control the government." See also John Stewart, *The Canadian House of Commons: Procedure and Reform* (Montreal: McGill-Queen's University Press, 1977), ch. 1. Of the several functions which the House performs, surveillance of government action is the main means by which the House holds the executive accountable.

7. Traditionally, there has been an exception to this rule, the position of the Leader of the Government in the Senate. This person sits as a member of Cabinet ostensibly to maintain liaison with the upper chamber. The Clark cabinet of June 1979 included several more exceptions. See discussion below.

8. See discussion in J.R. Mallory, *The Structure of Canadian Government*, (Toronto: Macmillan of Canada, 1971), ch. 2.

9. As Norman Ward states: "The members of cabinet are above everything else responsible to the House of Commons, not as individuals alone, but collectively as well. . . . This is the central fact of parliamentary democracy; for it is this practice which keeps the system both efficient and constantly amenable to popular control." In R. MacGregor Dawson, *The Government of Canada*, 5th ed. by Norman Ward (Toronto: University of Toronto Press, 1970), p. 175.

10. See "Responsibility in the Constitution. Part I," pp. 1-5 through 1-34, for detailed discussion.

11. See J.E. Hodgetts, *The Canadian Public Service 1867-1970: A Physiology of Government* (Toronto: University of Toronto Press, 1973), p. 59.

12. British North America Act, sections 53 and 54. See also Norman Ward, *The Public Purse: A Study in Canadian Democracy* (Toronto: University of Toronto Press, 1962), ch. 1.

13. H.V. Kroeker, *Accountability and Control: The Government Expenditure Process* (Montreal: C.D. Howe Research Institute, 1978), pp. 14-15. Reprinted by permission of the C.D. Howe Research Institute.

14. Ibid.

15. This feature is an important distinction between the Canadian parliamentary and the

American Congressional systems. See "Responsibility in the Constitution. Part I," pp. 1-55 to 1-59, for discussion.

16. See Kenneth Kernaghan, "Power, Parliament and Public Servants in Canada: Ministerial Responsibility Re-examined," in *Canadian Public Policy* (Summer 1979), vol. 3, pp. 383-96.

17. Ibid. In this article Kernaghan discusses how these conventions have been modified in the contemporary environment of government. See also discussion in Chapter 4 below.

18. These prerogatives are not contained in any statute or constitutional act. The only formal document that sets them out is a Minute of the Privy Council first passed in 1896 pursuant to a submission of Sir Charles Tupper, the Prime Minister of the moment. The Minute has been reissued on four subsequent occasions, the last time in 1935. Now, it is normally circulated by prime ministers to ministers upon the formation of a cabinet. See "Senior Personnel in the Public Service of Canada: Deputy Ministers," in *Submissions to the Royal Commission on Financial Management and Accountability*, p. 3-2.

19. See W.A. Matheson, *The Prime Minister and the Cabinet* (Toronto: Methuen, 1976), p. 22, where he states: "The Canadian cabinet, in addition to the functions normally expected of it in a parliamentary system, has also become a mechanism of accommodation, the truly federal body in Canada. . . ."

20. See Dawson, *The Government of Canada*, ch. 9—"The Cabinet: position and personnel"— for a discussion of this evolution.

21. Matheson, pp. 39-45.

22. Mr. Juneau's successor in the Communications portfolio was Jeanne Sauvé, a former media personality in Québec, with a strong substantive interest in the policy field.

23. See R. Van Loon and M. Whittington, *The Canadian Political System*, 2nd ed. (Toronto: McGraw-Hill Ryerson, 1976), pp. 315-24. The authors are critical of the lack of representativeness in the cabinet with respect to the socioeconomic backgrounds of cabinet ministers in comparison with Canadians as a whole. Their data do support the representation formula for provincial, ethnic and constituency interests. See also Matheson, pp. 22-46.

24. The subject of tours of duty for deputy ministers will be discussed in Chapter 4.

25. See W.T. Stanbury, *Business Interests and the Reform of Canadian Competition Policy, 1971-75* (Toronto: Methuen, 1977).

26. Jean Chrétien was the Minister of Indian Affairs and Northern Development from 1968 to 1974.

27. Data source: *Canadian Parliamentary Guide, 1978*. Ministers of state to assist not included in the sample.

28. J.E. Hodgetts, *Canadian Public Service*, ch. 5.

29. Ibid., p. 89.

30. Ibid., ch. 5.

31. Ibid., pp. 89-90.

32. The definition of ministerial portfolio used here is for purposes of identifying the types of responsibilities assigned to a minister. It is not to be confused with the "ministry concept" of portfolio relationships which will be discussed in a subsequent chapter.

33. See M.J. Kirby, H.V. Kroeker, W.R. Teschke, "The Impact of Public Policy-Making Structures and Processes in Canada," *Canadian Public Administration* (Fall 1978), Vol. 21, no. 3, pp. 407-17. On pages 411-12, it is noted that: "The first stirrings of this new policy

activism in Canada can be found in the Kingston Conference on National Problems in 1960. This Conference, besides providing Mr. Pearson with a sizeable portion of his government's program during the rest of the 1960s, established a pattern and created expectations for citizen involvement in the formation of future programs. . . . A further consequence of this new political consciousness was the public belief not only that the government was responsible for the detailed operation of the economy and the welfare of individuals, but that solutions did . . . exist for all problems if only adequate structures and processes were put in place to anticipate, to plan, and to co-ordinate government activity." (This excerpt is reprinted by permission of *Canadian Public Administration*.)

34. Canada, *Statutes*, 14-15 Eliz. II, 1966, ch. 24.

35. Canada, *Statutes*, 18 Eliz. II, 1969, ch. 28.

36. Canada, *Revised Statutes*, 2nd supplement, 1970, ch. 14. In the case of the Ministries of State for Science and Technology and for Urban Affairs, proclamations were issued pursuant to Part IV of the 1970 Act.

37. "Senior Personnel in the Public Service of Canada: Deputy Ministers," p. 3-22.

38. See P. Aucoin and R. French, *Knowledge, Power and Public Policy*, Science Council of Canada, Special Study no. 31 (Ottawa: Information Canada, 1974).

39. See G.B. Doern and R.W. Phidd, "Economic Management in the Government of Canada: Some Implications of the Board of Economic Development Ministers and the Lambert Report," a paper prepared for the Annual Meeting of the Canadian Political Science Association (Saskatoon: May 30, 1979), for a discussion of this committee and its secretariat. When the Board was established it was announced that it constituted a "super ministry" and would function as an inner cabinet (*Ottawa Citizen*, Saturday, November 25, 1978, pp. 1-2). In fact, it was to serve for a few brief months as a coordinating board that attempted to consult with business and industry interests and tailor government programs to better meet the latter's needs. The proclamation establishing the Ministry was declared in February 1979. See *Canada Gazette*, Part I, Order-in-Council, "Proclamation Establishing a Ministry of State For Economic Development" (February 3, 1979), p. 638.

40. The Government Organization Act (1970), section 23, states: "A Minister of State . . . (a) may be assigned by the Governor in Council to assist any Minister or Ministers having responsibilities for any department or other portion of the public service of Canada in the carrying out of those responsibilities; and (b) shall exercise or perform such of the powers, duties, or functions of any Minister or Ministers. . . ." Thus, "powers, duties and functions" may be transferred to such a minister, but departmental supervision and control must remain with the senior minister (section 24). Legally, a Minister of State appointed pursuant to sections 23 and 24 of the 1970 Act can have no independent authority. (The excerpt is reproduced by permission of the Minister of Supply and Services Canada.)

41. The anti-inflation program machinery was established in 1975 and other agencies such as Petro-Canada emerged, but no attempt was made to undertake a comprehensive policy-related reorganization after 1970.

42. Canada, *Statutes*, 1976-77, 25-26 Eliz. II, ch. 54, The Employment and Immigration Reorganization Act, 1977.

43. A Government Organization Act (Scientific Activities) had been passed in 1976 (Canada, *Statutes*, 1976-77, 25-26 Eliz. II, ch. 24) which rationalized the organizational and management structures of the key granting councils. The Government Organization Act of 1979 (Canada, *Statutes*, 1979, 27-28 Eliz. II, ch. 13) tidied up some leftover matters regarding the Councils' staff and executive offices from the 1976 Act; it repealed the Representation Commissioner

Act and provided for the division of the Department of Environment. All these matters had been pending or anticipated for some years prior to its passage. See also note 44.

44. The integration of the Department of Fisheries into a new Department of Environment in 1970 had not been a popular move with the fishing constituents on the East and West Coasts. There had been a Minister of Fisheries in the cabinet since Confederation and the loss of a full-time minister was not well received. In 1974, a Minister of State for Fisheries was appointed in the Environment portfolio "to assist" the senior minister in this area. When it became clear that the Fisheries minister would have to be the senior minister in the portfolio to satisfy constituency concerns, a Minister of State for Environment was appointed in 1976 and the title used by the senior minister was changed to Minister of Fisheries and Environment. The 1979 Act provided for the formal partition of the department that had thus begun some years previously.

45. See G.B. Doern, "Horizontal and Vertical Portfolios in Government," in G.B. Doern and V.S. Wilson (eds.), *Issues in Canadian Public Policy* (Toronto: Macmillan of Canada, 1974), pp. 310-36; and G.B. Doern, "The Cabinet and Central Agencies," in G.B. Doern and P. Aucoin (eds.), *Public Policy in Canada* (Toronto: Macmillan of Canada, 1979), pp. 43-59.

46. These would include: National Revenue, Public Works and, since 1969, Supply and Services.

47. Kirby, et al., "The Impact of Public Policy-Making Structures and Processes in Canada," pp. 407-10.

48. The classic references here are R.G. Robertson, "The Changing Role of the Privy Council Office", *Canadian Public Administration* (Winter 1971), vol. 14, no. 4, pp. 487-508; and G.B. Doern, "The Development of Policy Organizations in the Executive Arena," in Doern and Aucoin, *The Structures of Policy Making in Canada* (Toronto: Macmillan of Canada, 1971), pp. 39-78.

49. Robertson, "The Changing Role of the Privy Council Office," p. 495.

50. Kroeker, *Accountability and Control, op. cit.*, pp. 32-38. Prime Minister Clark, for his part, seemed to favour Jasper, Alberta, as a locale away from Ottawa to discuss matters of this nature with his colleagues.

51. Ibid.

52. Robertson, p. 495.

53. Once a committee report was issued, a minister could ask that the matter be placed on the main agenda of cabinet for reconsideration. If no questions were raised on such a report, it would be listed on the agenda addendum and formally approved by cabinet without further discussion. For an examination of the process of cabinet deliberations in this regard, see R.D. French, "The Privy Council Office: Support for Cabinet Decision-Making," in R. Schultz et al. (eds.), *The Canadian Political Process*, 3rd ed. (Toronto: Holt, Rinehart and Winston, 1979), pp. 363-94.

54. Ibid., p. 365.

55. Ibid., pp. 368-72.

56. Office of the Prime Minister, *Press Release* (June 4, 1979), p. 2.

57. Ibid., pp. 2-3.

58. See Mitchell Sharp, "Decision-making in the federal cabinet," *Canadian Public Administration* (Spring 1976), vol. 19, no. 1, pp. 1-8, for a discussion of this process.

59. For purposes of discussion, a distinction is being made between two types of collective management functions the cabinet performs. On the one hand, it is responsible for policy coordination—that is, the determination and collective approval of government policies and program proposals that support those policies. On the other hand, it is responsible for the determination and allocation of resources and the establishment of standards of administration across the service as a whole. These responsibilities have been delegated to one of its committees, the Treasury Board. The central agencies that support the former function are discussed here; the latter function, in the next chapter.

60. These committees and their secretariats are largely reactive to departmental submissions; hence, their role will be discussed more fully in the context of departmental policy development and planning. See R.D. French, "The Privy Council Office: Support for Cabinet Decision-Making," pp. 372-82, for his analysis of the same.

61. The near loss of the election and the formation of a minority government in 1972 quickly shifted attention to more immediate political concerns of the government. Long-range planning had little to offer the politician interested in reelection. After 1974 and the return to a majority situation, the influence of international events on domestic problems made effective long-range planning even more improbable.

62. See French, p. 367.

63. A Machinery of Government Secretariat was formally created in 1972 and was reconstituted as a Directorate in 1973. Its functions had initially been performed by one or two officers in the Plans Division of the PCO. Specifically, the staff engaged in the preparation of the organization acts of 1966, 1969 and 1970 could be said to have been the informal predecessor to the Directorate.

64. For example, the Green Papers on Freedom of Information and Control, Direction and Accountability of Crown Corporations of 1977 were prepared in this unit.

65. It had originally been proposed that the secretariat be located in the Treasury Board Secretariat, which is responsible for managing senior-executives policy on individuals subject to the Public Service Employment Act. However, given that Governor-in-Council appointments are a prerogative of the prime minister, the secretariat responsibility ultimately was situated in the Privy Council Office. When the Office of the Secretary to the Cabinet for Federal-Provincial Relations was created in December 1975, the responsibility for senior personnel went with the Secretary. At the time of the reorganization in 1976, the Senior Personnel Secretariat stayed within the PCO, but a dual reporting relationship was established for the Senior Assistant Secretary of the Directorate. In other words, on matters of government organization he reported to the Secretary to the Cabinet and Clerk of the Privy Council; on matters of senior personnel, he reported to the Secretary to the Cabinet for Federal-Provincial Relations. For administrative purposes, however, the Senior Personnel Secretariat was part of the Machinery of Government Directorate in the Privy Council Office.

66. Canada, Statutes, 1974, 23 Eliz. II, ch. 16, "An Act respecting the Office of the Secretary to the Cabinet for Federal-Provincial Relations and respecting the Clerk of the Privy Council."

67. The reorganization of the Office was essentially to establish a "matrix model" of management to provide for a better integration of activities. With respect to the Co-ordination Branch, provision was made for the establishment of a Constitutional Core Group, which was to have played a key role in the patriation and reform process planned by Prime Minister Trudeau if his government had been reelected.

68. See Marc Lalonde, "The Changing Role of the Prime Minister's Office," *Canadian Public Administration* (Winter 1971), vol. 14, no. 4, pp. 509-37.

69. Ibid., p. 526.

70. A recent study analyzed the role of the Privy Council Office, the Federal-Provincial Relations Office, the Prime Minister's Office, the Treasury Board Secretariat and the Department of Finance. On the basis of information gathered from interviews with senior officials in these agencies, an attempt was made to determine networks of influence among officials within and between central agencies. Unfortunately, a similar study of senior officials in departments and agencies has not been done to determine the accuracy of the perception that central-agency officials exercise as much influence as implied by the nomenclature "superbureaucrat." See Colin Campbell and George Szablowski, *The Superbureaucrats: Structure and Behaviour in Central Agencies* (Toronto: Macmillan of Canada, 1979).

3

The Administrative Setting

In the preceding chapter, we observed how the doctrine of ministerial responsibility provides the essential framework within which the public service must operate. Ministers, individually and collectively, are responsible for government policies and programs. The collective nature of the executive requires coordinated policy making at the highest level—that is, the cabinet and its committees. Support for these coordinative exercises, as we have seen, is provided by the central agencies that report to the prime minister.

The management of the public service is also a collective and individual exercise, although cabinet has delegated its collective responsibility in this regard to one of its committees, the Treasury Board. In the role of the central management arm of government, the Board and its Secretariat must seek to balance the interests of individual departments against those of the totality of government activities. The degree of centralization or, conversely, decentralization of management activities applied at one time in these operations will represent the administrative formula by which equilibrium is sought. Historically, one may discern periods in which departments exercised considerable independent management authority and others in which the Board and other agencies performing central-management functions exercised a high degree of centralized control.[1] In practical terms, these patterns may be said to represent a continual search for balance between central and departmental management needs.

In recent decades, a major reorientation in management in the federal public service resulted from the implementation of the recommendations of the Report of the Royal Commission on Government Organization (known as the Glassco Commission) which reported in 1962. The five-volume report became a seminal work in Canadian public administration. It provided the bases for major reform in the federal public service for over a decade. The diagnosis of the management problems in government at the time the Commission did its study was essentially that central agencies exercised excessive control over departmental operations. With the increase in the scope and nature of government activities that had occurred during and after World War II, it was considered impractical as well as inefficient and uneconomic for central controls to be stringently applied to administrative actions of departments. The formula recommended included a greater degree of decentralization of management responsibility and authority. "Let the managers manage" was a major theme of the report. The other half of the formula for management reform was to establish the Treasury Board Secretariat as a separate agency with its own minister. The role of the agency would emphasize central coordination rather than control and serve to provide administrative leadership in the management of the public service.

The Glassco reforms were in place by the late 1960s, but new developments during that and the ensuing period had a significant impact on the direction of change. On the one hand, government activities had continued to expand during this period. The ability of departments to obtain approval for programs before obtaining approval for resources necessary for those programs helped to contribute to a steady rate of increase of expenditure and a steady drain on the treasury.[2] It was not until the mid-1970s that an effort was made to tie the policy- and program-approval process to the resource-allocation process in a concerted manner. On the other hand, new centralizing forces emerged which provided a high profile for the Board and its Secretariat. The implementation of the Glassco recommendations and the introduction of the Program, Planning and Budgeting Systems (PPBS), collective bargaining and official-languages policy in the public service created a perceived and in some cases real need for more central management. The activities of the Secretariat expanded; its size in terms of numbers of employees nearly quadrupled in ten years.[3]

The expansion of the Treasury Board's responsibilities was not accompanied by measures that would effectively maintain a balance of central versus departmental interests in certain areas of management. The Royal Commission on Financial Management and Accountability, which reported in March 1979, diagnosed the problem of management in the public service in general terms as one of inadequate central control systems and ineffective accountability systems for departmental managers. In this vein, the Commission recommended changes to provide for greater centralization of management responsibility in the Treasury Board (to be reconstituted as a Board of Management) and for rigorous assessment processes for departmental managers.[4] A major concern was the need to contain levels of government spending and to provide effective means whereby performance could be measured.[5] The Commission attempted to design a "mutually compatible management system" that would balance the needs of central and departmental management.

Both these reports constitute major efforts to come to terms with what are often conflicting objectives in public-sector management. On the one hand, value for money—economy, efficiency and effectiveness—is a major objective for management, whether private or public funds are involved. On the other hand, the public service operates in an environment distinctly different from that of the private sector in which the profit motive is the primary objective. The principles of management in the public service must support the individual and collective responsibilities of ministers and hence the attainment of political objectives, which are often multifaceted and competitive. The needs of management therefore require a meshing of political, policy and administrative objectives. Thus, the pursuit of economy, efficiency and effectiveness must take into account the needs of responsible and responsive government. How best to organize and manage resources to achieve these ends is a continuing issue in a highly complex and politically sensitive environment. Let us begin our examination with a consideration of the size and the composition of the public service proper.

The Context

As noted earlier, the federal government has played an increasingly active role in Canadian society since World War II and particularly in the last decade. The effects of increased government activity are ably demonstrated in quantitative terms by increases in government spending and the size and the composition of the federal public service. In the first instance, growth in government spending provides a general indication of the scope of government activity. It is nevertheless often difficult to obtain easily corroborated statistics on the amounts of money spent and the manner in which they are disbursed.[6] Total federal government expenditures as set out in the Public Accounts of Canada provide the essential gross data on the magnitude of federal spending. (See Table 3-1.)

Considering the magnitude of funds at its disposal, it would not be far-fetched to suggest that the federal public service has been, and is, an active agent in shaping and influencing social forces. The growth of government spending has been significant and, while it has occurred in all

Table 3-1
Government Expenditures, in millions of dollars

Fiscal year	Net expenditures	Rate of increase over previous year
1966-67	9,884	
1967-68	11,338	14.5%
1968-69	12,482	11.0%
1969-70	13,486	11.0%
1970-71	15,788	17.1%
1971-72	18,020	14.1%
1972-73	20,655	14.6%
1973-74	23,779	14.3%
1974-75	29,213	22.8%
1975-76	33,977	16.3%
1976-77	39,011	14.7%
1977-78	42,882	9.9%

Source: The figures have been taken from the Public Accounts of Canada for each fiscal year.

areas of government activity, growth was especially noteworthy in the social-service areas. In particular, transfer payments from the federal government to the provinces for social services increased rapidly in the last decade.[7]

As noted earlier, the government's "Attack on Inflation" policy of 1975 provided for the introduction of a program of wage and price controls.[8] With respect to government spending, it was proposed that total spending by all governments should not rise more quickly than annual increases in the gross national product. Governments were encouraged to avoid tax rate increases and to limit borrowing. The *rate* of increase in expenditure began to decline in 1975-76; in addition to expenditure cuts in federal government programs in 1975 and 1978, changes were made to the Established Programmes Financing arrangements in 1977-78 in which the provinces were given additional revenues in lieu of direct transfer payments to cover part of the federal funding for hospital insurance, medicare and post-secondary education.[9] By reducing federal revenues in this way, it was also possible to maintain a reduced rate of increase in federal spending. In 1979-80, a modification was made to the Family Allowances program based on the same principle.[10] Thus, attempts to control the amount of government spending have included tax expenditures as well as expenditure reductions. The Conservative government's policy from June 1979 was for continued restraint.[11]

Table 3-2
Federal Government Employees

Fiscal year	PSEA[a]	Estimates[b]
1967-68	200,329	269,894
1968-69	200,321	269,644
1969-70	199,720	276,503
1970-71	198,701	272,174
1971-72	203,182	280,730
1972-73	223,264	291,174
1973-74	238,494	315,410
1974-75	258,590	333,003
1975-76	273,167	347,357
1976-77	283,169	352,836
1977-78	282,788[c]	354,892
1978-79	279,209	356,943

Note: It is difficult to find data from different public sources which can be corroborated. Each agency has its own reporting system. The sources used here were: (a) figures representing the number of *people* employed under the Public Service Employment Act as reported in the Annual Reports of the Public Service Commission for each of the years above; and, (b) the number of man-years or *positions* authorized by Parliament for federal departments as contained in the Estimates. It is even more difficult to maintain constant comparisons when agency methods of determining the data are changed, as represented by (c). The figures reported in the 1977 Annual Report of the Public Service Commission were calculated on a different basis from previous years and thus reflect a slightly different size of group. The decline indicated must therefore be qualified.

A major dilemma for federal governments attempting to control increased government spending has been the statutory commitments for many of its programs, particularly those involving the provinces, and the continued high rates of inflation and debt charges on borrowed funds. Furthermore, containment is not an easy policy to pursue when the determining factors are often international rather than domestic events. The perceived shift in public opinion from the mid-1970s away from support for big government was not followed by any clear demonstration that governments could dramatically affect their levels of spending regardless of political philosophy.[12] At best, they have tried to search for more effective use and control of moneys spent.

The rapid growth in federal expenditures, however, was not accompanied during this period by an equally rapid growth in the federal public service, contrary to popular belief. The federal government accounts for a small percentage of total public employees in Canada, although the public sector as a whole is a large employer.[13] The rate of growth in the federal public service in the last decade has been slow to moderate, as Table 3-2 shows.

Rapid increases did occur, however, in the size of certain occupational groups in the public service. The focus on policy and program formulation and coordination during this decade facilitated the advancement of employees in the professional categories.[14] Members of these groups were often promoted to senior-executive positions rather quickly, particularly in those departments that placed a high premium on creative policy development and on modern management practices. This trend created difficulties in the senior ranks, for officials often attained senior management positions without having obtained the requisite breadth of experience for the jobs.[15]

Table 3-3
Distribution of Employees by Selected Category

Year	Senior Executive		Scientific, Professional		Administrative, Foreign Service	
	Number	% Increase	Number	% Increase	Number	% Increase
1971	618		18,099		29,199	
1972	777	25.7%	19,165	5.9%	32,651	11.8%
1973	868	11.7%	20,855	8.3%	35,882	9.9%
1974	1,071	23.4%	22,097	6.0%	43,401	20.9%
1975	1,186	10.7%	23,444	6.1%	47,597	9.7%
1976	1,223	3.1%	24,623	5.0%	50,461	6.0%

Sources: Public Service Commission, *Annual Report* (each year, 1971 to 1976). Percentages were calculated from these figures. Entries were not made for 1977 and 1978 because the method of calculating figures from 1977 was conducted on a different basis. (See note to Figure 3-2.)

The rate of increase of the total number of employees under the Public Service Employment Act for the period 1971-76 was 6.6, 6.3, 4.5, 5.6 and 3.7 per cent, respectively. In comparison, the rate of increase in the senior executive, scientific and professional as well as administrative and foreign-service categories was considerably higher for the same years. (See Table 3-3.)

Other interesting patterns emerge when one examines the number of appointments to, promotions within and separations from the public service. As the figures in Table 3-4 show, the number of appointments from outside the public service for the most part surpassed the number of separations from the public service; the rate of promotions from within more than tripled.

The relatively uniform increases in appointments to and separations from the public service reflect a reasonably slow but steady growth in the overall size of the public service, with a decline setting in from 1976. The continuing increase in the appointments from within the public service signifies an increasing stability in the composition of the public service, especially in the last few years. Since a large number of these appoint-

Table 3-4
Public Service Appointments and Separations

Year	Appointments to Public Service	Appointments within the Public Service[1]	Separations from Public Service
1968	20,379	25,173	17,465
1969	20,733	25,609	17,512
1970	23,055	30,279	20,619
1971	27,706	38,969	23,202
1972	38,568	49,916	25,302
1973	38,979	59,536	33,239
1974	46,569	78,232	39,344
1975	36,251	90,920	31,783
1976	30,201	91,031	31,731
1977	22,437	112,543	32,503
1978	19,224	114,341	36,612

[1]Appointments within the public service include those made: from one occupational group to another; to a higher level within an occupational group; to a lower level within an occupational group; between subdivisions of an occupational group, no change in level; as lateral transfers both within and between departments; to level below position level, no change in occupational group/level/ department; and, of term employees for indeterminate period, no change in occupational group/level/department. Appointments of persons for a term of less than six months are not included in these figures. When such persons are subsequently appointed for a term of more than six months or for an indeterminate period, they are counted as "Appointments within the Public Service." In the latter case, therefore, it is possible to conceal a number of appointments within, as opposed to outside, the public service. For further explanation, see Public Service Commission, *Annual Report* (1976), pp. 45-47.

Sources: Figures were obtained from the *Annual Reports* of the Public Service Commission, 1968 to 1978 inclusive.

ments represent promotions, the figures support the trends noted earlier in the growth in the senior executive and professional categories.

During an expansionary period such as that represented by the figures from 1971 to 1975, increases in the public service will occur to provide new and extended services. In periods of restraint, the public service will also be directly affected and often will become a prime object of government policy. The 1975 restraint program called for a 1.5 per cent annual increase in the growth of the public service. To meet this commitment, the number of authorized man-years or positions for departments were reduced in that year to levels below that of the previous year. Staff increases were allowed only in operations related to new economic measures, police and penitentiary responsibilities and certain essential public services such as the post office.[16] In 1978, the government announced that it would eliminate 5,000 jobs, and in fact did so. The Progressive Conservative administration, upon taking office in June 1979, placed a temporary three-month hiring freeze on the public service and reiterated the election promise to eliminate 60,000 public-service jobs.

Thus, the public service and its activities are affected directly by changing economic and political circumstances. Governments, in providing leadership, will effect policies within their own administrations to provide examples to other jurisdictions and the private sector. Similarly, the composition of the public service can be an object of government policy. The representation of the two official language groups and minorities was a major element of recruitment and staffing practices from the late 1960s through the following decade. The purpose of these policies was to demonstrate another facet of responsiveness and leadership beyond the performance of economic functions and the provision of social services. The complexion of the public service was to reflect the complexion of Canadian society.

In representative terms, efforts to recruit francophones to the public

Table 3-5
Percentage Distribution of Francophones in the Public Service by
Occupational Category

	1974	1975	1976	1977	1978
Senior Executive	18.5	20.4	20.4	21.0	20.7
Scientific and professional	20.2	20.1	20.4	19.9	19.3
Administrative and foreign service	24.0	24.3	26.0	26.6	26.6
Technical	15.7	16.2	18.1	18.0	18.1
Administrative support	27.3	28.0	30.6	30.9	30.5
Operational	26.7	26.7	26.9	29.5	26.8
Total	24.6	24.9	26.2	27.2	26.2

Source: Public Service Commission, *Annual Report* (each year, 1974 to 1978).

service gradually changed its linguistic composition. The participation of French-speaking Canadians increased in most occupational categories to 20 per cent or more. (See Table 3-5.) In comparison, the percentage of francophones to the total population was, according to the 1971 census statistics, about 27 per cent.

The recruitment of women and other minority groups made less of an impact. Women constitute only a small percentage of the senior-executive positions and only a third of the total number of employees in the public service.[17] Native Employment and Black Employment Programs in the public service are not statistically significant.[18]

The regional composition of the federal public service was also a distinguishing feature that was given emphasis. The highly dispersed structure is reflected by the fact that in some areas federal regional offices closely approximate the size of the provincial public services. (See Table 3-6.)

In the interests of promoting sensitivity and responsiveness in the public service, the federal government announced in 1977 a formal policy of decentralization which, however, only involved the relocation of jobs. There was no official policy to decentralize authority. Thus, despite the highly dispersed nature of the public service, decision makers and decision

Table 3-6
The Size of the Public Service, by Province, 1977

Geographic Area	Federal public service	Provincial public services
Newfoundland	5,865	13,196
Prince Edward Island	1,507	4,735
Nova Scotia	16,803	19,637
New Brunswick	8,359	24,744
Quebec	52,918	92,424
Ontario	127,573	112,283
Manitoba	12,484	14,079
Saskatchewan	8,289	16,571
Alberta	18,085	47,112
British Columbia	26,636	41,928[1]
Yukon	924	1,702[2]
Northwest Territories	1,410	2,737[2]
Outside Canada	1,934	—
Total	282,788	391,148

[1]Figures obtained from Public Service Manual for the B.C. government; not otherwise publicly reported to federal statistics agencies.
[2]Denotes territorial government administrations.

Sources: The source of the figures for the federal public service is the Public Service Commission, *Annual Report* (1977).

The source of the provincial figures is Statistics Canada, *Provincial Government Employment* (Ottawa: October-December 1977). Exceptions noted.

making continue to be concentrated in the National Capital Region. In 1978, for example, 83.9 per cent of individuals in the senior-executive category were found in the National Capital Region, while only 26.5 per cent of the total number of employees in the federal public service were located there.[19] To date, no new measures have been proposed to modify this distribution.

In sum, the public service of Canada is a large, complex organization responsible for the management of enormous sums of public money. In the last several decades, it has experienced rapid expansion and, more recently, restraint in the level of its activities. The organization has responded accordingly in shifting management priorities to accommodate growth and, now, consolidation. The effects of expansion, however, served to provide a high degree of mobility for personnel within and from outside the public service, notably in the senior-executive and professional categories. Combined with efforts to recruit individuals representative of the society as a whole and to support a highly dispersed yet "sensitive" public service throughout the country, the professionalization of the public service has contributed to a changing environment in which management must be performed. Thus, providing leadership through the application of principles and practices promulgated from a central source to diverse components of a heterogeneous organization has become a highly complex and often difficult task. Let us turn, therefore, to an examination of the design and functions of the central-management system.

The Functions of Central Management

> The needs of effective management fall into two general categories: first, those associated with the administration of departmental operations; and second, those involved in the central direction and co-ordination of government activities as a whole.[20]

In an organization as large as the public service of Canada, effective management is a major challenge. The implications of the doctrine of individual and collective ministerial responsibility for the public service are nowhere more apparent than in the management design of the public service proper. The crux of that design is the relationship between central-management agencies and the departments. The departments must tailor their operations to respond to individual ministerial needs; the central agencies must provide for the effective collective management of the public service and its resources; these activities of departments and central agencies must be coordinated and mutually supportive.

In a historical perspective, the relationship between central management and the departments represents a struggle between centripetal and centrifugal forces. In the early years, departments played the dominant role in management and operated quite independently from the central managers. Generally speaking, effective central direction over matters of resource allocation and management was sporadic and often weak.[21]

The creation of the Treasury Board as a Committee of the Queen's Privy Council of Canada—first by Order-in-Council in 1867, then by statute in 1869[22]—represented an intention to have a central coordinating mechanism at the highest level of decision making. The responsibilities of the Board initially included "all matters relating to Finance, Revenue, Expenditure or Public Accounts, which may be referred to it by Council."[23] It consisted of the Minister of Finance as chairman and three (subsequently five) other members of the Privy Council; it was assisted by a small secretariat in the Department of Finance.

As the traditional role and mandate of the Department of Finance expanded, there was increasingly less time for the Minister to devote to the management functions of the Board. The prescription offered by the Glassco Commission to this problem was the separation of the Secretariat from the Department and the creation of a separate ministerial portfolio titled President of the Treasury Board.[24] The division of responsibilities between the Department and the Board served to distinguish the Department's responsibility in the broad areas of economic and fiscal policy[25] and the Secretariat's function as the management arm of cabinet. Thus, the Department's role as a central agency pertains to macro-economic management policy issues rather than to internal-management and resource-allocation questions, although the relationship between the Department and the Secretariat is, on related matters, reciprocal.

A succinct summary of the historical effectiveness of the Treasury Board is provided by Professor Hodgetts:

> In retrospect, the story . . . reveals a singular consistency in diagnosis of a problem and in the prescription for its cure. The problem was how to bring separate functioning entities into a co-ordinated, collaborative partnership that would bring real meaning to the term *the* civil service of Canada. The prescription proposed as early as 1867 was to inject a co-ordinating collegial body, the Treasury Board, into the top reaches of the system. For nearly one hundred years the prescription either did not take or was so irritating that supplementary and often competing palliatives were prescribed. What is surprising is that in the mid-1960s, following a much more meticulous but nevertheless similar diagnosis, the system has responded very rapidly to a prescription for top co-ordination to achieve the long-deferred objective of a unified civil service.[26]

The prescription for top coordination as set out in the Glassco Royal Commission report and as adopted with some modifications in 1966-67 marked the beginning of a new period in which the aims of central management became the dominant focus of administration in the public service. Despite the Glassco recommendations which were directed to "letting the managers manage," the development of the Board's new mandate[27] and the growth in the size and the activities of the Secretariat imposed a strong central mechanism onto the management system of the public service.

The aims of central management found expression through the activities of the Board as the Cabinet Committee on the Expenditure Budget on the one hand and as the Cabinet Committee on Management on the other.[28] Resource allocation, financial-management systems, administrative standards and practices and personnel management constituted the diverse range of matters that came within the Board's purview. The creation of the Cabinet Committee on Priorities and Planning in 1968, the introduction of Planning, Programming and Budgeting Systems (PPBS) in 1966, the introduction of collective bargaining in 1967, the revamping of the Civil Service Commission with the passage of the Public Service Employment Act in 1967 and the adoption of the Official Languages Act in 1969 served to enhance the central-management functions of the Treasury Board.

Within ten years of these reforms, however, the ability of the Board and its Secretariat to perform effectively was being questioned. Modifications were made and new measures were introduced to deal with emerging problems. In its review, the Royal Commission on Financial Management and Accountability (the Lambert Commission) assessed many of the problems as ones of inadequate control and accountability systems at the centre; it recommended a further enhancement of central responsibility. Whether changes of the kind recommended take adequate account of the complexity of the processes and the dynamics of the system is debatable: the search for balance between central- and departmental-management needs continues. Let us then examine the several key responsibilities of central management.

Resource Allocation

The spending of public money is at the heart of government activity. The allocation of financial resources between and among departmental programs is a competitive process that is mediated by the Treasury Board and its Secretariat. While it is the responsibility of the Minister of Finance to develop general economic policy, to determine tax changes and above all to present regular budgets of the government's revenue and overall expenditure position to the House of Commons, it is the responsibility of the President of the Treasury Board, assisted by the Board and its Secretariat, to determine the Expenditure Budget for the departments and agencies of the public service and to present it in the form of the Estimates to the House for approval.

Traditionally, departments requested and received funds on the basis of standard objects of expenditure. The budgeting system was control oriented, in that the main purpose of the exercise was to contain the increases from year to year in these objects of expenditure on a department to department basis. No consideration was given and little information generated on the objectives and rationale of the programs for which the money was spent. In 1962, the Glassco Commission recommended that departmental estimates be prepared on the basis of programs of activity and that long-term plans of expenditure requirements also be submitted by departments. While the Commission did not recommend the implementation of PPBS *per se*, the basic principles which would provide the basis for the implementation of the system were set out in the report.[29]

A main requirement for a budgeting system like PPBS is, in the first instance, top-down direction for the objectives and purposes of the activities to be undertaken. At the political level, this direction was to be provided by the Cabinet Committee on Priorities and Planning. The expenditure budgetary process would thus commence with the establishment of guidelines set by the Priorities and Planning Committee; the Treasury Board in turn would use these guidelines as a broad framework for establishing spending priorities. The link between these two committees was to be a crucial one for integrating policy and program objectives with spending decisions. In practice, however, this linkage was not effectively forged. As noted earlier, a change was made in 1976 in the cabinet committee procedure that required Treasury Board's consideration of new program proposals from operating committees before final consideration by cabinet. This practice pertained to new expenditures only, however, and was therefore limited in its effectiveness. Further reforms implemented in 1979 were related directly to linking policy and expenditure decisions.[30]

Within the public service, the impact of PPBS as a central coordinating technique began in 1966 with the reclassification of government expenditures into functional categories as opposed to standard objects of expenditure. These functions cut across government departments; thus, in theory, these functions provided a basis for comparative assessments of departmental spending activities. Departments were required to identify objectives as well as to delineate specific programs and activities to support those objectives through a process of cost-benefit analysis of alternative proposals; this requirement not only generated a great deal more information on government programs, but also provided the base from which the Treasury Board could exercise influence over the total resource-allocation process in the government. The requirement for long-term program forecasts facilitated further the centralization of the expenditure budgetary process.[31]

The increased emphasis on central coordination and the increased sophistication of the budgeting system, however, complicated and often forestalled the implementation of the new procedures at the departmental level. The elaborate process of coordination within central agencies and between the central agencies and the departments was often cumbersome. Moreover, difficulties arose from the practical constraints and limitations that bear on the implementation of a new scheme or system, particularly one that is highly "rational" in design. The identification and delineation of goals and priorities in a political setting is highly constrained. Politicians are not convinced easily that they should commit themselves to anything more specific than platitudes of objectives, such as "facilitating and fostering national unity, regional economic development, improved social services."[32] Broad objectives such as these created difficulty in establishing criteria for the evaluation of programs. That policy efficiency is ultimately measured by ministers intuitively further defies the application of precise measurement tools.

Efforts to refine the expenditure-planning process were also severely restricted by the large proportion of the budget that consists of previously committed moneys. Expenditure planning in the federal public service has been pursued within a three-year time frame. Departments are requested by the Treasury Board to prepare and submit program forecasts developed twelve to eighteen months in advance of the target fiscal year. They include that year plus the next two years as well as a review of the current and past fiscal year. The annual preparation of the program forecast ensures continual updating and revision.

The forecasts set out two projected levels of spending activity: the "A" budget, which represents the sums required to continue previously approved programs at the current level of service, and the "B" budget, which represents increased costs in financing the current level of expenditure plus new programs. However, the A budget expenditures normally constitute over 90 per cent of total expenditures, the so-called fixed costs of government.[33] The large items include: statutory commitments, continuing government services, public-service salaries and public debt.[34] As costs increase, the amount of money available for new programs is reduced proportionately.

Once the program forecasts have been reviewed and approved, departments are then required to prepare detailed estimates of their program expenditures for the coming fiscal year. These become the Main Estimates that are submitted to Parliament shortly before the beginning of the fiscal year for which they are to provide funds. Because not all expenditures can be foreseen and planned in advance, there is also a process of preparing and submitting Supplementary Estimates. While this exercise involves the lesser amount of money, it is often the Supplementaries that are contested most avidly.

The Treasury Board and its Secretariat—in this instance, the Program Branch—act as the central guardians of the public purse. The dynamics of the process place the departments (the spenders) in a defensive posture in maintaining existing programs and in an aggressive posture on obtaining new moneys. As resources become scarcer or as priorities shift and threaten existing programs, competition between and among departments increases and the role of Treasury Board as final arbiter—next to cabinet—is enhanced.

Table 3-7
Expenditure Budgetary Cycle for Program Forecasts and one set of Estimates, October 1975 to December 1978[35]

Stages	Time
Priorities set by the Cabinet Committee on Priorities and Planning	October-December 1975
Treasury Board request for Program Forecasts	December 1975
Departments prepare and submit Program Forecasts	January-February 1976
Treasury Board Secretariat reviews Program Forecasts	March-May 1976
The Treasury Board, Cabinet Committee on Priorities and Planning and the cabinet review Program Forecasts and establish expenditure guidelines	June-August 1976
Treasury Board request for Main Estimates	September 1976
Departments prepare and submit Main Estimates	September-October 1976
Treasury Board Secretariat reviews Main Estimates	November 1976
Treasury Board and cabinet approve Main Estimates	December 1976
Main Estimates tabled in Parliament by the President of the Treasury Board and referred to standing committees of the House of Commons	February-March 1977
House Committees review Main Estimates by departments	March-May 1977
Parliament votes interim supply on Main Estimates	March 1977
House debates and passes appropriation acts; Senate approval; royal assent obtained	May-June 1977
Supplementary Estimates requested by Treasury Board	September 1977
Supplementary Estimates prepared and reviewed by Treasury Board and cabinet	September-December 1977
Tabling of Supplementary Estimates	December 1977
Treasury Board requests Final Supplementaries	January 1978
Final Supplementaries prepared and reviewed	January-March 1978
Tabling of Final Supplementaries and procurement of supply	March 1978
Post audit by Auditor General	April-November 1978
Public Accounts and Auditor General's Report tabled and referred to Public Accounts Committee of House of Commons	November 1978
Public Accounts Committee examines Accounts and Report, then issues Committee report(s) on same.	December 1978-79

A recent examination of this "private government of public spending"[36] contends that the adversarial process underlying expenditure-budget formation and, indeed, resource-allocation decision making ultimately determines the content of the budget. While the introduction of PPBS and the development of sophisticated analytical techniques for measuring efficiency and effectiveness for government programs attempted to provide a more rational framework for ordering activities and allocating resources, they did not contribute substantively to improved planning and control of the resource-allocation process. In the final analysis, it has been the strongest interests, as mediated through the Treasury Board and its officials, that have "won" in the competition for resources.

The prevailing concern with developing ways and means of improving resource-allocation decisions represents, in certain respects, a recurring pattern. From 1968 to 1972, rational planning reigned supreme, in that there was a strong commitment to the application of budgetary tools and techniques that would promote efficient and effective allocation of resources. The Treasury Board Secretariat served as the fount of rational planning techniques and procedures respecting resource allocation. But PPBS failed the politician because it could not provide the flexibility needed to pursue political goals while achieving economically efficient results. Although the techniques could be considered useful to the political decision-making process in generating more and better information, they could not replace or significantly modify the political process. A minority government such as the one that existed from 1972 to 1974 has little need for rational long-range program planning.

As general economic circumstances began to change and resources became scarcer, particularly from 1975, the Board's role as mediator of competing interests nevertheless became even more critical. Its decisions on cutting programs and attempting to reduce expenditures were effectively nonnegotiable with the departments. The traditional process of forecasts and estimates proceeded, keeping in step with the parliamentary timetable, but innovative budgetary techniques were not pursued.

Given the experience of the government with the objective-setting, rational systems orientation of PPBS, it is interesting that the Lambert Commission in its analysis and review of budgetary systems in government concluded that the planning process had to be strengthened at all levels, beginning at the top. It recommended the development of a five-year Fiscal Plan by the Minister of Finance to "provide estimates of revenues, set expenditure ceilings and reflect the expected surplus or deficit."[37] The Plan would set the guidelines, particularly in terms of expenditure ceilings for departments and agencies, to apply to the preparation of their estimates. The Estimates could then serve as more specific and detailed short-term forecasts of expenditures.[38] Generally speaking, they would include more detailed information on expenditure activity and would contain more clearly defined objectives for each activity and subactivity.[39] In other words, the Fiscal Plan would serve to rationalize the budgetary process in government by providing clearer direction to departments of priorities and resource availability; departments would therefore be assisted in defining objectives and outlining program activities in specific and detailed terms. It would also enhance the role of the Minister and the Department of Finance in establishing the broad financial framework for government operations and would ensure tighter integration of policy priorities, program activities and resource-management functions through the coordinative efforts of the Privy Council Office, the Treasury Board Secretariat and the departments.

The importance of priorities and objectives and, indeed, limited long-range planning to a budgetary process cannot be disputed. The extent to which they can be refined and serve as a definitive and specific framework for determining and evaluating government activities will be limited by practical political considerations. Priorities can never be so precisely defined as to depoliticize the process by which departments compete for funds; objectives can never be so precisely defined as to provide indisputable criteria for performance measurement.[40] Long-range planning will always be affected by political and economic exigencies. Accurate and timely information is essential, nevertheless, and improvements can always be made in the systems that generate and coordinate the acquisition of that information. Competition for resources remains an essential feature of the budgetary process and in that respect the role of the Treasury Board as the central mediator is paramount. New techniques can facilitate or add to the complexity of the process, but its basic institutional features will invariably influence the effect of any attempt at reform.

Financial Management and Control

The Glassco Commission had been generally critical of the myriad of central controls on departmental administration, particularly in the area of financial management. Once Parliament had authorized the appropriation of funds, it was argued, departments should have the necessary financial authority for the detailed expenditure of program funds and "be held accountable for the effective management of the financial resources placed at their disposal."[41] To that end, the traditional pre-audit responsibility of the Comptroller of the Treasury for the certification and authorization of departmental expenditures was delegated to departments.[42] The Comptroller's responsibility for maintaining the accounts of the government was transferred to the newly created Department of Supply and Services, and his Office was formally abolished in 1969. The Treasury Board was to continue to oversee and develop policies on financial matters for the public service as a whole, but in a less restrictive manner. Guidelines rather than controls would be the main vehicle of supervision. A Financial Administration Division was created in the Treasury Board Secretariat for that purpose.

As a result of these changes, the central financial-control feature became the post-audit function of the Office of the Auditor General which is, and functions as, an agent of Parliament and not as an arm of management. The Auditor General audits the Public Accounts of Canada (the actual expenditures as opposed to the proposed expenditures, the Estimates) and submits his report to Parliament as a final stage in the expenditure budgetary cycle.

A combination of factors, including the significant increases in government expenditures generally during the late 1960s and early 1970s, served to render the proposed decentralized system of financial management and control inadequate. In the Auditor General's view, however, a primary cause of the unsatisfactory state of affairs which he found in 1975 was the fact that certain key recommendations of the Glassco Commission were not implemented. As he stated:

> Perhaps they were not understood, although the recommendations relating to the decentralization of financial authorities were fully implemented. . . . Unfortunately, the concurrent and equally important Glassco recommendation that new counterbalancing controls be instituted and that existing ones be strengthened was not implemented—certainly not in the manner and to the extent visualized by Glassco. Thus, it is apparent that the situation which now causes my concern has not developed overnight. Control over public funds would appear to have been deteriorating for at least the last 15 years.[43]

For its part, the government's response to the Auditor General's criticisms[44] was threefold. First, the role and function of the Financial Administration Division within the Treasury Board Secretariat was elevated in 1976. The Division became a full-fledged branch with its own deputy secretary of the Board. With this change, a new emphasis was placed on the development of financial-management guidelines for departmental use. In December 1977, the President of the Treasury Board released a paper on Performance Measurement to demonstrate further that measures were being taken within the Secretariat to improve assessment and audit of programs.[45]

Second, the Lambert Royal Commission on Financial Management and Accountability, as noted earlier, was established in December 1976. The Report, *inter alia*, examined the financial system in government and recommended a tightening of central control over financial-management practices through improved reporting systems from departments to the central agencies. Value-for-money criteria—economy, efficiency and effectiveness—were to be applied in the evaluation of all government activities.[46] In general, its recommendations in this area were consistent with and supported the concerns expressed earlier by the Auditor General.

Third, the government agreed to create an Office of Comptroller General. The Act establishing this Office was passed in April 1978.[47] The Comptroller was given the full status of a deputy minister with a direct reporting relationship to the President of the Treasury Board. He monitors the quality and integrity of financial-control systems and related administrative practices. He also advises on policies to ensure that satisfactory procedures are established to measure and to report on the efficiency and effectiveness of government programs. Hence, the determination of accounting principles for the financial statements of the government of Canada, the form and content of financial reports, internal-audit procedures and evaluation mechanisms for programs and projects fall within the purview of his mandate.[48]

The creation of this Office divided the staff of the Treasury Board Secretariat. The Efficiency Evaluation Branch (formerly a division of the disbanded Planning Branch) and the Financial Administration Branch were transferred to the Comptroller General. In the Comptroller's words, he became responsible for the "How" of financial management; the Secretary of the Treasury Board remained responsible for the "What"—priorities, resource allocation, review and control.[49]

The significance of the creation of this Office from the standpoint of central management cannot be overemphasized. The Glassco Commission's reforms of decentralized financial management did not take. Within a decade, the need to reinstitute a central controller had become clearly evident, at least to the Auditor General. The location of that office in the Treasury Board Secretariat reinforces the role of the Board and the Secretariat as the central management body and, indeed, controller of departmental administration. The extent to which the Office can develop systems of accounting and evaluation centrally and on a department-by-department basis is a major challenge.[50]

Administrative Improvement

In concert with its proposals for the decentralization of financial management in the public service, the Glassco Commission had also recommended greater delegation of responsibility to departments for matters of general administrative concern. The Treasury Board, for its part, was to be responsible for the development of policies and guidelines; to that end, it established an Administrative Policy Branch within the Secretariat. The functions of the Board in this regard were explained by a former Secretary of the Board in this way:

> It is the Treasury Board which attempts to give leadership to
> departments in the development and use of such important and

expensive inputs as computing and data processing equipment and which prescribes guidelines or regulations as to the standards which ought to apply in respect of other inputs such as accommodation, travel, entertainment expenses and employee benefits such as parking. It is the Board which has determined what contract methods should be used by departments in acquiring services, equipment and capital structures, and when materials and supplies should be acquired through central agencies.[51]

It was intended that, as in the area of financial management, the control orientation of the Board would be shifted to one of leadership and coordination. The Board would develop its administrative policies in the form of guidelines to departments rather than regulations. Prior approval by the Board of the application of those guidelines would not be required. Thus, leadership in standard setting would be provided by the Board; departments would comply within the general policy framework set by the guidelines. Control would be maintained through review and evaluation by the Board and through post-audit by the Auditor General.

In this area, the Auditor General, in successive reports from the mid-1970s, criticized the laxity in the application of guidelines and the deficiencies in the level of standards achieved in departmental program operations. Studies were conducted on ways and means of improving performance. For its part, the Royal Commission on Financial Management and Accountability recommended a rationalization of practices by departments for the provision of common administrative services. In particular, the responsibility of the Treasury Board for common-service policy across government was reiterated, including appropriate accounting and cash-management systems for those services.[52] In discharging its responsibility in this area in the future, the Board must be wary of a return to overly centralized controls in improving administrative practices. The balance between central- and departmental-management needs in this area may be a difficult one to achieve but, as in other areas, should provide for operational effectiveness within the framework of general standards and practices.

Personnel Management

If the allocation and control of financial resources need to be coordinated centrally to provide for effective management in the public service, it follows that the effective management of public-service employees requires central coordination to ensure that high standards of performance and productivity are achieved. However, the history of the development of a unified public service[53] represents a more complicated struggle of central agencies and institutions against departmental organizations than that involved in the control of financial resources. In general, conflicts have existed and continue to exist between the requirements of the public service as a whole and those of individual departments and programs as well as between the needs of organizations and those of employees working in them. The continuing challenge in personnel management is to strike workable balances among these often conflicting objectives.

In 1967, the role of the Treasury Board was expanded considerably in this area, even though the Glassco Commission had recommended a highly decentralized structure for personnel management in the public service. The management design involved essentially: the Treasury Board as the central manager of personnel policy and manpower needs; the Public Service Commission to continue as the central staffing agency reporting to Parliament; and the departments, which would "be given the requisite authority to manage their own personnel and be held accountable for efficient performance."[54] With the introduction of collective bargaining and official-languages policy, the Board expanded its horizons of responsibility. The responsibility for developing personnel policy was also a new undertaking and necessitated a new set of relationships with the Public Service Commission. The Commission, for its part, provided the operational support for the Board. For example, the Board would set policies on job qualifications; the Commission would be asked to respond with special recruitment and training programs, which in turn it would have to coordinate with the departments. Over time, conflicts between its role as an independent agent of Parliament and as an operational arm of management led the Commission to prompt a review of its roles and relationships.[55]

Of the several examinations made of the role and relationships of the agencies engaged in the personnel field, the Lambert Commission, in its review of central-management functions, proposed the transfer of staffing and training responsibilities from the Public Service Commission to the Treasury Board (Board of Management),[56] thus consolidating financial- and human-resource-management functions in a single agency. In practical terms, this model represented a significant further extension of central-management control as well as a significant increase in the size of agency operations.[57] Considering the responsibilities the Board has assumed in the personnel field in the last decade, it is questionable whether the assumption of additional responsibilities could be realistically accommodated from an organizational perspective. Let us consider three key areas in which the Treasury Board's influence in personnel management was previously expanded—manpower planning, collective bargaining and official-languages policy.

Manpower Planning

The Treasury Board controls the number of jobs or positions available to departments and agencies of the public service through the expenditure budgetary process. Departments are required in the preparation of program forecasts and estimates to identify the number of positions or man-years as well as the amount of funds required to operate programs. Thus, in the first instance, it is the Program Branch of the Secretariat that reviews overall levels of manpower requirements in the public service. Its recommendations, both in the case of the forecasts and in the case of the estimates, are considered by the Treasury Board and cabinet. Once approval has been obtained in each stage, information on man-year allocations is given to the Manpower Division of the Personnel Policy Branch of the Secretariat, which is responsible for monitoring the deployment of employees in the departments.[58]

However, two exercises occur outside the regular expenditure planning process: the authorization of supplementary man-years and funds relative to the Official Languages Programme and the authorization of Senior Executive (SX) and Equivalent (SXE) positions. The first exercise is undertaken to reconcile the requirements of the government's official-languages policy with the requirements of other programs in allowing individuals to be replaced temporarily while on language training. The second exercise is a control over departmental managers.

Generally, deputy ministers have authority to determine the internal structure of their departments, in that they have delegated authority for the classification of positions. However, when changes such as reclassifications or new-position requests are made or internal reorganizations are undertaken, submissions must be made to the Treasury Board Secretariat and the Treasury Board for approval. The services of the Organization Division of the Planning Branch and the Classification Section of the Personnel Policy Branch (now the Organization and Classification Division of the Personnel Policy Branch) would be used extensively by departments to assist them in preparing these submissions. The key positions, nevertheless, are those in the management structure—senior-executive (SX) category—and these are the positions most avidly sought by deputies, for they strengthen their departments' ability to perform and, indeed, to extend their mandates.[59]

The Co-ordinating Committee on Organization—which was initially chaired by the Director of the Organization Division and included representatives from the Personnel Policy Branch (Manpower and Classification Sections) of the Secretariat, the Executive Staffing Programme of the Public Service Commission and the Machinery of Government Directorate in the Privy Council Office—acts as the control mechanism on SX deployment. It is this Committee that reviews, recommends and rejects departmental requests for reclassification or increase in the number of executive positions. These positions are key for, if they are obtained, they can provide the basis for submissions for additional man-years to support the newly acquired line or executive post. In no instance, however, can the total number of positions exceed that authorized in the Estimates;

the classification and allocation of these positions are controlled by the Board, not by the departments themselves.

The effectiveness of this central control was demonstrated in Table 3-3, which showed a high rate of increase in the number of senior executives from 1971 to 1974, then a dramatic reduction from 1975. Both the increases and the reduction were the result of the work of the Co-ordinating Committee. Because the government had committed itself in its White Paper, "Attack on Inflation" (October 1975), to a reduction in the rate of growth of the public service, it was incumbent upon the Committee that that policy directive be followed up as reflected in the 1975-76 figures.

In sum, the Treasury Board and its Secretariat control the total number of positions authorized for departments and agencies in the public service through the expenditure budgetary process. In order to contain departments' internal growth or structure, the Board more particularly controls the number of senior-executive positions allocated to any one department and monitors and reviews changes in the classification of other positions. The reclassifications of other positions result from the collective-bargaining process.

Collective Bargaining

The introduction of collective bargaining into the federal public service in 1967 constituted a complete and comprehensive revision of employer-employee relations. Until the passage of the Civil Service Act of 1961, civil servants were paid as a matter of privilege of the crown rather than of right. The granting of full bargaining rights with the right of strike, then, marked a significant stage of development of the public service. A commitment had been made by each of the three main national political parties before the 1963 general election to introduce collective bargaining in the public service if elected. Following the election, the Liberal government established a Preparatory Committee on Collective Bargaining in the Public Service. The Committee reported in 1965[60] and the legislation was passed in 1967.

Essentially three pieces of legislation were involved. First, amendments were made to the Financial Administration Act, establishing the Treasury Board as the "employer" for purposes of collective bargaining. Former responsibilities of the Civil Service Commission for manpower requirements, pay, classification and training policy were transferred to the Treasury Board.[61] Second, the Public Service Employment Act was passed, reconstituting the Public Service Commission as the central staffing agency without any direct "management" responsibilities.[62] Finally, the Public Service Staff Relations Act was enacted to provide for the machinery of collective bargaining.[63] The authority to certify bargaining units and to administer dispute settlements through either arbitration or conciliation processes was vested with the Public Service Staff Relations Board.

The first step in implementation was the classification of employees into occupational categories and groups. (See Table 3-8.) This task was undertaken by the Treasury Board Secretariat in conjunction with the Public Service Commission and the public-service unions. Employees were classified into six main occupational categories and some seventy occupational groups across the public service as a whole; public-service unions were established as bargaining agents for those groups. The structure for a unified public service had been aspired to but never achieved in such a concerted fashion by the former Civil Service Commission, with its responsibilities for personnel administration.

The second step was the conduct of the collective-bargaining process itself. Bargaining takes place between officials of the Negotiation Groups

Table 3-8
Occupational Categories and Groups

Senior Executive
  Nonbargainable: terms and conditions of employment determined by cabinet on recommendation from the Advisory Group on Executive Compensation in the Public Service. (See Chapter 4.)

Administrative and Foreign Category
  Examples of Occupational Groups: Administrative Services (AS), Commerce (CO), Foreign Service (FS), Organization and Methods (OM), Personnel Administration (PE), Program Administration (PM), Translation (TR), Welfare Programs (WP).

Scientific and Professional Category
  Examples of Occupational Groups: Actuarial Science (AC), Agriculture (AG), Auditing (AU), Chemistry (CH), Dentistry (DE), Economics, Sociology and Statistics (ES), Historical Research (HR), Nursing (NU), Physical Science (PC), University Teaching (UT).

Technical Category
  Examples of Occupational Groups: Air Traffic Control (AI), Educational Support (EU), Engineering and Scientific Support (EG), General Technical (GT), Photography (PY), Radio Operation (RO), Social Science Support (SI), Technical Inspection (TI).

Administrative Support
  Examples of Occupational Groups: Clerical and Regulatory (CR), Communications (CM), Data Processing (DA), Secretarial, Stenographic, Typing (ST), Telephone Operation (TE).

Operational Category
  Examples of Occupational Groups: Correctional (CX), Firefighters (FR), General Services (GS), Hospital Services (HS), Lightkeepers (LI), Ship Repair (SR), Ships Crews (SC).

Source: Selected from the list in Public Service Commission, *Annual Report* (1978).

of the Staff Relations and Compensation Division of the Personnel Policy Branch and designated bargaining agents representing employees. The Treasury Board proper establishes the guidelines for the Secretariat in terms of the amounts of money the government is prepared to offer and, given this mandate, the Secretariat officials proceed with the negotiations. In the event of an impasse, bargaining agents have a choice of two dispute settlement options: binding arbitration or conciliation, the latter course offering in certain circumstances the right to strike.

The centralized control the Board exercises over salary and benefit awards to groups across the service is noteworthy. Departmental managers, for their part, may find themselves in a totally ineffective role in the case of disputes, for most often bargaining groups cut across several departments. In the case of the post office where union members are localized in one department, the deputy is in an even more awkward position when disputes arise, for he is effectively a secondary management figure.

The introduction of collective bargaining on such a comprehensive scale was not without growing pains. The Staff Relations and Compensation Division became one of the larger units in the Treasury Board Secretariat. Bargaining is a continuous process from the negotiation of an agreement with one group to that of another. Given the number of groups and the short terms of the agreements (two years is the normal length of time), a backlog often develops. Moreover, public-service salaries and salary increases are issues of political concern. Whereas the government can be seen to be a "good employer," it will be criticized if public-service salaries are or are perceived to be higher than those in other sectors of the economy.[64] Collective bargaining contributed to significant increases in particular occupational groups' salary levels during the decade, although differing opinions exist about whether the levels were comparatively that excessive.[65]

In an endeavour to more effectively contain the evolution of collective bargaining, in March 1978 the government introduced Bill C-28 to amend the Public Service Staff Relations Act. Following several years of independent study,[66] parliamentary review[67] and internal consideration, the key changes put forward in the bill included:

- The definition of individuals working in a managerial or confidential capacity was broadened to exclude more employees from the bargaining process; in particular, employees earning $33,500 or more were removed from the bargaining process. The Governor-in-Council was to have authority to amend this salary level.
- "Lockout" rights for the employer were provided.
- Remuneration for public-service jobs was to be determined on the basis of total compensation benefits and of job comparability with other sectors.

- The Pay Research Bureau was given a statutory base and was to be responsible to the Chairman of the Public Service Staff Relations Board; the establishment of an Advisory Committee on Pay Research was recommended.

There was strong opposition by public-service unions to this bill, for it was accurately interpreted (with the exception of the provisions for the Pay Research Bureau) as a restriction of their bargaining rights. The bill died on the order paper for that session of Parliament. In the next session, a revised bill (C-22), which dealt with the proposals for the Pay Research Bureau only, was introduced but it, too, died on the order paper. In philosophical terms, these attempted changes to the collective-bargaining process raised several questions about the status of public servants as employees. Unlike the private sector, public-service salaries come from public funds that in theory are controlled by the elected representatives of the people. The government—in particular its delegate, the Treasury Board—has to be responsible for the efficient and effective use of those funds. Thus, the political environment of public-service bargaining places some very real constraints on the determination of salaries and work benefits. While it is the Board's responsibility to represent the "employer" for purposes of bargaining, there is considerable ambiguity in the exercise of that responsibility in a public-service context.

Official-Languages Policy

The Glassco Commission had issued a minority report on some aspects of bilingualism in the federal public service and included some proposals in its recommendations.[68] However, the report of the Royal Commission on Bilingualism and Biculturalism provided the basis for government policy in this area.[69] In 1966, a statement on bilingualism in the public service was made in the House of Commons by Prime Minister Pearson, setting out the objectives of promoting the use of the French and English languages in, and the recruitment of francophones and anglophones to, the public service on the basis of equality of rights for both English-speaking and French-speaking Canadians. Bilingualism would be considered an element of merit in recruitment and staffing of the public service, but the requirement of such a qualification would not discriminate against individuals already in the public service.[70]

In 1969, Parliament passed the Official Languages Act, which provided a statutory basis for the policy. The responsibility for its implementation within the public service was divided among the Treasury Board (policy and program development), the Public Service Commission (recruitment, staffing and language training), the departments (identification of needs, classification and planning of positions in conjunction with the Treasury Board) and a new Office of the Official Languages Commissioner.[71] The Commissioner acts both as an ombudsman and as an auditor through an annual review of measures taken and results achieved by departments in their efforts to implement the policy.

The attempt to transform a largely unilingual English-speaking public service into a bilingual institution over a short period of years was ambitiously undertaken.[72] The Treasury Board provided the management guidelines to be followed by departments in the development of bilingualism in the public service. Target percentages were set for the bilingualization of positions in the public service by 1975. A two-pronged approach was undertaken to meet these goals through recruitment of francophones to the public service and language training in both official languages. The Public Service Commission assumed the operational responsibility for language training and, in conformity with Treasury Board policy, developed recruitment programs for francophones and incorporated bilingualism into the merit system for candidate selection and promotion.

Despite concerted efforts to effectively implement the policy, Parliament was asked in 1973 to pass a Resolution[73] that recommended the establishment of guidelines for the identification of language requirements for all positions in the public service by 1978. Under these guidelines, all positions in the public service were identified as requiring knowledge of English, French, or both and designated levels of language skill required for different occupational groups were established. The Resolution also reiterated that bilingual capability be considered an element of merit in staffing positions in the public service.

The implementation of the bilingual policy in the public service was highly controversial and highly criticized. In its capacity as central manager and administrative coordinator, the Treasury Board and its Secretariat were faced with the task of reconciling conflicts between stated policy objectives and the actual means of policy implementation. In 1974, the Board commissioned Dr. Gilles Bibeau of l'Université de Montréal to undertake an independent study of the effect of bilingual training in the public service. His report[74] exposed a broad range of deficiencies; in response, the Treasury Board issued new guidelines—Revised Official Language Policies in the Public Service of Canada—in September 1977.

In practical terms, the revised guidelines placed greater emphasis on the acquisition of language skills before entry to the public service and before application for a bilingual post. It is intended that "conditional" appointments and universal basic language training will be phased out by 1983. Departments are being required to make special recruitment efforts in areas of their operation where francophone representation is found to be low, although they will have greater flexibility in selecting measures suited to their particular needs to achieve these objectives. Opportunities for francophones to work in French are being expanded through placing a greater emphasis on the use of unilingual French positions. Bilingualism is to be a requirement only where needed for the effective delivery of services, both to the public and to employees. Official-languages policy now applies to crown corporations as well as departments of the public service.

The task of introducing what amounted to radical social change in the public service placed the Treasury Board Secretariat in a high-profile policy role. Language concerns cut across every aspect of the Secretariat's responsibilities, from resource allocation to pay and classification matters. The high priority that was assigned to the program by the cabinet and in particular by the Prime Minister gave the Secretariat the support it needed at the political level to introduce change. However, top-down coordination, in the brief time frames allowed, created difficult problems in the departments and agencies that were expected to follow central direction. While it is evident that the intended transformation of the public service is now taking hold, it has been perhaps one of the most difficult changes that central management has been required to effect.

In the broad perspective, the evolution of the role of the Treasury Board and its Secretariat over the past decade or more has been characterized by a steady expansion of its mandate and responsibilities. As *the* central-management arm of the executive, it provided for the initiation and implementation of management reforms in all areas of administration. As its responsibilities were extended, so too was its importance in the broader framework of government activities. The application of the Glassco formula for a greater degree of decentralization, however, was not balanced during the initial years of reform by effective coordination and monitoring efforts by central management. This imbalance was particularly true in the area of financial and materiel management. The new centralizing forces which resulted from changes in the budgeting process, personnel policy and employer-employee relations created a more elaborate and complex system of central management, but one which became increasingly difficult to coordinate at the centre and between the centre and the departments. The prescriptions put forward in recent years reflect, on the face of the record, a return to more centralized control. Thus, a pattern of management which emphasizes central rather than departmental interests is apparent and could be said to represent a recurring cycle in the continuing search for balance of management needs.

Management Principles and Administrative Leadership

Public-sector management is, by its very nature, distinct from private-sector management. Nevertheless, there have been continued efforts to make government more businesslike—that is, more efficient. The management philosophy that permeated the Glassco Commission's studies was a reflection of this attitude. The guiding principles of the Commission as set out in its terms of reference were to consider changes which "would best promote efficiency, economy and improved service in the despatch of public business."[75] Although the pursuit of these principles in the practice of administration has evolved over the years in response to changing circumstances, they continue to be a main preoccupation of management.[76] The Lambert Commission reiterated their importance, for as its Report states: "The quality and effectiveness of government programs can only be maintained if greater economy and efficiency in their administration can be attained."[77] Thus, the assumption that effectiveness is synonymous with economy and efficiency persists.

As a primary principle of public-service management, however, efficiency in government is conditioned by the constitutional framework and the political nature of the central-management body. Efficiency, defined as a measure of performance and results obtained, must be considered in at least two different contexts in the public service. As Al Johnson has commented:

> "Administrative efficiency"—what the Glassco Commission concerned itself with primarily—consists of good organization, efficient procedure, effective financial control, proper inventory control, appropriate paperwork and systems management and the rest. "Policy efficiency", on the other hand, is a matter of making the right policy decisions, of selecting the appropriate programs in order to achieve the government's objectives.[78]

Policy efficiency therefore has to be measured in more than economic terms. Policy efficiency may be uneconomic if the political choices made reflect a measure of administrative inefficiency as part of the price for achieving political objectives. Administrative efficiency, on the other hand, pertains directly to ensuring that programs and services are provided and managed in the most economical terms possible. Techniques such as PPBS, cost-benefit analysis, operational-performance measurement and financial reporting and accounting systems become important management tools for ensuring that efficiency in this sense is achieved. Thus, the relationship between policy and administrative efficiency can be mutually supportive or conflicting. Efficient program administration can, on the one hand, serve to facilitate and to promote efficient policy decisions. On the other hand, conflicts may arise where an efficient policy decision may be highly inefficient in administrative terms and result in inordinate costs for the benefits actually achieved.

The partner of efficiency in government is effectiveness. Effectiveness may be measured by the extent to which an activity achieves the objectives set for it. The measurement of effectiveness requires evaluation techniques that take into account both economic and noneconomic criteria. The latter are often difficult to establish. Thus, efforts to develop and to

Figure 3-1
Organizational Evolution
Treasury Board Secretariat

1. Glassco Model (implemented in 1967)

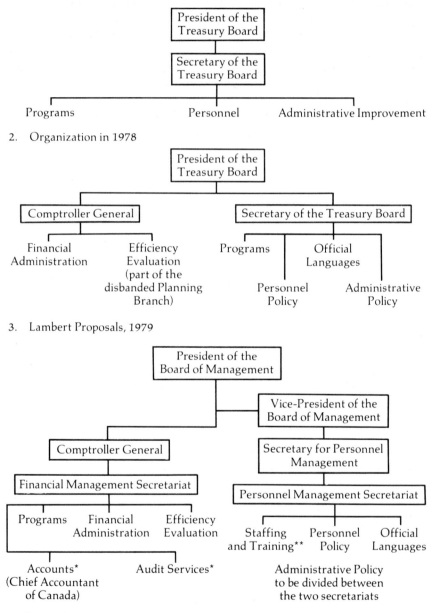

2. Organization in 1978

3. Lambert Proposals, 1979

*To be transferred from the Department of Supply and Services
**To be transferred from Public Service Commission

improve measures of effectiveness—particularly in the implementation of public programs—constitute a continuing exercise.

Responsiveness is another primary principle of public-sector management. It is perhaps an overriding one, for the business of government might be construed essentially as providing the services the public wants.[79] It may also be considered as another form of efficiency in government, "service efficiency."[80] In the last few years, the principle of sensitivity has been added to responsiveness to support more fully the government's public-service objectives. Sensitivity to local and regional needs will ensure that those needs are met within the requirements of the particular locale or setting. This principle may also be put into operation through the promotion of "representative bureaucracy." Special recruitment programs for francophones, women and natives can be cited as an example of this approach.

The Treasury Board and its Secretariat have played the central role in determining the principles on which management in the public service is based and in developing policy guidelines and measures by which they can be achieved. The several functions of the Treasury Board as central manager of the public service provide the essential vehicles for promulgating the theories of management. In providing administrative leadership, it must also pay attention to the development of managers. In this regard, the Secretariat shares responsibility with the Public Service Commission. The Commission's Executive Staffing Program and Executive Training Program have played major supporting roles. The development of managerial skills therefore represents the need for a sensible balance between the "hard" tools of efficient administrative performance and the "soft" tools of effective personnel recruitment and development.[81]

The needs of central management require that the central agencies responsible play an instrumental role in providing leadership and in instilling appropriate management philosophies in the public service. At the same time, the needs of departmental administration must be honed. The changing role and responsibilities of the public service have changed the role of the public-service manager. The public service does not operate in a vacuum and, when subject to often conflicting demands, must be capable of reconciling those demands in a politically acceptable and accountable fashion. In the next chapter we will consider the task of the public-service manager.

Notes

1. J.E. Hodgetts, *The Canadian Public Service, op. cit.*, pp. 241-309; and J.E. Hodgetts et al., *The Biography of an Institution* (Montreal: McGill-Queen's University Press, 1972).

2. R. French, "The Privy Council Office: Support for Cabinet Decision-Making," in R. Schultz et al. (eds.), *The Canadian Political Process*, 3rd ed. (Toronto: Holt, Rinehart and Winston, 1979), pp. 380-81.

3. In 1967, the Secretariat employed approximately 200 people. In 1978, it had a position authorization of more than 750.

4. See Canada, Royal Commission on Financial Management and Accountability, *Report*, pp. 111-18.

5. Ibid., pp. 71-109.

6. The best analysis of government spending can be found in R.M. Bird, *The Growth of Government Spending in Canada* (Toronto: Canadian Tax Foundation, 1970). In particular, an exhaustive and critical analysis of data definition and corroboration is provided in appendices A to D. The problem of methodology in data collection by public agencies is not inconsiderable, in that not only are different systems used by different agencies, but also changes made in reporting systems within an agency can invalidate data for comparative purposes. See note to Table 3-2.

7. R.M. Bird, pp. 58 and 60.

8. See Government of Canada, "Highlights of the Government of Canada's Anti-Inflation Program" (October 1975), pp. 16-17.

9. See Government of Canada, "Briefing on Federal Expenditures," a Joint Statement by the Hon. Sinclair Stevens, President of the Treasury Board, and the Hon. John Crosbie, Minister of Finance (Ottawa: July 20, 1979), p. 3.

10. Ibid.

11. Ibid.

12. The 1975 restraint program had little visible impact. As noted earlier, by 1978, cutbacks were being made in a piecemeal fashion. For its part, the Conservative government in 1979 quickly realized that simplistic solutions were not feasible. Its attempt to make a marginal impact in reducing government expenditures resulted in its defeat on its first budget in December 1979.

13. See R. Bird and D.K. Foot, "Bureaucratic Growth in Canada: Myths and Realities," in G.B. Doern and Allan M. Maslove (eds.), *The Public Evaluation of Government Spending* (Toronto: Butterworth, 1979), pp. 121-48.

14. One might note also that the introduction of collective bargaining and with it the classification of occupational categories and groups in 1967 helped to give a distinct identification to professional employees and assisted in their recognition in departments and agencies.

15. For discussion, see Chapter 4 below.

16. Government of Canada, "Highlights of the Anti-Inflation Program," *op. cit.*

17. Public Service Commission, *Annual Report* (1978), vol. II, Table 12, p. 12.

18. Ibid., vol. I, p. 33.

19. See Public Service Commission, *Annual Report* (1978), Table 13, p. 14.

20. Canada, Royal Commission on Government Organization, *Report* (1962), p. 48.

21. J.E. Hodgetts, *The Canadian Public Service*; see ch. 11.

22. Order-in-Council PC-3 was passed on July 2, 1867. The Department of Finance Act was passed in 1869. See Canada, *Statutes* 1869, 32-33 Victoria, ch. 4.

23. *Statutes*, ibid.

24. Canada, Royal Commission on Government Organization, *Report*, vol. 1, pp. 64-66.

25. See R.W. Phidd and G. Bruce Doern, *The Politics and Management of Canadian Economic Policy* (Toronto: Macmillan of Canada, 1978), ch. 7, "The Role of the Department of Finance," for a discussion of its current role in these and related areas.

26. J.E. Hodgetts, *The Canadian Public Service*, p. 262.

27. Canada, *Statutes*, Financial Administration Act, 1966-67, sections 5 and 7.

28. See A.W. Johnson, "The Treasury Board of Canada and the Machinery of Government of the 1970s," *Canadian Journal of Political Science* (1971), vol. IV, no. 3, pp. 346-56; and Michael Hicks, "The Treasury Board of Canada and its clients: five years of change and administrative reform", *Canadian Public Administration* (Summer 1973), vol. 16, no. 2, pp. 182-205.

29. Royal Commission on Government Organization, *Report*, pp. 96-102.

30. In August 1979, the Conservative government announced the implementation of a new expenditure-management system which in fact had been in various stages of development even before the election in May. The recommendations of the Lambert Commission Report had been considered in part in determining the design of the system. The essential feature of the system was the identification of nine policy areas referred to as "envelopes," representing key government spending functions. Each envelope was assigned to one of the cabinet committees or inner cabinet as the case may be. The committees were to prepare initial work plans for each policy area, establish priorities, identify new programs and review existing ones. The work plans, combined with assessments of the economic situation from the Minister of Finance and the expenditure situation provided by the President of the Treasury Board, would form the basis for the proposed allocation of funds. In theory, this system represents a tight integration between policy and program development and resource allocation processes at the highest decision-making level along with significant enhancement of the role of cabinet committees in those processes. See Office of the Prime Minister, Press Release, "New Expenditure Management System". (Jasper, Alberta: mimeo, August 30, 1979), pp. 1-6. See also Chapter 8 for discussion.

31. See W.L. White and J.C. Strick, *Policy, Politics and the Treasury Board in Canadian Government* (Don Mills: Science Research Associates, 1970), pp. 128-40; and G.B. Doern, "The Budgetary Process and the Policy Role of the Federal Bureaucracy," in G.B. Doern and P. Aucoin, *The Structures of Policy-Making in Canada*, pp. 79-112.

32. See H.V. Kroeker, *Accountability and Control*, pp. 32-33 and 41-48.

33. Kroeker, ibid., p. 34, and Canada, Treasury Board, *Federal Expenditure Plan: How Your Tax Dollar Is Spent* (Ottawa: Supply and Services, 1977).

34. Currently more than 52 per cent of federal spending is in the form of transfer payments; 28 per cent is for operating and capital expenditures of government; about 16 per cent represents the costs of public debt. See "Briefing on Federal Expenditures" (Ottawa: July 20, 1979), p. 4.

35. This table was drawn from material in: Canada, Ministry of State for Urban Affairs,

74 / The Machinery of Government

Discussion Paper, "The Federal Urban Domain: Vol. I" (Ottawa, 1973), pp. 23-26; J.C. Strick, *Canadian Public Finance*, 2nd ed. (Toronto: Holt, Rinehart and Winston, 1978), p. 33; and Kroeker, *Accountability and Control*, pp. 33-37. Reprinted by permission of Holt, Rinehart and Winston of Canada, Limited.

36. This phrase is an allusion to the work by H. Heclo and A. Wildavsky, *The Private Government of Public Money* (London: 1974). Bruce Doern in Doern and Aucoin (eds.), *Public Policy in Canada*, notes on p. 101 that the sense of community observed by Heclo in describing the resource-allocation process in the British public service is not entirely approximated in Canada. However, an internal process is certainly distinguishable in the Canadian context. See D.G. Hartle, *A Theory of the Expenditure Budgetary Process* (Toronto: University of Toronto Press for the Ontario Economic Council, 1976), and *The Expenditure Budget Process in the Government of Canada* (Toronto: Canadian Tax Foundation, 1978), for a former insider's assessment of the dynamics of the process. The author concerns himself with four sets of "games" played by key actors and affected individuals: he demonstrates how interpersonal relations and vested interests serve to affect the budget process.

37. Royal Commission on Financial Management and Accountability, *Report*, p. 80.

38. Ibid., pp. 94-102.

39. Ibid.

40. See D.G. Hartle, "The Report of the Royal Commission on Financial Management and Accountability," *Canadian Public Policy* (Summer 1979), vol. 3, pp. 366-82; and A. Wildavsky, "A Budget for All Seasons? Why the Traditional Budget Lasts," in G.B. Doern and A.M. Maslove (eds.), *The Public Evaluation of Government Spending* (Toronto: Butterworth, 1979), pp. 61-78.

41. Royal Commission on Government Organization, *Report*, vol. I, p. 105.

42. The Office of the Comptroller of the Treasury was created in 1931 and housed within the Department of Finance. The Comptroller had two main responsibilities: to maintain the accounts of the government; and to certify the legality and to authorize the release of funds appropriated by Parliament to departments. This pre-audit practice ensured that no expenditure could be made that was not authorized by Parliament.

43. Report of the Auditor General of Canada to the House of Commons for the fiscal year ended March 31, 1976 (Ottawa: Supply and Services, 1977), p. 11. Reproduced by permission of the Minister of Supply and Services Canada.

44. His criticisms were blunt. In his report for the fiscal year ending March 31, 1975, he observed: "The present state of the financial management and control systems of departments and agencies of the Government of Canada is significantly below acceptable standards of quality and effectiveness." See Report, 1975, p. 4.

45. Canada, Treasury Board, "Performance Measurement," a report to the House of Commons by the President of the Treasury Board (December 1977).

46. Royal Commission on Financial Management and Accountability, *Report*, pp. 130-32.

47. Canada, *Statutes*, An Act to Amend the Financial Administration Act, 1977-78, 26-27 Eliz. II, Bill C-10. Harry Rogers, a senior executive of Xerox Co. Ltd., was appointed as the first Comptroller General.

48. Harry Rogers, "Program Evaluation in the Federal Government," in Doern and Maslove, *The Public Evaluation of Government Spending*, pp. 79-89.

49. Ibid., p. 81.

50. Ibid., p. 89.

51. A.W. Johnson, "The Treasury Board and the Machinery of Government," pp. 360-61. Reprinted by permission of the *Canadian Journal of Political Science*.

52. Royal Commission on Financial Management and Accountability, *Report*, pp. 159-71.

53. See in particular J.E. Hodgetts et al., *The Biography of an Institution: The Civil Service Commission of Canada*, and *The Canadian Public Service*, ch. 12, "The Public Service Commission."

54. Royal Commission on Government Organization, *Report*, vol. I, p. 259.

55. In February 1977, the government established a Special Committee on Personnel Management and the Merit Principle to review personnel-management problems in the public service. The establishment of the Committee had initially been proposed by Mr. John Carson at the end of his term as Chairman of the Commission. His proposal had been strongly supported by the public service unions. The Special Committee was a tripartite body chaired by Mr. Guy D'Avignon and represented on the official side by Mr. Bruce Brittain, deputy minister of Veterans Affairs, and on the staff side by Mr. Des Davidge, union representative. The Committee released a Working Paper in November 1978 setting out its findings and a final report in the fall of 1979. Its focus and concerns emphasized the human-relations side of personnel management in contrast to the approach by the Lambert Commission in its review of personnel-management structures.

56. Royal Commission on Financial Management and Accountability, *Report*, pp. 111-26.

57. Ibid. The transfer of staffing and training and development responsibilities from the Commission to a newly constituted Secretariat would involve the transfer of roughly 2,000 positions.

58. The information is also shared with the Public Service Commission in support for its staffing responsibilities.

59. This kind of growth phenomenon in government organization is described more cynically as empire building.

60. See Canada, Civil Service Commission, *Report of the Preparatory Committee on Collective Bargaining in the Public Service* (Ottawa: Queen's Printer, 1965).

61. Financial Administration Act, section 7.

62. Public Service Employment Act, section 5.

63. Canada, *Statutes*, Public Service Staff Relations Act, 1967, 14-15-16 Eliz. II, ch. 72.

64. As a percentage of total government expenditures, public-service salaries have constituted roughly 15-20 per cent of overall government costs. Given the labour-intensive nature of the "industry," this proportion might not be considered excessive.

65. Numerous internal and independent studies have been undertaken by the Treasury Board Secretariat and outside firms, respectively, to determine pay comparisons in the public and private sectors. The main charge generally made against the public sector is that, in terms of total compensation (wages plus benefits), the public sector is higher than the private sector. For a good recent study, see David K. Foot (ed.), *Public Employment and Compensation in Canada: Myths and Realities* (Toronto: Butterworth, for the Institute for Research on Public Policy, 1978).

66. See J. Finkelman, "Employer-Employee Relations in the Public Service of Canada," Parts I and II (Ottawa: Information Canada, 1974 and 1975).

67. See Canada, Parliament, Special Joint Committee on Employer-Employee Relations in the Public Service of Canada, *Sixth Report* (February 1976), 1st session, 30th Parliament 1974-75-76.

68. Royal Commission on Government Organization, *Report*, vol. I, pp. 265-67.

69. The Commission was established in 1963 and issued a preliminary report in 1965. The final report on the public service and background studies were publicly released in 1969.

70. Canada, House of Commons, *Report of the Proceedings of Debates* (April 6, 1966), p. 3915.

71. Other affected agencies included the Privy Council Office (policy coordination), the department of the Secretary of State (translation services and bilingual programs outside the public service) and the Bilingual Districts Advisory Board established to designate bilingual districts across Canada. The latter were never effectively established.

72. See V.S. Wilson, "Language Policy," in G.B. Doern and V.S. Wilson (eds.), *Issues in Canadian Public Policy* (Toronto: Macmillan of Canada, 1974), pp. 253-85.

73. Canada, "Official Languages in the Public Service of Canada," Resolution adopted by Parliament (mimeo, June 1973).

74. Gilles Bibeau, *Report of the Independent Study on the Language Training Programmes of the Public Service of Canada* (Ottawa: 1976).

75. Royal Commission on Government Organization, *Report*, vol. I, p. 19.

76. See K. Kernaghan, "Changing concepts of power and responsibility in the Canadian public service," *Canadian Public Administration* (Fall 1978), vol. 21, no. 3, pp. 389-406, for a discussion of "values" of public service.

77. Royal Commission on Financial Management and Accountability, *Report*, p. 10.

78. A.W. Johnson, "Efficiency in Government and Business," *Canadian Public Administration* (September 1963), vol. 6, no. 3, p. 248. Reprinted by permission of *Canadian Public Administration*.

79. As the Glassco Commission observed, "But even greater [than efficiency and integrity] is the importance of a service responsive to public wants and expectations. No plan of management and no system of checks and balances can, by themselves, offer guarantees of this responsiveness. This is the test, not merely of the machinery of government, but also—and principally—of the political process by which its goals are set." *Report*, p. 63.

80. Al Johnson describes "service efficiency" as "a heterogeneous group of public service objectives, including service to the public, responsiveness to public opinion, and the preservation of parliamentary control." See Johnson, "Efficiency in Government and Business," p. 249.

81. The role and activities of the Public Service Commission in personnel management has been given limited attention in the discussion, for the focus has been on central *management*. While the Commission is an independent agency, it does play an important role in supporting the executive in personnel-management activities, as noted in the text. The philosophy and orientation of the Commission in the last decade in the personnel-policy field could be distinguished from that of the Board and Secretariat, in that the Board has emphasized the quality of human-relations skills, while the Secretariat has been more concerned with performance and performance measurement. In this sense, the Commission has played a useful role in providing balance to the more technically oriented approach of the Secretariat. For example, see the submission of the Public Service Commission to the Special Committee on Personnel Management and the Merit Principle, Canada, Public Service Commission, "Public Service and Public Interest" (June 1978).

4

Public-Service Managers and Their Departments

The design of management in the federal public service represents at any one time a formula for balancing the interests of central and departmental needs in support of collective and individual ministerial responsibilities. The formula recommended by the Royal Commission on Government Organization in 1962 emphasized the importance of "letting the managers manage," while at the same time it stressed the need for effective central coordination. The new central-management structure discussed in Chapter 3 included the establishment of a separate agency, the Treasury Board Secretariat, that supported the collective-management responsibilities exercised by the Treasury Board.

On the side of departmental management, the effects of the changes brought about by the implementation of the Glassco reforms were essentially twofold. On the one hand, activity was increased within departments in response to initiatives by the Treasury Board Secretariat in the several areas of management reform.[1] On the other hand, the "loosening" of financial, personnel and materiel management controls gave departmental managers more flexibility than before in using resources to meet the objectives of their mandates. In addition, the emphasis placed on policy development during the late 1960s and early 1970s expanded the scope of activities within and between departments as well as between departments and central agencies. Thus, increased management *and* policy responsibilities contributed to a changing environment for departmental management.

These changes brought pressure to bear on senior departmental officials from a number of different sources. For example, as ministers' workloads increased and greater demands were made on their time, they delegated more responsibilities to their deputies, particularly in the area of policy development. Second, the decentralization of certain management functions to departments was accompanied, as noted, by a continuing and pervasive central-agency influence in the form of guidelines, directives and procedures with which departments had to comply. Finally, pressures came from within the departments themselves. The redefinition of mandates and the reorganization of departments constituted a major challenge to departmental managers, who had to ensure that the internal structure of their organizations could provide for the effective performance and delivery of policies and programs. As a result, a high premium was placed on policy expertise—substantive and procedural. Organizational and administrative skills were also in strong demand.

Collectively, senior personnel in the public service represented a highly professional, highly educated senior cadre of career public servants.

Despite the increased professionalization of the public service, particularly within the senior management group, however, the rate and scope of growth and change during this period strained the management system. Quality control was often difficult to maintain. For his part, the Auditor General criticized deficiencies in the area of financial management. On the basis of his studies and reviews of departmental spending, managers were found to be lacking in their ability to maintain control and account for financial resources at their disposal. This issue was pursued by the Royal Commission on Financial Management and Accountability. In the Lambert Commission's view, if the managers were going to manage they also had to be held accountable. The assessment of managers' performance was therefore a primary condition of maintaining effective accountability.

One might argue that in many respects the changes and reforms of the Trudeau administration had the most dramatic impact at the departmental level. Efforts at top-down coordination activated a number of different developments and processes within departments. At the same time, departmental mandates were pushed outward as the range of activities increased and became increasingly differentiated. Lines of responsibility and hence accountability for senior officials often became blurred. From the perspective of the deputy minister in particular, the job environment became both more complex and more constrained.

The Deputy Minister—Responsibilities and Relationships

Deputy ministers provide the link between the political executive and the neutral public service. As the senior managers of agencies who report directly to ministers, they play a key role in ensuring that political decisions are translated into government action. To this end, they exercise considerable influence in the policy and management processes in the public service. The extent of that influence, however, is qualified by a number of factors respecting the sources of their authority and their relationships with their ministers.

As noted in Chapter 2, constitutionally the minister alone is responsible for the policies and administration of a department. The departmental act provides the legal basis for the minister's position and sets out in broad terms the department's mandate. The "powers, duties and functions" and "supervision and control" or "management and direction" of a department are the minister's exclusive responsibility.[2] The departmental act will also provide for the position of the deputy minister, but duties and responsibilities will not normally be assigned to the position.[3] The deputy receives his authority for departmental policy and management functions, in the main, on delegation from the minister. The Interpretation Act, section 23(2), provides the legal basis for this delegation.[4]

The Financial Administration Act and the Public Service Employment Act also provide bases of authority for deputies. Several sections of the Financial Administration Act assign responsibilities to deputies rather than to ministers as, for example, in the areas of financial management,[5] contract performance,[6] and public-property management.[7] This Act also provides for the delegation of personnel-management responsibilities to deputies by the Treasury Board.[8] Under Section 6(1) of the Public Service Employment Act, the Public Service Commission may delegate to deputies authority "to exercise and perform, in such manner and subject to such terms and conditions as the Commission directs, any of the powers, functions and duties of the Commission under the Act" other than those responsibilities relating to appeal and inquiries. In other legislation, such as the Official Languages Act, the deputy head of the department is identified and designated as the individual to whom the Commissioner will direct a complaint or request for corrective action.[9]

The statutory delineation of these responsibilities was the result by and large of the implementation of the Glassco recommendations and, in the case of language policy, subsequent government measures. While the statutes provided specific terms of reference for deputies in support of collective management needs and of particular departmental interests, they also established more limited parameters for the exercise of individual ministerial responsibility. In theory, ministers are responsible for both policy and administration in their departments.

While the formal responsibilities of the position are received by delegation from either the minister or the Treasury Board and Public Service Commission, the nature of the appointment of the deputy minister also has an influence on the exercise of those responsibilities. The selection of deputy ministers, like ministers, is the prerogative of the prime minister. Their formal appointment is made by the Governor-in-Council on the recommendation of the prime minister.[10] Although most deputy ministers are career public servants appointed from among the senior-executive ranks in the public service, upon appointment they become part of the "Governor-in-Council group" of public servants separate from the public service proper.[11]

Deputies are appointed "at pleasure" and may be changed or re-appointed as the prime minister sees fit. The term of the appointment and the lack of tenure associated with it provides the prime minister with the means of ensuring that deputy-ministerial skills are deployed to the best advantage during any particular period of time. This deployment may involve, during the life of a particular administration, the matching of personal and technical skills between minister and deputy. For example, when Mr. Chrétien was moved from the portfolio of President of the Treasury Board to that of Minister of Industry, Trade and Commerce in 1976, Mr. Osbaldeston (who served under him as Secretary of the Treasury Board) was shifted to the position of deputy minister of Industry,

Trade and Commerce a few months after the ministerial move was made. On the other hand, following a change of government such as occurred in 1979, there may be a desire to replace certain deputies who, because of the long term of office of the previous administration, may be perceived to be identified too closely with the latter administration's policies.[12] Technically speaking, however, there is no automatic removal or call for resignations of deputies with a change in government. Professional, not partisan, considerations are the primary criteria for appointment of these senior managers.[13]

On appointment, a deputy normally receives a letter of instruction from the prime minister: it sets out particular goals and objectives for the policy orientation or organization of the department and any other items of priority concern to the government. Because the selection of the deputy is normally conducted in consultation with the minister affected, the instructions to the deputy from the prime minister help to reinforce the collegial nature of the executive and to communicate the government's priorities and objectives to deputy heads. As a result, the prime minister can ensure that the collective interests in government policy are pursued in a balanced and coordinated fashion. His prerogatives to assign responsibilities to ministers and to organize government departments to support such assignments, combined with his prerogative to appoint ministers *and* deputy ministers, are primary instruments by which collective responsibility is exercised. Deputies, like their ministers, are part of a team. By managing individual departments, they also support the collective efforts of the government. During periods of major policy change and government reorganization such as those which occurred in the last fifteen years, the ability of deputies to respond to new directions and to support changing collective interests is a crucial element of good performance.

Thus, the formal and informal bases of the deputy's responsibilities serve to demonstrate how the principles of individual and collective ministerial responsibility pertain to him. On the one hand, he is responsible to his minister, to whom he owes his first loyalty. It is the minister who by and large delegates the responsibilities of office to the deputy. On the other hand, deputies have a collective responsibility for the management of the public service on the basis of delegation from the central-management body, the Treasury Board, and the central staffing agency, the Public Service Commission. Their collective allegiance to the prime minister and the cabinet is best reflected in the nature of their appointment. Thus, the position of a deputy is conditioned by a number of vertical and horizontal relationships with individuals and institutions that define and influence his responsibilities.

It is interesting to note, from the several excellent appendices to the Lambert Commission Report, which responsibilities the majority of deputies perceived as being the most important. They included:

- managing my executive team
- assuring economy and efficiency in operations
- supporting my minister
- ensuring that my department is responsive to the policy thrusts of the government
- providing the government with sound policy advice.[14]

One can see in this list a mix of those responsibilities that might be said to fall into the category of supporting individual ministerial responsibilities and those supporting collective ministerial responsibilities. However, in indicating persons and organizations to whom deputies considered themselves responsible for these specific subjects, responsibility to the minister ranked highest. There was also a high ranking of the responsibility of the deputy to himself, especially for subjects relating to management and management practices in his departments. The Treasury Board Secretariat and the Public Service Commission were ranked low overall for all subjects. However, while responsibility to their minister was recognized as paramount, deputies did acknowledge varying degrees of influence that central agencies can have on departmental policy and programs and departmental management.[15]

The primary duties and functions of the deputy therefore derive from his relationship with his minister. The deputy serves as chief policy adviser to his minister and senior administrative officer of his department.[16] Although the minister may seek out advice and consult with the political advisers in his office,[17] officials in the central agencies and, occasionally, representatives of external policy advisory groups, the deputy and the department provide the main source of policy advice on day-to-day matters and long-term issues. With respect to the operation and management of departmental programs, the minister relies almost exclusively on the deputy minister.

It is widely accepted that a minister should not be expected to try to be involved in the purely administrative aspects of his department, but the deputy must be involved in both policy and administrative activities.[18] Policy cannot be formed and measures to give it effect cannot be determined without the knowledge and experience the department possesses. At the same time, the department is dependent in executing policy on continuous guidance, direction and authority from the minister. The relationship is therefore one of partnership—complementary, not competitive, in nature.[19] In this way, policy and administration are melded in the functions and responsibilities of the deputy.

The extent of the power and influence a deputy can wield in that relationship nevertheless cannot be definitely determined. There are those who would argue that, given the professional expertise and resources of the department and the continuity and permanence of appointed (as opposed to elected) officials, the deputy does play a dominant role in relations with his minister.[20] The minister is prevented from exercising a strong personal influence because of the complexity of policy and program development resulting from the need for coordinating different departmental and agency activities, the numerous actors involved in different parts of the federal public service and, often, in the public services of other jurisdictions. The deputy is often much better situated to orchestrate the performances required to get results in his department as well as in other parts of the public service. The minister is the "outsider" to the bureaucratic world and its established rules and norms of operation.[21]

Much of what transpires between ministers and deputies nevertheless is cloaked in secrecy. Confidentiality is of the essence. There are no Canadian equivalents of the Crossman diaries,[22] which appeared in Great Britain several years ago and which documented in minute detail the difficulties one minister experienced in attempting to get his own way in his ministry. The evidence that we do have from biographies, autobiographies and other writings of and by former ministers and deputies in the Canadian government suggests that, generally speaking, the partnership concept is appreciated and pursued by both parties.[23] Deputies are recognized to have influence by virtue of the positions they hold, but their authority is checked because it is delegated, usually from the minister. In the final analysis, it is the minister, not the deputy, who makes the decisions, even though much of the detail of the decision may be left to the deputy.[24]

It is important to a deputy to have a strong minister, an individual who is not easily led by his advisers but one who takes an interest in the affairs of his department. Leadership in the first instance comes from the minister and the role of the deputy is facilitated greatly if his minister exerts a strong influence on the direction of activities in the department and, even more importantly, represents his department's interests effectively in cabinet. The political strength of a minister in cabinet, from the deputy's point of view, is often a key factor in determining how well the department may be able to execute policies and programs.

It is also important that the deputy be able to work effectively with his peers in the bureaucracy. He must work in concert with the Privy Council Office, especially with the Office's senior officials and the officials in the cabinet secretariats; these officials serve the cabinet committees to ensure that appropriate coordination between and among government policies and programs occurs and, indeed, that the government's policies are followed. The deputy must work in concert with senior officials in the several branches of the Treasury Board Secretariat to ensure that central-management policies and guidelines are complied with and that appropriate resources are obtained for departmental operations. He must also work with senior officials in the Public Service Commission to ensure that the staffing and the development of employees meets his department's needs.[25]

The individual and collective processes in respect to the responsibilities of deputies form an intricate and complex web of relationships with a number of different individuals and agencies in government. Lines of responsibility overlap and occasionally intersect, but, as indicated above, deputies understand their primary responsibility to their ministers well. The problem of accountability, as currently defined, pertains in large part to developing appropriate systems of accountability based on the lines of responsibility. In practical terms, the complexity of the relationships of which deputies are a part creates a highly constrained environment within which they must work.

The changing context of public-service management and the accelerated pace of activity in government served to broaden the scope and to increase the burdens of office for deputies. The focus on policy making that pervaded the structuring and reorganizing of government departments during the last decade or more, for example, served to enhance the deputy's responsibility for the provision of policy advice and to extend his authority for departmental administration. He was no longer anonymous in the traditional sense of public-service anonymity, in that he was known to play—and was often responsible for playing—a significant role in policy making and in managing his department.[26]

The changing context of public-service management also had an impact on the composition of the senior cadre. The demand for new skills and specialized knowledge was reflected in the types of individuals appointed to these positions. As a group, deputies had a high level of formal education. In 1967, 93 per cent of deputies had one or more university degrees; in 1977, the percentage had increased to 96.7 per cent.[27] Of the latter group, over 80 per cent had two or more degrees. The disciplines in which these degrees were received were concentrated in the social and management sciences and economics, as contrasted with the humanities and law or particular specialized fields in the sciences represented in deputy-minister groups of earlier decades.[28] In 1977, the average age of deputies was 49.8 years; the average age on appointment was 45.4 years.[29] Furthermore, an overwhelming majority—73 per cent in 1967 and 70 per cent in 1977—had spent their entire career in the federal public service.[30]

This profile represents the highly professional nature of senior management in the public service as well as the complementary nature of the skills required for the jobs undertaken. The scope of the demands on deputies requires a broad range of skills in both the management and policy areas. Let us examine some of these activities.

The Deputy Minister and His Senior Managers

The effectiveness of a deputy's performance is in large part a function of his ability to select and to manage individuals in his department. His management team may be defined as those individuals who occupy

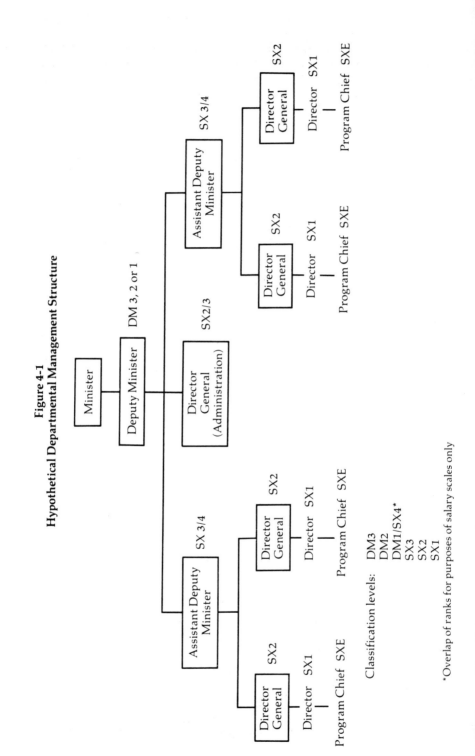

Figure 4-1
Hypothetical Departmental Management Structure

Minister

Deputy Minister   DM 3, 2 or 1

Director General (Administration)   SX2/3

Assistant Deputy Minister   SX 3/4

Assistant Deputy Minister   SX 3/4

Director General   SX2

Director   SX1

Program Chief   SXE

Director General   SX2

Director   SX1

Program Chief   SXE

Director General   SX2

Director   SX1

Program Chief   SXE

Director General   SX2

Director   SX1

Program Chief   SXE

Classification levels: DM3
DM2
DM1/SX4*
SX3
SX2
SX1

*Overlap of ranks for purposes of salary scales only

senior-executive positions in his department.[31] While the deputy is appointed by the Governor-in-Council, the senior-executive positions below him are filled by appointment under the Public Service Employment Act.

As discussed in Chapter 3, the authorization for jobs or positions in the several departments and agencies of government is obtained through the expenditure budgetary process. Departments request the number of positions required to carry out departmental activities, along with the funds required, in the program estimates submitted to the Treasury Board Secretariat and subsequently directed to the Treasury Board and cabinet. Formal approval is obtained when the Estimates are passed by Parliament.

The actual deployment of the positions thus authorized involves other stages of planning and organization in the department. Deputies receive authority to organize their departments and to classify positions up to the senior-executive level on delegation from the Treasury Board pursuant to the Financial Administration Act. Departmental reorganizations that required the reclassification of senior-executive posts would involve the Organization and Classification Division of the Secretariat and the Co-ordinating Committee of Officials.[32] Since most departmental reorganizations will affect senior-executive positions, the Treasury Board in effect can exercise control over the deputy for the internal organization of his department and the number of senior-management positions in it.

The staffing of the senior management positions is done by the Public Service Commission. The Commission has delegated authority to deputies for staffing departmental positions *except* those in the senior-executive (SX) category to maintain high standards in the selection of executive manpower and to provide for the effective deployment of executives across the public service as a whole. The Executive Staffing Programme maintains an inventory of all individuals in the SX category as well as an inventory of those individuals in the top two levels of some twenty or more occupational groups from which senior-executive candidates may be drawn.[33]

For his part, the deputy must seek out individuals with a variety of different skills in assembling his management team. If the mandate of his department is mainly policy oriented, he will need to recruit senior executives who have had policy experience—preferably in the substantive policy field in which the department is involved or in a related area. Organizational and administrative skills are also important. Organization and personnel are key instruments which may be used to assist in the achievement of policy goals. Finally, "process" expertise is advantageous. In particular, experience in a central agency or in intergovernmental relations is a useful asset, for it can assist an individual's ability to gain support for policy initiatives on an interdepartmental and intergovern-mental level. Substantive policy expertise can be provided by professional staff if the manager lacks specialization, but process skills cannot be delegated in the same way.

If the mandate of the department is program oriented, then the deputy must seek out individuals with experience in the administration of program operations. In recent years, experience in regional field operations has been considered an important asset. Since the operation of programs and the development of new programs require resources, experience in the Treasury Board Secretariat—especially the Programme Branch—is often highly valued.

The rapid growth in the senior-executive ranks reflected by and large the impact of policy orientations of departments and agencies as well as the expansion of government programs. Given the high premium placed on policy skills, however, individuals engaged in these activities were often promoted to fill executive positions and moved rapidly within those ranks. This upward mobility was nevertheless accomplished at a cost of not fully developing individual managerial skills.[34]

In the first instance, the emphasis placed on recruiting individuals with general administrative skills in areas such as financial and personnel management varied from department to department. Given the decentralization of authority in these areas recommended by the Glassco Commission, the Commission also proposed the appointment of senior financial officers and chief personnel officers in the departments to be responsible for these functions. In practice, the creation of these positions in the departments did not always situate the incumbents of these posts at very senior levels in the departmental hierarchy, nor were they involved in a meaningful way in overall planning activities in the departments. In his 1976 report, the Auditor General directed scathing criticism at the lack of financial-administrative expertise among senior managers in the departments generally. Not only was financial management being neglected as a specific area of departmental activity, but also few senior managers had gained any expertise in this area before reaching a senior level. The Lambert Commission echoed the concerns of the Auditor General and recommended measures for improving financial- and personnel-management activities in departments that in some ways approximated those put forward by the Glassco Commission seventeen years earlier.[35]

Second, the difficulties of recruiting individuals with a balanced combination of policy and administrative skills were not easy ones to address. The complexity of departmental activities often required that so-called generalists be specialized to some degree. For example, the policy manager required not only a broad understanding of policy issues and processes across the public service but also a good grasp of the particular policy field of his department. The amount of time devoted to these activities left little room for acquiring general administrative skills. Similarly, the program manager had administrative experience that might have been concentrated in one or two areas of management. Moreover, he might have had little or no experience in policy activities. Unless an individual's career was carefully planned or directed, he could reach and indeed advance through the executive ranks without gaining a broad range of policy and administrative experience.

Thus, the deputy's role in assembling his management team could be fraught with frustration not only by the control exercised by the Treasury Board Secretariat and the Public Service Commission in the authorization of positions and the staffing of the positions, but also by the lack of control over the development of management potential in the executive ranks and in those ranks immediately below the executive level. The system of career advancement that existed within these groups could appropriately be described as entrepreneurial in nature.

Opportunities for career advancement in the public service are perhaps unique to most institutional settings. A public servant is an employee of a single organization (department) that is only one part of the total organization (the public service) in which he may be eligible for employment and advancement. The mobility of personnel between departments and agencies was facilitated by the classification system put into place with the introduction of collective bargaining, which provides for common occupational categories and groups across the public service. Individuals in professional categories, for example, can move easily from department to department. From the deputy's viewpoint, however, this contributes to considerable turnover in his department and reduces his ability to develop managerial expertise in his staff.

The desirability of identifying a middle-management group was first expressed by the Advisory Group on Executive Compensation in the Public Service in 1971. While initially the proposal was put forth as a measure to enlarge the size of the group excluded from collective bargaining,[36] the idea was pursued subsequently as a means of improving the development of managerial skills and enhancing career development generally.[37] The development of manpower inventories by the Treasury Board Secretariat and the Public Service Commission facilitated the gradual development of such a group, although deputy-ministerial involvement has been limited. For its part, the Lambert Commission recommended that deputies be responsible for developing departmental-management-succession and career-development plans and for promoting other measures of career development.[38] Generally speaking, managerial development has received greater attention in recent years than previously.

While career planning is desirable from the point of view of developing skilled managers and improving managerial performance, it must be balanced against a system of selection and advancement based on competition for positions. Management-succession plans, if rigorously developed and administered, could be perceived as closing the ranks at the senior-management level. The development of an elitist senior cadre has been resisted in the past, despite periodic efforts to establish a formal process to select individuals for executive positions and to control individual advancement thereafter. Until recently, only a select group of outstanding senior executives, commonly referred to inside the public service as the "high flyers," have had directed career paths. If career management were extended systematically and rigorously throughout the senior- and middle-management ranks, it could reduce managerial flexibility in staffing and individual choice in career development, which in turn could result in organizational rigidity.

For the deputy, the recruitment of qualified and experienced managers is essential to the effective operation of his department and to the fulfillment of the departmental mandate. His role in the development of these skills and expertise is important, but often the time needed to devote to these activities is superseded by other demands. On the whole, however, the quality of management skills in the public service is and has been considerable given the size and scope of activities. The following discussion will demonstrate how these skills have been applied in particular areas.

Departmental Policy and Planning Structures

It has been stated that departments' activities in general tend to be policy oriented or program oriented. Nevertheless, in fulfilling their mandates, most departments have developed some combination of policy and program functions. For example, a department such as National Health and Welfare—which is mainly responsible for operating health and welfare programs—maintains a policy-planning capability in its organization. In contrast, a Ministry of State such as Science and Technology allocates most, if not all, of its resources to policy functions.

The pervading philosophy of departmental operations in the last decade, whatever their orientation, focused on the need for planning—that is, the establishment of objectives—the development of appropriate courses of action and, where possible, the measurement of results of activities within a given time frame. The extent to which public services, functioning as they do in highly charged political environments, can rigorously and systematically engage in planning processes is debatable,[39] but that does not deny the basic administrative need to organize resources and to plan activities towards the achievement of a given set of goals.

The impact on departments of organizational changes and management innovations undertaken in response to central agency initiatives in planning and administrative reform during the late 1960s and early 1970s was significant. The creation and reorganization of a large number of departments mentioned earlier and the concomitant redefinition of and addition to their mandates generated a high level of activity within departments directed toward developing new policy directions, designing new programs and providing new services. Coordination and liaison activities between and across departments also increased in an endeavour to ensure complementarity between related policies and programs. The implementation of PPBS and other related management techniques such as management by objectives and operational-performance measurement systems similarly generated a high degree of activity in departments.

In an effort to respond to these changes and reforms, departments adapted their internal organizational structures in a variety of ways.[40] At the senior-management level, three types of organizations emerged: corporate branches under an assistant deputy minister, small staff groups which reported directly to the deputy minister and single advisers who also normally had a direct reporting relationship to the deputy. At the program level within the department, planning and evaluation units were established as: staff groups to programs, units within the programs themselves and, in regional operations, staff groups to regional-program operations. Thus, these units functioned mainly in a staff role to line management.[41]

The functions these units have performed cover a broad range of activities influenced by the general orientation of the department. A planning unit or branch in a policy-oriented department, for example, may in fact concentrate on policy development—that is, the development of objectives and proposals that may provide the framework for the development of different kinds of programs. Planning in this context is focused at a fairly high level in the organization and usually encompasses a broad overview of departmental activities.

For program-oriented departments, the planning function is often more specifically focused on program design and program evaluation. Planning in this context involves the development of departmental objectives in support of its mandate and the development of departmental strategies or approaches for achieving those objectives. The development and adaptation of programs would follow from these activities. Program evaluation would involve analyzing departmental programs to determine if they succeeded in achieving the intended objectives. In both types of departments, one would also find strategic and/or long-range planning as well as research, coordination and liaison functions as components of the policy and program activities in the planning units.

While distinctions may be made to describe the several organizational designs and the types of functions that the planning units perform, in practical terms the manner in which organization and function are integrated in any one departmental setting can include a number of combinations of forms and activities.[42] For example, one "basic" model for a policy-oriented department, such as a ministry of state, could include a number of special single advisers and separate policy and research, coordination and liaison as well as evaluation branches at the corporate level.

Figure 4-2
Policy-Oriented Department: Model 1

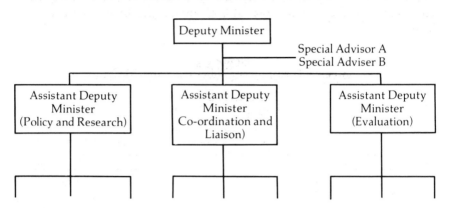

Program-oriented departments tend to concentrate planning units at the program level in both staff and 'within program' locations. For example, one model for a program department might include: a policy or planning staff group reporting directly to the deputy minister, and staff groups for programs, as well as planning and evaluation groups within programs, plus program and evaluation groups in the field operations:

Figure 4-3
Program-Oriented Department: Model 2

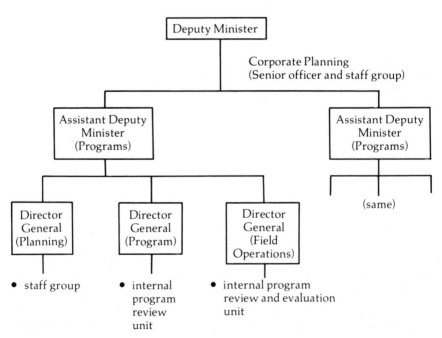

An integrated model is conceivable for departments attempting to fulfill a major policy mandate as well as program responsibilities. One could combine the various units at both the corporate and the program level:

Figure 4-4
Integrated Program and Policy Functions: Model 3

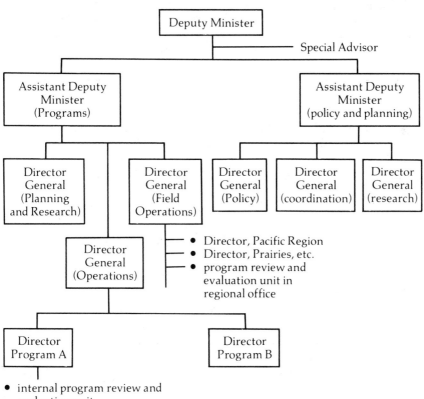

The policy and planning structures can thus constitute the total structure of the department in the case of a policy-oriented department or be superimposed and/or integrated in a program-oriented department. In the case of a program-oriented department, there was also a trend to identify the program units with the program activity structure. That is to say, a department, in identifying its major program activities as community employment services, manpower centres, and manpower retraining, for example, would establish within the department a community-employment division or branch, a manpower division or branch and so on. In this way, the internal organization of a department would visibly support and be focused on the several objectives in the departmental mandate.

The establishment of planning units in their various policy and program forms within departments gave rise to a veritable "boom" in the planning business in government. The technical skills in greatest demand for these positions were those held by individuals in the ESS (Economist, Sociologist and Statistician) and PM (Program Manager) groups. Economists topped the list of the classifications of positions in these units.[43] Support staff for the professionals was drawn mainly from the SI (Social Science Support) and AS (Administrative Support) groups. The total community of individuals engaged in these activities, however, was not large. In 1975, it was estimated that they numbered about 3500 in twenty-eight departments.[44] The SX and SXE/man-year ratio in these units was high. As noted earlier, most of the growth in the SX ranks during the early 1970s was attributed to the creation of these units.

In sum, in undertaking policy- and program-planning activities, these units performed several functions as staff structures reporting to line management. On the average they have probably been most successful in those departments that placed a premium on policy functions and in which they did not have to compete with other parts of the organization in gaining recognition for the services they might render. Firefighting activities, while not integral to broader planning activities, provided opportunities for establishing the credibility of the units in the departments.[45] The manner in which they were incorporated into the departmental structure was nevertheless determined by the nature of the departmental mandate. Above all, they provided bases of expertise used by senior managers to discharge their policy- and program-planning functions.

Departmental Policy and Planning Activities

As noted above, the internal departmental policy and planning structures were in large measure responses to changes in central-agency processes. They provided the capability for departments to respond to top-down direction, which in the first instance was provided by cabinet and its committees. The political goals and policy priorities established by cabinet set the framework within which departments would determine their priorities and develop proposals and plans of action. Thus, the process represented both a top-down and bottom-up exercise. By far the major portion of cabinet business was and continues to be departmental initiatives. A critical feature of these interactions between cabinet and the central agencies on the one hand and the departments on the other was the need for coordination. The particular instruments and processes by departments to develop their proposals and communicate them to ministers and central agency officials are discussed below.

Policy Advice

There are several instruments by which policy advice is transmitted from the department to the minister. Although the deputy may meet daily with his minister for oral exchanges on immediate and short-term problems, he will normally have one or several "briefing notes" prepared in advance or in concert with his meetings with the minister to discuss policy issues affecting the department. The briefing note will contain a concise description and assessment of an issue, including recommendations on courses of action to be taken. Given the large number of issues arising at any one time and the high degree of technicality of most matters, the briefing note is likely to be used extensively in most departmental settings and will occupy a considerable portion of the time of professional staff.

Departments also undertake in-depth analyses and long-range research studies as bases for establishing policy objectives and proposals for the department. The results of these studies may be reviewed at the senior-management level and/or provide background material for a cabinet memorandum. The cabinet memorandum is *the* formal policy instrument that is prepared in the departments and presented by the deputy to the minister. The format of the document is structured in such a way to provide ministers with an assessment of a problem or proposal (purpose, background, factors), a range of possible alternatives, relevant considerations (federal-provincial relations, public relations, caucus considerations) as well as a set of recommendations. As the process of cabinet and cabinet committee consideration of departmental memoranda became formalized after 1968, there was a tendency to increase not only the number of memoranda that a department might prepare, but also the size of the documents—particularly on highly technical matters. Many of them were fairly lengthy treatises.[46] In an endeavour to reduce the volume of the material that ministers were required to read, the format of the document was changed in 1977 to include two parts: the political memorandum that sets out the essential issues to ministers; and an accompanying technical document of greater length providing detailed analyses of issues and alternatives.[47]

A large portion of time—second only to that required for planning and research—that goes into the preparation of a cabinet memorandum is devoted to interdepartmental meetings, which are held while a policy proposal is being formulated by departmental officials. Consultation and coordination may lead to compromises on the proposal to accommodate conflicting interests between departments. The result may often be a watered-down facsimile of the original proposal.[48] Coordination and liaison are essential activities, however, in preparing a cabinet memorandum—particularly one on a major policy issue. In supporting a minister, it is incumbent upon the deputy and his officials to ensure that, to the greatest extent possible, interdepartmental conflicts are resolved before the document reaches the minister for final approval. Any outstanding issues will be resolved at the political level.

In the consultations during the preparation of a memorandum, the deputy and departmental officials will also liaise closely with officials in the Privy Council Office. Departmental officials working on a document are well advised to contact cabinet committee-secretariat officials when the memorandum is in the early drafting stage. A Privy Council officer can be asked to attend departmental or interdepartmental meetings in the course of the memorandum preparation. A draft of the document may be sent to the Privy Council Office before it is submitted by the deputy to the minister, as a final check that there are no outstanding issues or conflicts which might be resolved before the minister proposes the recommendations he approves to cabinet committee. The secretariats of the operational cabinet committees play an important role in smoothing the way and preparing the ground for the consideration of a departmental policy proposal.

Ministerial involvement in the process of cabinet memoranda preparation may vary from subject to subject. On major issues, the minister would likely request the deputy to prepare a document and provide general direction on its substance. Depending on its importance, he could be consulted at different stages of its development and exchange views with the deputy on the nature of the recommendations. Thus, a memorandum presented by a deputy to his minister would reflect the minister's views before the latter formally approved. In cases in which close consultation had not taken place beforehand, the deputy could run the risk of having his advice rejected by the minister, even though he may have obtained support for it on an interdepartmental basis. The general rule that officials can provide expert advice but ministers make the decisions is an important one.

The stages of cabinet committee and cabinet consideration can involve a minister's sponsoring a major policy proposal in a lengthy process. For example, a minister could present a memorandum to his colleagues for approval in principle of a new policy orientation for his department (resulting from a major departmental policy-review exercise, for example). If approval was obtained, a second document setting out concrete courses of action to be taken could be required. This document could include specific program proposals or a more detailed statement of the policy. If legislative change was required, particularly if it involved the drafting of a new bill, a third document including the draft bill would be necessary, unless the legislation had been prepared and attached to an earlier memorandum. In other words, in the case of major policy reviews, it would be possible that three documents and three separate rounds of cabinet committee and cabinet review would be required.[49]

The importance of these documents to departmental activities is self-evident. They are the formal instruments of confidential policy advice from the deputy to the minister. In turn, the minister sponsors these proposals in cabinet committee and cabinet to seek approval from his colleagues. The resulting cabinet decision provides an authoritative base for departments to undertake recommended courses of action. Thus, individual departmental initiatives require collective support of the executive. While the range of matters brought to cabinet may be broad and vary in importance, even relatively insignificant housekeeping issues may be critical to a department's overall policy and program activities.

Expenditure Plans

Expenditure planning, in contrast to policy development, is focused more directly on management and administrative activities in the department. Expenditure planning serves as a mechanism for internal coordination and control as well as for ongoing program development and program delivery. The Glassco Commission, in stressing the need for planning in departments, recommended that the program forecasts and program estimates serve as the key planning documents in the departments. The preparation of long-range forecasts and annual budgets would be an integrated activity to provide basic plans for resource needs and resource deployment for departmental operations.

It was intended that the establishment of government priorities by cabinet and of expenditure guidelines by the Treasury Board would provide the necessary first step in this planning process. The establishment of departmental objectives would mainly take into account the departmental mandate, the government's priorities and the expenditure guidelines. Departmental objectives in turn would provide the framework within which departmental program activities would be organized and developed. To that end, the introduction of PPBS was envisaged as the critical management tool to facilitate and coordinate these activities. As one author has commented:

> PPBS is, in theory, the answer to a manager's prayer. It is a system designed to rationalize the whole resource management spectrum from setting objectives and the logical selection of alternative courses of action to the measurement of returns for expenditures made. Objectives are formulated in a hierarchy, descending from national, to federal, to departmental, to program, to sub-program, to activity, to sub-activity objectives.[50]

In practice, PPBS had an uneven impact in its application in departments. Of the several key-activity stages,[51] efforts were often concentrated on objective-setting and program-design activities. In addition the application of PPBS was limited by and large to the budgetary process in the department and not integrated into broader departmental planning activities.

Thus, departmental planning took the form of two separate sets of activities. At the corporate level, planning activities focused on policy and program design. Proposals emanating from these activities would go forward to the minister for consideration and in some cases be presented to cabinet for approval if new undertakings were involved. At the program level, planning was focused on program activities and resource-allocation matters; these were coordinated through senior departmental administrative officers who coordinated the preparation of budget submissions to Treasury Board. Program evaluation was often absent or a minor activity at the corporate level and applied in a limited way at the program level.

The lack of integration between the two kinds of planning activities in departments contributed to the anomalous situation, referred to earlier, in which departments would seek approval from cabinet for new programs. Once approval in principle was obtained, departments would then use the expenditure budgetary process (often the supplementary-estimates route) to obtain resources. Since cabinet approval in principle was in a manner of speaking already obtained, it was difficult for ministers to deny the department the resources required.[52] Changes made in 1976 required departments to identify resources needed for new program proposals in the original submission to cabinet, and Treasury Board review of the same before final cabinet consideration. This approach to integrating program proposal and resource allocation consideration was carried further in 1979 with the introduction of the resource-envelope system, which required that departmental plans for program activities and resource requirements be scrutinized simultaneously by appropriate cabinet committees.[53]

The several processes involved with these activities bring departmental officials into regular contact with central-agency officials, particularly those in the Treasury Board Secretariat. Central agency assistance and support may be needed in preparing departmental plans and program estimates to ensure consonance with government priorities and expenditure guidelines. The implementation of new management techniques to improve planning processes and practices in turn requires consultation between departments and the Secretariat. The competitive process— which underlies resource-allocation decision making in particular—influences the pattern of interactions and relationships between and among the officials in the different agencies.

The term "planning" has been used rather loosely in this discussion, in that it has been applied to corporate planning and expenditure planning in the department. Both exercises relate to program design and implementation but, as noted above, have not always been integrated undertakings. The expenditure-planning process provides one kind of time frame in which the planning of departmental activities can be pursued with some degree of regularity. However, constantly changing political and economic circumstances—even during periods of majority government—may require continual reformulation of new and ongoing program activities.

A main value of planning activities is that they do require the establishment of goals and objectives and the compilation of information that can be applied in decision making and used in evaluation and assessment of performance. However, there are limits to these activities. The Lambert Commission recommendations on the preparation of a five-year Fiscal Plan for overall government activities and departmental strategic plans, for example, may be viewed as means of obtaining better (and perhaps different) information than that obtained under the expenditure-guideline and program-forecast exercises; the recommendations can also be viewed as a means of ensuring a greater degree of integration between and among the several policy, program and resource-allocation functions of departments and central agencies. However, given the multiple objectives of most government policies and programs and the competitive process of resource allocation, it is unlikely that any major changes can be made to make objectives easier to define or methods of measurement easier to develop.[54] Efforts for coordinated departmental planning can provide improved integration of related activities within the department and in turn between the department and other agencies, but these efforts must be continuous and sustained to have much impact.

Accountability and Performance Assessment

The numerous policy and administrative reforms initiated during the period of rapid expansion of government activity in the late 1960s and early 1970s contributed to the development of a highly complex environment for public-service management. In many respects, the senior departmental official and his subordinates bore the brunt of the reforms because they were required to respond to increased demands from their minister on policy and program needs as well as from the central management on planning and administrative matters. In the process, their role in supporting the individual and collective responsibilities of ministers was complicated by an increasingly complex network of vertical and horizontal relationships. As attention became focused on accountability in government through criticisms made by the Auditor General and the subsequent Royal Commission on Financial Management and Accountability, the role of public-service managers came under careful scrutiny. In considering the means by which deputies are held accountable for their actions, therefore, a reexamination of responsibilities and relationships is in order.

In the first instance, deputy ministers—and departmental officials through their deputy—are accountable to their ministers for the actions and activities they undertake on his behalf. Traditionally, ministerial accountability has pertained to both policy and administrative responsibilities. In practice, however, responsibility for the administration of the department has been assumed primarily by the deputy minister. Moreover, the deputy also supports the exercise of collective responsibility and is accountable to central authorities such as the Treasury Board for the performance of particular responsibilities delegated or assigned to him. Thus, the deputy's relationship with the Treasury Board and its Secretariat on administrative matters of resource allocation and financial and personnel administration requires some balance of accountability to the minister individually and to the government collectively.

Second, responsibility to the minister for departmental matters can be affected by the need for coordination and collaboration with other departments on related policies and programs. Normally, one department will act as a "lead agency" on such undertakings, but direct accountability to the minister may be diluted in these cases. Thus, the onus often falls on the deputy to ensure that the department's and hence the minister's primary responsibility in such a case is well protected.

For their part, deputies are held accountable to their ministers on a daily basis in the support that they are required to provide ministers on policy and administrative matters. In broader terms, deputies are held accountable by their ministers and by their peers through an annual process of performance assessment. In its first report in 1968, the Advisory Group on Executive Compensation in the Public Service recommended that a Committee of Senior Officials be established for the purpose of evaluating senior personnel performance.[55] This Committee, which was created in 1969, is chaired by the prime minister's senior adviser on executive personnel and comprises four permanent members and four rotating members. This process of peer-group evaluation of deputy-ministerial performance takes into account ministerial assessments of the deputy and assessments made by the Secretaries to the Cabinet, the Secretary of the Treasury Board and the Chairman of the Public Service Commission as well as other senior colleagues.[56] Thus, all aspects of the deputy's responsibilities from policy to administration are considered. This type of appraisal is an important instrument for ensuring that deputies comply with central-administrative standards of performance as well as those of the minister. It is important to note, however, that evaluations of effectiveness will vary with the evaluator. There are, as discussed in Chapter 3, different kinds of efficiency and effectiveness in the affairs of government. The results that may be satisfying to a minister may not be satisfying to central-management officials or vice versa. In such cases, if problems arise, the prime minister makes the final assessment.

The development and increasing sophistication of the performance-appraisal process has not been considered by some to meet the needs of improving deputy-ministerial accountability, particularly as it pertains to the discharge of administrative responsibilities. The principle of ministerial responsibility presumes that the minister alone and the cabinet collectively are accountable to the House of Commons for their actions. The argument has been made that, since the deputy has assumed the major portion of responsibility for departmental administration, he should be held accountable in an appropriate fashion to the House. In particular, the Lambert Commission recommended that the deputy be designated as the Chief Administrative Officer of the department and "be liable to be called to account directly for their assigned and delegated responsibilities before the parliamentary committee most directly concerned with administrative performance, the Public Accounts Committee."[57] The idea of designating the deputy minister as chief administrative officer is borrowed from the British practice of permanent heads of departments' being designated as accounting officers and appearing before the Public Accounts Committee.[58] However, British and Canadian practice differ, in that the former system is well established and governed by accepted rules and procedures, while the latter system is less developed. Policy and administrative issues are raised before the Public Accounts Committee in the Canadian House, but its proceedings could not be construed as entirely nonpartisan as in the British case.[59]

Deputies and other senior officials *do* appear before standing committees of the House to assist ministers in answering questions on administrative matters. So long as the exercise of ministerial responsibility is not called into question—particularly on matters of policy—the deputy's responsibility to his minister and his minister's responsibility to the House are maintained in appropriate fashion. There is nothing to prevent standing committees including the Public Accounts Committee from developing more systematic and formal practices of scrutiny of departmental administration if they so choose, to improve the means of ministerial accountability to the House for departmental matters.[60]

In the final analysis, perhaps the best guarantee for ensuring that the accountability of senior officials can be maintained effectively lies in the development of sound policy and managerial skills in the senior-executive ranks. It has already been noted that increased emphasis has been placed on executive development in recent years. The increased professionalization of the senior ranks combined with the emphasis on specialized training programs and experience in all facets of management has evolved and continues to develop. Considerable experience has been gained in applying effective means to foster this development.

For example, the Glassco Commission recommended the regular rotation of deputy ministers as a means of developing senior managerial skills. This practice, which was adopted by the Trudeau administration, was premised on the assumption that the several functions of departmental administration were common throughout the public service and

that the skills needed for departmental administration could be characterized as generalist rather than specialist.[61] For the period 1968-79, rotation
was fairly frequent, as seen in Table 4-1. The total population of the
individuals who were appointed to these thirty positions was eighty-three.
Thus, while the rate of rotation during the period was fairly high, the
turnover of personnel was moderate.

The effect of the fairly high rate of rotation of deputies was double-
edged. On the one hand, rotated tours of duty assisted deputies in developing expertise across a broad range of departmental activities and in

Table 4-1
Rotation of Deputy Ministers, 1968-79

Deputy-minister position	Number of incumbents, 1968-79
Secretary to the Cabinet	2
Secretary to the Cabinet for Federal-Provincial Relations	1
Agriculture	3
Communications	3
Consumer and Corporate Affairs	5
Defence	3
Employment and Immigration	4
Energy, Mines and Resources	6
Environment	3
External Affairs	4
Finance	4
Indian Affairs and Northern Development	3
Industry, Trade and Commerce	5
Justice	3
Labour	4
National Health and Welfare	3
National Revenue (Taxation)	4
(Customs)	5
Post Office	3
Public Works	5
Regional Economic Expansion	4
Science and Technology	3
Solicitor General	4
State	5
Supply and Services (Supply)	3
(Services)	2
Transport	3
Treasury Board	5
Urban Affairs	3
Veterans Affairs	3

Sources: These figures were drawn from a listing made of deputy-minister appointments from
1968 to 1979. The listing was based on information obtained from the *Canadian Parliamentary
Guides* for the period as well as press releases from the Prime Minister's Office and was
checked against orders-in-council appointments published in the *Canada Gazette*.

the process honed their general administrative skills. On the other hand, a change in job every two years on the average provided a very short time frame in which to pursue with some degree of continuity the development and consolidation of departmental activities and undertakings. In recognition of this problem, the rate of rotation was reduced from the mid-1970s, in advance of the Lambert Commission recommendation for a tour of duty of at least three to five years.[62]

A critical and continuing issue respecting the performance of senior departmental officials pertains to the broad scope of responsibilities they are expected to discharge. Efforts to improve individual management abilities will have limited impact if the time required to discharge policy and administrative responsibilities is not available. Priorities must be set and, in the case of the deputy minister, they will be determined by the needs of the minister.

The problems of the increased burdens of office of the senior departmental official might be addressed by splitting the policy responsibilities from the position and appointing a senior policy adviser. It would be expected that he would maintain a formal reporting relationship through the deputy to the minister. The deputy would be able to devote his full time to management and administrative matters. This suggestion was in fact made in 1968 by the Fulton Committee on the Civil Service in Great Britain.[63] The idea is an attractive one in the sense that it would relieve the deputy of his main policy responsibilities. In practice, however, the possibility of conflicts between and among the minister and his two senior officials could be substantial if concerted efforts were not made to delineate responsibilities precisely, as difficult as that might be.

In the final analysis, the current dilemma of the deputy minister is similar to that of the minister. Increased burdens of office forced ministers to delegate greater responsibilities to their deputies in both policy and administrative spheres. The deputy in turn has inherited the problem and must seek ways and means of delegating responsibilities while maintaining effective accountability for them.

Notes

1. See H.L. Laframboise, "Administrative Reform in the Federal Public Service: Signs of a Saturation Psychosis," *Canadian Public Administration* (1971), vol. 20, no. 4, pp. 303-25.

2. These are the normal statutory phrases designating the responsibilities of ministers. They provide the authoritative framework for all aspects of policy and administrative responsibilities.

3. In the case of two departments, Justice and National Defence, provision is also made for the position of Associate Deputy Minister, which is a G-i-C appointment.

4. Canada, *Revised Statutes*, 1970, Interpretation Act, ch. I-23, section 23(2) reads: "Words directing or empowering a Minister of the Crown to do an act or thing, or otherwise applying to him by his name of office, include a Minister acting for him, or if the office is vacant, a Minister designated to act in the office by or under the authority of an order-in-council, and also his successors in the office, and his or their deputy, but nothing in this subsection shall be construed to authorize a deputy to exercise any authority conferred upon a Minister to make a regulation as defined in the Regulations Act."

5. Canada, *Revised Statutes*, 1970, Financial Administration Act, ch. F-10, sections 7(3), 24 and 25.

6. Ibid., sections 25 and 27.

7. Ibid., section 53.

8. Ibid., section 7(2).

9. Canada, *Revised Statutes*, 1970, Official Languages Act, ch. O-2, sections 27 and 31(2).

10. See Chapter 2, note 18. The prime minister receives advice on appointments from the Prime Minister's Office and the Privy Council Office as well as from affected ministers in the selection of candidates. The formal instrument of appointment is an Order-in-Council.

11. See Privy Council Office, "Senior Personnel in the Public Service of Canada: Deputy Ministers," *op. cit.*

12. When Mr. Clark assumed office in June 1979 he asked for and received the resignation of Michael Pitfield, Clerk of the Privy Council and Secretary to the Cabinet, within twenty-four hours of officially becoming Prime Minister. This removal was an exception and in any case Mr. Pitfield's successor was another career public servant, Mr. Marcel Massé. Other changes and reassignments followed but were made gradually over several months.

13. See "Senior Personnel in the Public Service of Canada: Deputy Ministers," pp. 3-15. The professionalization of the senior ranks of the public service could be said to have started during the 1930s and early 1940s. Currently, over 70 per cent of deputies have spent their entire working lives in the federal public service; the remainder have been recruited from provincial public services and the private sector. It is an exception rather than a rule for a purely political appointment to be made.

14. Royal Commission on Financial Management and Accountability, *Report*, p. 453. There was, however, no uniformity in the ranking of those responsibilities by deputies. Generally speaking, it was observed that deputies of policy-oriented departments chose policy advice and deputies of operational or program-oriented departments chose administration.

15. Ibid., pp. 471 and 486.

16. This role has been discussed in both the Report of the Royal Commission on Government Organization in 1962 and the Report of the Royal Commission on Financial Management and Accountability. See also, Lord Bridges, "The Relationships between Ministers and the Permanent Departmental Head", *Canadian Public Administration* (1964), vol. 7, no. 3, pp. 269-81.

17. The role of ministerial office staff has been the subject of limited, yet critical, analysis. The support these officers provide to ministers can serve to facilitate liaison with their ministers' departments as well as other ministers' offices and agencies in the public service. See J.R. Mallory, "The Minister's Office Staff: An unreformed part of the public service," *Canadian Public Administration* (1967), vol. 10, pp. 25-34; Gerald Lenoski, "Ministers' Staff

and Leadership Politics", in T.A. Hockin, *Apex of Power*, 2nd ed. (Scarborough: Prentice-Hall, 1977), pp. 165-75; and Blair Williams, "The Para-Political Bureaucracy in Ottawa," in Harold D. Clarke, Colin Campbell, F.Q. Quo, and Arthur Goddard (eds.), *Parliament, Policy and Representation* (Toronto: Methuen, 1980), pp. 215-230.

18. Bridges, pp. 271-72.

19. As Bridges has noted: "The knowledge, the experience, the acquired skill which the Minister brings to his duties differ from those of the Permanent Head. This contrast is not only one of the chief characteristics of the partnership . . . it is one of the sources of strength since the experience and outlook of the partners is complementary." Ibid., p. 270.

20. See R. Van Loon and M. Whittington, *The Canadian Political System: Environment, Structure and Process*, 2nd ed. (Toronto: McGraw-Hill Ryerson, 1976), pp. 380-415. For a summary of the proceedings of a recent seminar on this question, see D.M. Cameron, "Power and responsibility in the Public Service: Summary of Discussions," *Canadian Public Administration* (Fall 1978), vol. 21, no. 3, pp. 358-72.

21. See, for example, Van Loon and Whittington, *The Canadian Political System*, pp. 382-83.

22. Richard Crossman, *The Diaries of a Cabinet Minister, vol. I, Minister of Housing, 1964-66* (London: Hamish Hamilton, 1975).

23. Numerous articles testify to the nature of this working relationship. In particular, see H.R. Balls, "Decision-making: the role of the deputy minister," *Canadian Public Administration* (1976), vol. 19, no. 3, pp. 417-31; A.W. Johnson, "The Role of the Deputy Minister," *Canadian Public Administration* (1961), vol. 4, no. 4, pp. 363-69; J.W. Pickersgill, "Bureaucrats and Politicians," *Canadian Public Administration* (1972), vol. 15, no. 3, pp. 418-27; M. Sharp, "The Bureaucratic Elite and Policy Formation," in W.D.K. Kernaghan (ed.), *Bureaucracy in Canadian Government*, 2nd ed. (Toronto: Methuen, 1973), pp. 69-73; and Arnold Heeney, *The Things That Are Caesar's* (Toronto: University of Toronto Press, 1972).

24. See the testimony of Mr. R. Bryce, "The Cabinet and the Public Service Establishment," in T.A. Hockin, *Apex of Power*, 1st ed. (Scarborough: Prentice-Hall, 1971), pp. 116-21.

25. See "Senior Personnel in the Public Service of Canada: Deputy Ministers," pp. 3-1 to 3-3.

26. K. Kernaghan, "Power, Parliament and Public Servants in Canada: Ministerial Responsibility Re-examined," *Canadian Public Policy* (Summer 1979), vol. V, no. 3, pp. 383-96 generally and p. 392 in particular.

27. "Senior Personnel in the Public Service of Canada: Deputy Ministers," p. 3-12.

28. Ibid., pp. 3-12 and 3-13.

29. Ibid., pp. 3-11 and 3-12.

30. Ibid., p. 3-14.

31. Public servants up to the level of deputy minister in the departments are, for purposes of appointment and promotion, covered by the provisions of the Public Service Employment Act. Executives up to the rank of deputy, therefore, constitute the group of "public service" executives distinct from those appointed by the Governor-in-Council. For purposes of classification and pay administration, the two groups have been integrated into a six-level salary and classification structure as proposed by the Advisory Group on Executive Compensation in the Public Service in its first report in 1967.

32. See Chapter 3.

33. This group has been referred to as the "30K" group because its members were receiving

salaries in the $30,000 salary range. Recently a new classification, the "SM," has been instituted for middle-level managers.

34. The 1976 Annual Report of the Public Service Commission contained a critical review of the effects of rapid growth in the public service. With respect to those effects on senior management, it was noted: "The period of rapid growth appears to have had particular impact on managers in the Public Service. It is unquestionable that the vast majority are highly motivated and have high levels of integrity. It is probable, however, that many of the problems they encounter are due in part to an inadequate understanding of the often special characteristics of Public Service management and inadequate familiarity with the intricate management systems necessitated by the size and diversity of the Public Service. During the growth years, many have risen to management ranks without extensive experience at lower levels, precisely in a period when the substantial delegation of administrative responsibility requires a much greater and more detailed knowledge of the managerial environment in the Public Service." Public Service Commission, *Annual Report* (1976), pp. 7-8. Reproduced by permission of the Minister of Supply and Services Canada.

35. Royal Commission on Financial Management and Accountability, *Report*, pp. 232 and 241.

36. Advisory Group on Executive Compensation in the Public Service, *Second Report* (January 13, 1971), pp. 10-11.

37. Advisory Group on Executive Compensation in the Public Service, *Fifth Report* (March 3, 1977), p. 11.

38. Royal Commission on Financial Management and Accountability, *Report*, pp. 229-32.

39. See D.G. Hartle, "A Proposed System of Program and Policy Evaluation," *Canadian Public Administration* (Summer 1973), vol. 16, no. 2, pp. 243-66; *A Theory of the Expenditure Budgetary Process* (Toronto: University of Toronto Press, 1976); and "The Lambert Report," *Canadian Public Policy* (Summer 1979), vol. V, no. 3, pp. 366-82.

40. See Treasury Board Secretariat, *Departmental Planning and Evaluation Groups in the Federal Government* (Ottawa: July 1976); and Michael J. Prince, "Policy Advisory Groups in Government Departments," in G.B. Doern and P. Aucoin (eds.), *Public Policy in Canada* (Toronto: Macmillan of Canada, 1979), pp. 275-300.

41. Prince, ibid., p. 276.

42. The models set out here are hypothetical organizations based on composites of individual departmental structures.

43. Treasury Board Secretariat, *Departmental Planning and Evaluation Groups*, p. 31.

44. Ibid., p. 22.

45. "Firefighting" is the term used to describe day-to-day crisis handling. For example, a minister may request immediate information on a story reported in the morning newspaper before he goes to the House for Question Period. A quick response that satisfies the minister's query may lead to further requests of a more significant nature. Over time, a unit can develop the reputation of being able to serve the minister's and the deputy's needs and will acquire a high profile in the department and in turn qualify itself for priority policy or planning activities. In other words, establish a reputation for short-term policy issues, then seek larger undertakings for your unit.

46. On highly technical subjects, documents could run over a hundred pages in length. See also, R. French, "The Privy Council Office: Support for Cabinet Decision-Making," p. 369.

47. Ibid.

48. Professor Hartle's case study, "The Draft Cabinet Memorandum" (Case Program in Canadian Public Administration, Institute of Public Administration of Canada, 1976), captures the essence of interdepartmental negotiations on cabinet proposals and the often unintended results, albeit in somewhat facetious terms.

49. For full discussion see French, "The Privy Council Office," pp. 381-82.

50. H.L. Laframboise, "Administrative Reform in the Federal Public Service: Signs of a Saturation Psychosis," p. 322. Reprinted by permission of *Canadian Public Administration*.

51. The six concepts common to PPBS include: objective setting, analysis, program-activity structures based on the objectives, cost projections over several years, annual plans, and information systems for monitoring. See Treasury Board Secretariat, *Planning Programming Budgeting Guide* (Ottawa: September 1969), p. 8.

52. French, "The Privy Council Office," pp. 381.

53. See Chapter 8.

54. For a particularly poignant discussion of this and related issues, see A. Wildavsky, "A Budget for All Seasons? Why the Traditional Budget Lasts," in G.B. Doern and A.M. Maslove, *The Public Evaluation of Government Spending* (Toronto: Butterworth, 1979), pp. 61-78.

55. Advisory Group on Executive Compensation in the Public Service of Canada, *First Report* (December 2, 1968), p. 8.

56. "Senior Personnel in the Public Service of Canada: Deputy Ministers," pp. 3-32 to 3-41.

57. Royal Commission on Financial Management and Accountability, *Report*, p. 189.

58. See Privy Council Office, "Responsibility in the Constitution," pp. 3-51 to 3-55, for discussion of Westminster practice.

59. Ibid., p. 1-51.

60. Ibid., pp. 1-54 and 1-55.

61. Royal Commission on Government Organization, *Report*, vol. I, p. 60.

62. Royal Commission on Financial Management and Accountability, *Report*, p. 194.

63. Great Britain, Prime Minister and Chancellor of the Exchequer, "The Civil Service," vol. 1, *Report of the Committee*, 1966-68, Chairman: Lord Fulton (London: H.M.S.O., 1968), Cmd no. 3638, pp. 58-60. See also G.B. Doern, "A Critical Evaluation of the Report of the Lambert Royal Commission on Financial Management and Accountability" (Ottawa: 1979), p. 6, where the suggestion of a senior policy adviser is discussed.

5
The "Private" Public Sector: Nondepartmental Bodies

The preceding chapters have focused on the central core of the machinery of government—the cabinet, with the departments and agencies that report directly to ministers. In strictly quantitative terms, this inner core of executive structures is the smallest part of the federal-government organization. Approximately thirty bodies may be described as ministerial departments. Outside this inner core, however, an elaborate satellite system of nondepartmental bodies emanates from cabinet and from departments.[1] The "structural heretics"[2] include hundreds of different kinds of agencies, which in varying degrees operate independently from direct ministerial control and direction.

Generally, it is contended that the resort to structures other than the conventional departmental form is a function of two main considerations: to lighten the workload of a department and hence its minister; and to use organizational designs more appropriately suited to performing certain functions than the departmental form.[3] Although ministers are not directly responsible for the management of these bodies, they will in some fashion bear indirect responsibility and will therefore have to involve themselves in the coordination of the activities of the agencies within their portfolio. Hence, their workload on matters of the day-to-day operation of these bodies may be lightened, but their general responsibility for these structures will require their time and attention. The second consideration is more compelling in explaining the growth and proliferation of nondepartmental organizational forms. As mentioned in Chapter 1, government has historically been an active agent in nation building in Canada.[4] The development of a welfare state and a public-finance system that encouraged a high degree of government involvement served as a major impetus in extending the federal government's role as provider and procurer of goods and services as well as general manager of the economy. To these ends, organizational designs were developed to regulate and to promote economic growth and social development. Public ownership, regulation, arbitration, external advice and research were activities that have been deemed to require distinct organizational forms.

Unlike a department, the powers necessary to carry out the functions of these bodies are vested in the individual who, or board that, heads the body, rather than the minister. Within the framework of cabinet-parliamentary government, nevertheless, any organization that is created by the executive and that serves as an instrument of government must ultimately be accountable to the body that sanctions its establishment—Parliament. Thus, while Parliament may delegate its authority to an agency to operate independently or semi-independently from direct government control, it cannot abrogate its responsibility. Ministers provide the necessary link in the accountability chain from the management structure of these agencies to Parliament. At minimum, ministers serve as spokesmen for these agencies in Parliament.[5]

Within this context, it is not surprising that efforts to classify these organizations have focused traditionally on the degree of autonomy or independence from ministerial and administrative control accorded to them. Moreover, the creation of a fairly large number of crown corporations during and after World War II centred attention on the corporate form of organization. In the main, these were government-owned businesses established to support the war and post-war reconstruction efforts. The Financial Administration Act (1951) set out the basic classification scheme based on different categories of corporations.

The Act provided for three main categories of corporation—departmental, agency and proprietary—as well as an undesignated category.[6] It established requirements for administrative and reporting practices considered appropriate to each type. As new agencies emerged, the general practice adopted by the government in establishing the Parliament-minister-agency relationship was to list them in one of these categories in the schedules of the Act. In many cases, these categories imposed an artificial classification on an agency. For example, the National Energy Board, a regulatory commission set up in 1959, was described in the Act as "a branch designated as a department for purposes of the Act."

In its review of nondepartmental organizations, the Glassco Commission emphasized the need to clarify the relationships of these agencies with ministers on the one hand and with Parliament on the other.[7] The presumption was that an appropriate degree of ministerial control was necessary and that efforts should be taken to ensure that they were provided for adequately in legislation. The political reasons for employing different organizational forms were generally acknowledged and major reforms in this area were not put forward.[8]

During the 1960s and 1970s, the use of nondepartmental organizations was extended further in other areas of government activity. As government began to consult more widely and solicit expert opinions outside of government, several advisory councils and committees were formally constituted. Regulatory commissions, marketing boards and administrative tribunals as well as crown corporations increased in numbers. The creation of these several kinds of bodies was undertaken with relative ease. Although legislation was required in most cases to establish these bodies formally, the structural proposals were sometimes only a part of a legislative bill; thus, they were not always the main focus of debate. Since the creation of these types of administrative units did not involve the creation of a new ministerial portfolio, there was often limited interest in their creation. The extent of the growth and proliferation of government-owned and government-controlled agencies was starkly revealed before the Public Accounts Committee in 1977 when Treasury Board officials reported that there were several hundred different agencies in existence at that time.[9] The Financial Administration Act listed only fifty-four agencies in its schedules.[10]

The growth and development of nondepartmental bodies raised two sets of distinct but related issues. As public agencies, these bodies support the activities of government. Despite the independence accorded to them in varying degrees, their activities must complement the broader framework of government policy. Thus, it has been argued that the government should provide policy directions to these agencies. A second and related issue has been the problem of the control and accountability of these agencies to government. As the number of agencies has increased, the means by which appropriate control and accountability can be obtained has often been a critical issue.

In 1974, a comprehensive internal review of nondepartmental bodies was undertaken and resulted in several efforts to define the different types of agencies and to determine the kinds of direction and control that would pertain to them. In 1977, the government issued a Green Paper on Crown Corporations which included legislative proposals.[11] A key feature of these proposals was the recommendation to include a policy-directive power in agency legislation. For its part, the Royal Commission on Financial Management and Accountability devoted considerable attention to the role and functions of nondepartmental bodies. It addressed the issue of classification and accountability and attempted to provide a more comprehensive and all-inclusive framework for identifying and listing agencies on the basis of the authority delegated to them, their internal organization and their management and decision-making processes.[12] Its recommendations were focused on means whereby tighter and more effective control of agency operations could be exercised.

In sum, a primary issue in considering nondepartmental forms of organization pertains to the degree of independence accorded to them. The rationale for establishing the different types of agencies has been premised in varying degrees on the need for some degree of autonomy from government and from administrative controls.[13] Nevertheless, the "independence" of nondepartmental bodies may be considered a relative term. In differing contexts and capacities, they do operate as policy instruments of government and represent some mix of public and private interests in relationships that are essentially government controlled or determined.[14] A consideration of the nature of those relationships and their importance to the processes of government must therefore begin with an examination of the main types of nondepartmental bodies, based on the nature of the functions they perform and the key aspects of their operation and management.[15]

Crown Corporations

A crown corporation has been defined as a corporation that is ultimately accountable through a minister to Parliament for the conduct of its affairs and is wholly owned by the government of Canada either directly or indirectly.[16] Such corporations have a long-established history.[17] The basic rationale offered by governments in creating public companies has been pragmatic rather than ideological.[18] For example, the creation of a public company has been justified in the case of a high-risk undertaking for which private capital was not forthcoming (Petro-Canada, 1975) and in a case in which national security was of primary concern (Atomic Energy Control Limited, 1952). The federal government has also established commercial undertakings for purposes of promoting efficiency through the creation of a government monopoly (Air Canada, 1937). Alternatively, a federal-government presence has been considered necessary in a competitive industry for purposes of achieving broad social and cultural goals (Canadian Broadcasting Corporation, 1936). In other cases (such as the Central Mortgage and Housing Corporation, 1946) a mix of economic and social goals has also provided the primary rationale. In essence, the creation of these bodies represents an attempt to combine the operational advantages of private-sector business practices with the assistance of public funding and government direction. Therefore, they are and may be considered to be essentially commercial undertakings.[19]

Mandates

Most Crown corporations have been established by specific enabling legislation.[20] The act or other statutory authority will set out with varying degrees of specificity the particular objectives of the corporation. These objectives constitute the policy mandate of the organization. Since corporations will normally be required to report to Parliament *through* a minister, the statute must delimit as clearly as possible the exercise of authority of the corporation in the parent statute. Unlike departments, corporations have no authority to adjust their policy objectives or priorities on their own. Any change of this nature would require legislative amendment or statutory revision.

The objects for which crown corporations have been established are as varied as the types of corporations themselves. The Canadian Broadcasting Corporation, for example, is charged with providing a national broadcasting service "that is predominantly Canadian in content and character" and that should:

(i) be a balanced service of information, enlightenment and entertainment for people of different ages, interests and tastes covering the whole range of programming in fair proportion;
(ii) extend to all parts of Canada as public funds become available;
(iii) use both official languages, serving the special needs of geographic

regions and actively contributing to the flow and exchange of cultural and regional information and entertainment; and,

(iv) contribute to the development of national unity and provide for a continuing expression of Canadian identity.[21]

The major object of the Central Mortgage and Housing Corporation is to administer the National Housing Act. Under this Act, the Corporation is authorized to insure mortgage loans made by approved lenders for new and existing homeowner housing, new rental housing and dwellings built by cooperative associations. The extension of the mortgage-lending function to social housing programs occurred in the early 1970s.[22] The creation of Petro-Canada in 1975 represented a major federal-government venture into the resource-development sector. The enabling legislation established a crown-owned company with authority to:

> ... explore for hydrocarbon deposits, to negotiate for and acquire petroleum and petroleum products from abroad to assure a continuity of supply for the needs of Canada, to develop and exploit deposits of hydrocarbons within and without Canada in the interests of Canada, to carry out research and development projects in relation to hydro-carbons and other fuels and to engage in exploration for, and the production, distribution, refining and marketing of fuels.[23]

In looking at these examples of policy objectives, it is evident that they involve the delegation of broad discretionary authority to the respective corporations. The exercise of this discretionary authority can become a contentious political issue. The history of the Canadian Broad-casting Corporation, for example, is fraught with cases of objections raised about its programming activities.[24] Given the importance of house construction to the state of the economy, it is important that the housing corporation's programs are integrated closely with other fiscal instruments of government.[25] In the case of Petro-Canada, the issue has focused on the basic question of government intervention in the private sector. The means by which the government has attempted to improve its control over policy and policy-related matters respecting crown corporations are discussed below.

Management Structure

The corporate form of public enterprise closely parallels that of private-sector firms. It normally consists of a chairman and chief executive officer who are responsible to a board of directors. The power and authority of the corporation is vested in the board. This collegial form of management is typical, contrasting with a hierarchical structure of departments in which the senior officer reports directly to a minister.[26]

Despite the collegial form, however, normally only the chief executive officer and/or chairman are full-time positions; directorships are part-time posts. In the case of the full-time positions, appointments are made for the most part by the Governor-in-Council "during good behaviour" and are subject to a definite term that on the average runs five to seven years.[27] In the case of part-time appointments, which are also made by the Governor-in-Council, the term varies from two to five years. The full-time status of the chief executive officer combined with the tenured term appointment give these officials significant influence and independence in the management and conduct of the corporation's affairs.

The directors of public corporations serve a representative function. They are there to represent the public interest as determined by the government. To this end, appointments to these boards will normally include a mix of public officials and private-sector members.[28] Furthermore, boards of directors of crown corporations do not represent shareholder interests in the same way as they do in private corporations. For those corporations with a share structure,[29] for example, the shares are vested in the crown. The trustee shareholder will be the minister or the Governor-in-Council as the case may be.

The minister's role in the management of a corporation is an arm's length relationship. He is required to approve budgets and regulations passed by the corporation and receive annual reports of operations. However, the responsibility of the chief executive officer is to the board of directors and ultimately to Parliament.

Controls

The degree of independence enjoyed by a corporation or, conversely, the degree of administrative control exercised by the government over a corporation has been a function of the status of the corporation as defined in the Financial Administration Act.[30] Administrative requirements have varied, therefore, with the category of corporation.

To begin, corporations performing purely commercial functions may in theory be expected to be self-financing. Public funding may be required at the time of their creation, but they are expected to operate on a corporate profit-and-loss basis. In fact, few public corporations, even those established for strictly economic purposes, have proven to be totally self-financing and are required to submit annual requests for funds. The Financial Administration Act sets out the procedure for budgetary control. Some corporations are required to provide operating budgets;[31] all corporations must submit capital budgets.[32] The form of these budgets is prescribed by regulation by the Treasury Board, on the joint recommendation of the President of the Treasury Board and the appropriate minister.[33] In turn, the budgets are viewed by the appropriate minister and then by the Minister of Finance and the President of the Treasury Board before being considered by cabinet committee. Finally, corporations are required to submit annual financial statements.[34] In considering the measures of financial control, the government and the Lambert Commission both recommended that corporations, in addition to submitting budgets, be required to submit corporate plans annually to set out statements of objectives and corporate strategies for achieving those objectives as well as policies and financial plans for implementing those objectives and strategies.[35] In this way, performance assessments would be easier to make and hence the accountability for their operations would be improved.

The ability to hire staff without the restrictions imposed by the Public Service Employment Act, the Financial Administration Act and the Public Service Staff Relations Act is another measure of independence that may be accorded to a crown corporation. All proprietary corporations have independent authority to hire staff, although they can take advantage of providing employee benefits under the Public Service Superannuation Act. Thus, these corporations have the freedom to determine and control the types and numbers of staff employed as well as the salary and classification schedules applicable to the employees.

Crown corporations report to Parliament through a designated minister. The requirement to report annually is contained in the enabling legislation and the Financial Administration Act, but the contents of these reports are determined by the corporations themselves. In the past these reports have not been very elucidating. The Auditor General, the government and the Lambert Commission recommended that the contents of these reports become more comprehensive and detailed.[36] In general, the thrust of the proposals put forward on corporations' operations has been to require more and better-quality information.

The provision for an annual audit of a corporation's accounts and finances is also contained in the majority of corporation acts as well as the general requirements set out in the Financial Administration Act. The Auditor General may be the designated auditor for a corporation or an outside auditor may be appointed by the Governor-in-Council. The number of cases in which the Auditor General has not been designated as corporation auditor is small. The practice has been, partly on the Auditor General's suggestion, to designate him as the chief auditor for corporations.[37] As these audits are reported to Parliament, the Auditor's ability to scrutinize and control are enhanced.

Directives

The inclusion of a directive power in enabling legislation of crown corporations is not new. For example, the initial Central Mortgage and Housing Act contained the provision that: "The Corporation shall comply with any directions from time to time given to it by the Governor in Council or the minister respecting the exercise of the performance of its powers, duties and functions."[38] The Canadian Commercial Corporation

Act (1946) also contained a directive power to the effect that: "The Corporation shall comply with any general or special direction given by the Governor in Council or the Minister with reference to carrying out its purposes."[39] More recently, directives have been included in enabling legislation with specific reference to policy matters. For example, the Act providing for the creation of Petro-Canada contained the provision that: "In the exercise of its powers, the Corporation shall comply with such policy directions as may from time to time be given to it in writing by the Governor in Council."[40]

The distinction that can be drawn between these two kinds of directive powers is readily apparent. The recent directives specify "policy" rather than "general" or "special" directives. In clarifying the relationship between corporations and the designated or appropriate minister responsible, the distinction between policy and administration is a critical one. The policy directives focus ministerial responsibility for corporation policy and more clearly identify the corporation's responsibility for administration and management. Thus, a policy directive would not be issued to a corporation to modify particular recruitment procedures, but it could give direction to a corporation to implement a program of bilingualism in support of the official-languages policy.[41]

In its review of crown corporations, the federal government recommended in 1977 that provisions be made in a new Crown Corporations Act for the inclusion of directions to crown corporations listed in the schedules of the Financial Administration Act. The Green Paper proposed that these directions be issued by the Governor-in-Council and be subject to tabling in Parliament "by the appropriate Minister within fifteen days after the direction is given to the Crown corporation."[42] The directive power was intended to serve two main purposes. First, it would focus and enhance the government's responsibility for defining public policy and the corporation's responsibility for the day-to-day management of its affairs and operations. Second, it would enhance the government's control over the corporation on major policy issues and thus improve accountability. In these ways, the directions would serve to clarify the relationship between the corporation and the government on the one hand and the corporation and Parliament on the other.[43]

In the broader sense, the government study undertaken by the Privy Council Office presented a full set of proposals for reform in the draft legislation. All major areas of corporation performance were covered.[44] The Lambert Commission, for its part, endorsed most of these proposals in principle but went further in recommending other reforms, such as the accountability of corporation chief executive officers before the Public Accounts Committee of the House of Commons and a systematic review of annual reports of crown corporations by standing committees of the House of Commons [45]

It would not be far-fetched to say that, under the guise of account-ability, what in fact has been occurring is an extension of government control over corporate activity. The distinction is perhaps a fine one but, if a corporation is performing effectively and is reporting its administrative practices adequately, the need for directives, for example, should be minimal. On the other hand, the public nature of these agencies provides the opportunity to ministers for achieving political objectives through direction and control. Independence, therefore, may be tempered by political and economic needs and circumstances.

Privatization

In addition to the preoccupation with improving the accountability of crown corporations, attention has been focused in recent years on the "privatization" of government functions, particularly those performed by crown agencies. The 1976 "The Way Ahead" document suggested the need for new policies that would provide alternatives to "increasing expenditure and expanding bureaucracies." The Speech from the Throne in October 1978 promised a review of all federal programs that could be transferred to the private sector without reducing the quality of service to the public.[46] In addition to examining the possibility of transferring services to the private sector (or contracting out), the possibility of "privatizing" government-owned companies and corporations came under scrutiny.

Theoretically, privatization could involve dismantling a corporation, selling shares in it, or its outright sale. A major inhibiting factor is obvious. If a government corporation is performing effectively, a government will want to take credit for that performance. Thus, there is no incentive to dismantle the operation. Moreover, there may be strong external pressures to maintain government involvement. It is generally easier for government to intervene than it is to withdraw its activities in opposition to the interests the agency serves.

A classic and current example of the issue of privatization is Petro-Canada. A major promise of the Progressive Conservative party during the 1979 election campaign was to dismantle the corporation. Upon the formation of a minority government, however, it became readily apparent to the Clark administration that it would be difficult to implement the promise. In response to mixed reaction within the party and strong opposition from without—particularly from the opposition parties—a more piecemeal approach was adopted. A task force was established to "review" the fate of the corporation and a modified policy was announced just before the government was defeated in December 1979.

The critical problem in pursuing measures of privatization is a political one in the broad and narrow sense. As noted above, ministers are unlikely to approve action that will divest them of important levers of influence and authority with groups and individuals. Second, the organizations themselves develop their own vested interests and will use any means (including clientele support) to ensure their continued existence.

Regulatory Commissions

A regulatory commission is an independent agency. Within the policy parameters established by Parliament, it regulates economic and occasionally noneconomic activities "in the public interest." To that end, it may serve to promote monopolies (regulation of air services by the Canadian Transport Commission, 1967) on the one hand or promote limited competition (broadcasting licences granted by the Canadian Radio-television and Telecommunications Commission, 1968, 1975) on the other, or to engage in a strictly policing function (health and safety standards regulation by the Atomic Energy Control Board, 1946).[47] As a policy instrument, a regulatory commission has certain political appeal, in that the costs and consequences of its activities compared to spending or service undertakings tend to be indirect and hence hidden from the public view.[48]

Regulatory processes establish sets of rules or standards with which individuals and groups are expected to comply.[49] Economic regulation may be said to be directed at adjusting private-sector behaviour in a way in which the benefits of economic activity can be more generally distributed throughout society as a whole.[50] Social regulation by and large pertains to areas such as occupational health and safety, environmental protection and consumer product safety.

The choice of an independent commission rather than a departmental form as a vehicle for implementing regulation has traditionally been justified by the need for impartiality in the making of regulatory decisions.[51] Activities such as granting licences, setting prices and standards of service and fixing tariffs and fees involve the adjudication of individual rights in the marketplace, which are presumed to require protection from direct political pressures or interference. The independence of these commissions is tempered, nevertheless, by the nature of the parliamentary system which requires accountability to Parliament. As in the case of crown corporations, regulatory commissions are government bodies and are therefore subject to certain direction and controls.

Mandates

The main functions of regulatory commissions are legislative and adjudicative, although administrative, investigatory and advisory functions may also be performed. For example, they are normally empowered to make regulations or rules governing the activity being regulated and to decide which individuals or groups will receive the benefit (licence) and pay the price of undertaking the activity (fee). As Schultz has noted,[52] the focus of regulation has undergone a relative shift from what might be described as a policing function to one which promotes economic development. One might say that the policing function has pertained to noneconomic regulatory processes respecting environmental protection, health and safety standards, and consumer services; economic promotion has pertained to regulating those industries, most of which are a mix of public and private enterprises, in the provision of some good or service (transportation, broadcasting, resource exploration).[53]

A common characteristic of the enabling legislation of many regulatory commissions has been the absence of precise objectives governing their operation.[54] The National Energy Board Act (1959), for example, sets out the Board's jurisdiction on hearings and the determination of any matter of regulations, certificates, licences or permits and provides the Board with the authority to determine actions that may be necessary "in the public interest" within its jurisdiction.[55] The policy objectives of the Act are implicit but not explicitly stated. Conversely, the legislation governing the Canadian Radio-television and Telecommunications Commission includes a list of policy objectives the Commission is responsible for implementing through its regulatory and supervisory authority. Similarly, the National Transportation Act sets out a list of policy objectives the Canadian Transport Commission must strive to implement. In both of these latter cases, however, the general nature of the objectives as set out in the legislation leaves a broad scope of discretionary authority to the bodies in terms of actual implementation.

Although their quasi-judicial function is the distinguishing feature of regulatory commissions, several of the bodies have also been delegated advisory and research functions (National Energy Board, Canadian Radio-television and Telecommunications Commission) ostensibly on the basis that they have the expertise and experience required for promulgating such advice. In the case of a quasi-regulatory body such as the Foreign Investment Review Agency (1973) and the former Anti-Inflation Board (1975), the primary purpose was to advise the minister in the first case and the Anti-Inflation Administrator in the second. Their functions are therefore to negotiate and to advise rather than to adjudicate.

The question of the extent and nature of the policy-advisory role of regulatory commissions is a controversial one. On the one hand, an argument can be made that in performing the adjudicative function, a commission will in the course of deciding cases develop precedents and guidelines that may in turn provide the basis for policy and policy advice. Thus, a policy role will be performed whether it is required by statute or not. On the other hand, an argument can be made that regulatory commissions should not have a policy-advisory role, for that function is more appropriately performed by departmental officials who report directly to a minister. In particular, a regulatory commission should not be in a position to develop policy on matters it will adjudicate; that is, it should not be a judge in its own cause.

It has already been noted that, in cases such as the Foreign Investment Review Agency, the regulatory body has been constituted as a negotiating and advisory forum. The policy role is monitored directly by the minister responsible. However, in the case of those commissions constituted as courts of record (National Energy Board, Atomic Energy Control Board and the Canadian Radio-television and Telecommunications Commission, the latter for hearings only), it is difficult to justify a policy-advisory role except for its own internal operations.[56] It would seem that policy advice and direction should be provided by the department through the appropriate minister to maintain appropriate lines of accountability on these matters.

Management Structure

The management structure of regulatory commissions is also collegial, in that it will normally consist of a chairman who serves as chief executive officer, one or more vice-chairmen and a panel of board or commission members. Members may be full-time or part-time and for the most part plan an active role in the deliberations and hearings of the commissions. In the case of the Canadian Transport Commission, several "modal" committees (such as air transport, railway transport, water transport) have their own committee chairmen and operate independently of each other.[57]

The tenure of commission officers varies according to the type of regulatory agency in question. Appointments are made by the Governor-in-Council. In the case of regulatory agencies such as the Canadian Radio-television and Telecommunications Commission, the Canadian Transport Commission and the National Energy Board, officers are appointed for fixed terms and can only be removed for cause. In the case of the Atomic Energy Control Board, the Foreign Investment Review Agency and the Anti-Inflation Board, officers serve at pleasure. Thus, in the former cases there is a larger degree of independence accorded by the nature of the appointments.[58]

For the appointment of members of commissions, the representation of interests (particularly regional interests) is also taken into consideration. It would not be far-fetched to say that the composition of the commissions serves to determine the type of definition of "public interest" the board or commission may from time to time delineate.

The relationship between ministers and the commissions for which they are responsible is normally an arm's length one except in those cases in which the commission serves an advisory function. A shift to greater ministerial direction and hence control of policy activities of regulatory commissions is discernible. The proposed revision of the broadcasting and telecommunications legislation (introduced in the House of Commons in November 1978 but never passed) contained clauses that allowed ministerial directions to the commission on policy and research activities.[59] In 1979, the Lambert Commission recommended a series of proposals for the inclusion of goals and public policies in enabling statutes, the requirement of Governor-in-Council approval for the promulgation of regulations, the provision of policy directives from the Governor-in-Council in enabling statutes and the regularization of the term and the requirement to evaluate the chief executive officers of the commissions.[60] These kinds of measures would serve to strengthen ministers' involvement in providing direction and maintaining accountability of these agencies.

Controls

The degree of independence from administrative controls accorded regulatory commissions is mostly a function of the extent of their adjudicative responsibilities. These bodies are required to submit annual requests for funds and operating budgets, which are reviewed by the Department of Finance and the Treasury Board Secretariat, in the same way that crown corporations do. Quasi-judicial regulatory commissions are normally accorded full authority in their enabling statutes to obtain expert staff and to determine their own operating procedures. They are also required to present annual reports to the minister responsible and, through him, to Parliament. Their operations are audited in most instances by the Auditor General. As a means of strengthening their accountability to Parliament, the Lambert Commission recommended that the annual reports of these bodies be "automatically and permanently referred to the appropriate standing committees of the House of Commons" and that their contents be comprehensive and detailed.[61] In other words, it was the Commission's view that regulatory bodies should be scrutinized by Parliament in the same manner as prescribed for crown corporations for administrative purposes.

Hearing Processes

In granting licences and setting fee schedules for an industry, a commission will normally be required to provide for a public hearing. The extent to which the rules of natural justice and legal procedures will apply in the proceedings is, if the act is silent, left to the discretion of the commission. For purposes of hearings, the National Energy Board, the Canadian Transport Commission and the Canadian Radio-television and Telecommunications Commission are courts of record and have established formal procedures for their hearings. Formal submissions are made to the commissions for certificates or licences. Depending on the workload of a particular commission, however, it may develop categories among its applications for those to be heard publicly or not.[62] Right of hearing presumes right of notice and subsequent right of decision. The Canadian Radio-television and Telecommunications Commission is required by its statute to gazette its decisions on station licences in the local newspapers.[63]

In the conduct of its adjudicative functions, a regulatory commission is expected to act in the public interest. In determining the public interest, a regulatory commission will be influenced in large measure by the private interests that are heard as well as the attitudes of staff members to what the public interest may be in any given circumstances at any one time.[64] If there is no provision for the hearing of a broad cross-section of views on an issue, the definition of the public interest may be narrowly construed. In recent years, demands for a public intervener have been made.[65] To ensure that adequate representation of different private interests is effected, recommendations for the subsidization of private groups and individuals have been put forward.

Appeals on quasi-judicial decisions of regulatory agencies can be made to the Governor-in-Council or to the designated minister in certain cases. Decisions of the Canadian Transport Commission[66] and the Canadian Radio-television and Telecommunications Commission[67] for example, may be appealed to the Governor-in-Council. In the case of orders made by the former Anti-Inflation Administrator, the Act provided for an appeal to the Governor-in-Council or the Anti-Inflation Appeal Tribunal.[68] In the cases of the National Energy Board and the Foreign Investment Review Agency, the Governor-in-Council is empowered to make the final decisions, thus removing the possibility of appeal to the political level.

Regulatory commissions such as the National Energy Board, the Canadian Radio-television and Telecommunications Commission and the Canadian Transport Commission can, in the exercise of their legislative and adjudicative functions, be subject to judicial review pursuant to section 28 of the Federal Court Act. Judicial review mainly involves an examination of the procedures by which decisions or regulations of regulatory agencies have been set aside by the superior courts. Perhaps the better-known examples of judicial review have been cases brought against the National Energy Board that have resulted in the court's declaring particular regulations passed by the Board as *ultra vires* and that have required subsequent amendment by the Board.[69]

Appeals from and judicial review of regulatory commission rulings are inherent means of control of administrative actions. In this regard, the Lambert Commission, for example, recommended the establishment of regularized practices in the exercise of judicial control.[70] The right of appeal and the process of judicial review have frequently been recommended. In the past, it seems that the problems of implementation have been ones of lack of consistency and care in drafting legislation.[71]

Deregulation

In the search for means of reducing the scope of government activities and intervention, deregulation has become a counterpart to privatization. Whereas privatization has meant the return to the private sector of the provision of a service or the undertaking of a commercial enterprise, deregulation connotes the reduction of red tape (administrative procedures) on the one hand and the elimination of government regulation on the other. Concern with excessive regulation was expressed initially in "The Way Ahead" document in 1976. In July 1978, Prime Minister Trudeau transmitted a reference to the Economic Council of Canada, requesting the Council to examine the entire area of regulation in government and to provide reports to the First Ministers' Conference.[72] Thus, this issue is one which has been reviewed at both federal and provincial levels.

The major preoccupation in this area has been with the first aspect of deregulation—that is, the reduction of the number of regulations and the elimination of overlapping and duplicative regulations. For example, the appointment of a federal Minister of State for Small Businesses in 1976 was in large part an attempt to address the problem of reducing the number and kind of forms businessmen are required to complete and return to different government agencies. In the province of British Columbia, a Ministry of Deregulation was established in 1978 to conduct a service-wide review with the intent of reducing and eliminating duplicative and redundant laws and regulations and of improving administrative procedures. The ministry existed for one year and then was disbanded.

The second aspect of deregulation—the removal of government regulation in a particular economic or social sector—would involve major policy changes and has not yet been implemented in any major area of government regulation. There are philosophical as well as economic arguments which need to be considered. The issue of efficiency of free-market competition is at the heart of both sets of arguments. Nevertheless, areas such as communications and transportation have been reviewed as fields in which deregulation could be considered.[73]

Advisory Councils

While crown corporations and regulatory commissions may be considered as instruments to implement government policy, advisory councils are bodies which initiate policy proposals and monitor government activities. Ostensibly their purpose is to provide independent and/or external policy advice and research. Many different kinds of organizations could be classified as advisory councils, from the formally constituted advisory and research institutions that operate under their own legislation and have been accorded crown-corporation status to "consultative bodies" that have been established by order-in-council or cabinet decision. The several categories could include: central advisory agencies such as the Economic Council of Canada; functional advisory councils such as the Fisheries and Oceans Research Advisory Council, the National Research Council, or the Medical Research Council; granting councils such as the Canada Council and the Social Science and Humanities Research Council; and consultative bodies such as the Advisory Council on the Status of Women and the Advisory Committee on Multiculturalism.[74]

Generally speaking, advisory councils combine a number of different functions in their operations. As bodies composed of representatives from the private sector, they serve as vehicles for channelling public opinion on particular issues. Conversely, they assist the government in this capacity by generating support for the latter's policies. As independent research centres, they can serve as counterweights to bureaucratic expertise in the departments. Thus, they can serve as critics and consensus builders in the policy process. In providing a link between governmental and private interests, advisory councils can become engaged in the reciprocal exchange of information and opinions. In the case of granting councils, such bodies also serve to define and focus policy issues in applied research and provide technical knowledge in pure research undertakings.

Mandates

Advisory councils established by statute have their terms of reference set out in legislation. These terms may be detailed and comprehensive. For example, the Economic Council of Canada is charged with "advising and recommending to the Minister how Canada can achieve the highest possible levels of employment and efficient production in order that the country may enjoy a high and consistent rate of economic growth."[75] A long list of functions is then set out in the Act, including a provision (referred to in passing earlier) for references by the minister for the undertaking of studies or inquiries on any matter related to its duties and functions.

In the case of nonstatutory bodies, the terms of reference may be found in the program description for the council as contained in the Estimates. For example, the Advisory Council on the Status of Women is charged with the responsibility of making "recommendations to the Government on legislation on programs to improve the status of women; research on matters pertaining to the status of women in Canada; and, publications of reports on areas of concern and an annual report on the progress being made in improving the status of women."[76]

The main means by which central and functional advisory agencies fulfill their mandates are the publication of annual reports and special research studies. In the case of the granting councils, the subsidization of research projects has indirect benefit to the government in that the kinds of research undertaken are often more directly beneficial to the institutions where the research is conducted. In the case of the consultative bodies, meetings of the members and other public conferences which they sponsor are perhaps more important means of fulfilling their mandates than any reports or briefs they might prepare. As noted above, most of these kinds of agencies fulfill a number of different functions, although, in terms of mandates, advice and research are primary. A critical issue in all these cases is the degree of independence the agencies have for allowing them to develop and recommend policies that may in fact be critical of or contrary to government policy.

It is difficult, however, to assess quantitatively or qualitatively the impact that reports of advisory agencies have on the executive. The Economic Council of Canada is a case in point. For the first decade of its existence, it held a prestigious position.[77] While its reports were not formally endorsed by the government, they usually received widespread attention at the political and administrative level. During the mid-1970s, there was a move by the then Chairman of the Council to more closely integrate the outputs of the Council with the cabinet process. Such a move would have considerably diminished the independent role of the Council, for it would have required compromises necessary to any process of consensus decision making. The attempt was not successful and the chairman subsequently resigned to take an active part in the political process. In other instances, government priorities have influenced the efficacy of a council. When government interests shift, for example, funds for particular agencies' activities may not be readily forthcoming. On the other hand, if an advisory process has become entrenched, new structures may be created—if it is not possible to disband the old—to develop an improved process.[78]

Management Structure

If they can, advisory councils will normally seek crown-corporation status. The reason, quite simply, is to ensure permanent funding and to protect themselves from direct government intervention. An interesting example of concern with formal status can be demonstrated by the legislation passed in 1976 that formalized the corporation status of the Medical Research Council, the National Research Council, the Natural Science and Engineering Research Council and the Social Sciences and Humanities Research Council. The first two councils had initially been established as corporate bodies. When the latter two were considered, the expectations were that they would have similar benefits accorded to them.

Generally speaking, in the case of both formally constituted and nonstatutory bodies, the structure of management is collegial. The bodies normally comprise a full-time chairman, vice-chairmen and varying numbers of part-time board members, all of whom are appointed by the Governor-in-Council. The appointments are usually for a specified term: "not to exceed five years" in the case of full-time officers; normally two years for a board member.

The representative nature of the board may be provided in the enabling statute, as in the case of the Economic Council or the Science Council, or on the basis of a representation formula determined by the principal officers of the agency in consultation with the minister, as in the case of the Advisory Council on the Status of Women. In some instances, external organizations or associations may be asked to nominate candidates. Normally, different organizations will lobby for appointments to these boards, whether the organizations are consulted or not. The representative nature of the board is balanced in the case of the formally constituted agencies by expert staff. The staff is responsible to the board, but in reality may carry greater influence, in concert with the principal full-time officers, in determining the contents of reports.

These agencies provide advice directly to designated ministers. This relationship is one step removed, but one must acknowledge the exchange between the minister and the agency which can and does occur about the direction of the work a council may be doing. As in the cases of crown corporations and regulatory commissions, proposals have been made to provide ministers with greater authority to provide policy direction than has been practised in the past.[79]

Controls

The degree of independence accorded advisory bodies has varied widely. As noted above, an advisory agency will prefer corporation status to protect itself from political interference. In the case of professional advisory councils, independence has been avidly sought and jealously guarded by professional associations to allow these bodies to take critical, nonpartisan stances. Thus, a regular budgetary vote and independent authority to hire staff, for example, are often viewed as essential. Little independence can be claimed by these bodies if they are dependent on discretionary funds. However, formal status can result in other kinds of costs. The case of the Canada Council is a good example of how a change in status can result in greater, not less, government control. When the Council was required to go to the government for money after its initial endowment fund was depleted, the Council's granting activities were affected in substantive ways as a result of becoming part of the regular government budgetary process.[80]

In addition to budgets, advisory councils submit annual reports on their activities to Parliament through the designated ministers. They are also subject to audit by the Auditor General. The Lambert recommendations on these bodies proposed a systematic application of policy and administrative controls.[81] It was envisaged that these bodies should be treated in every respect as government entities.

Lobbying Activities

Although advisory councils are considered to be primarily policy advisory and/or research agencies, their role as interest groups is an important and significant feature of their operations. They are established to advise and in so doing will seek to promote the interests of the profession or clientele they represent. As noted above, the selection of board members can be a highly political process. From the government's point of view, concern with representation may quite openly focus on interests to be co-opted; from the point of view of groups and individuals, the motivation may be to gain representation and hence access to a decision-influencing forum. C.L. Brown-John's study has demonstrated both propositions.[82]

Besides being responsible for the issuing of reports and studies, the senior officials of these agencies will attempt to operate in the informal networks of political and administrative information exchange. It is regular practice of agency principals to hold press conferences when reports are released and to speak publicly on recommendations and findings. In this regard, advisory councils are more active policy agents than either crown corporations or regulatory commissions. Control by removal and replacement of senior officials can be effected, but such action cannot be exercised too blatantly because these bodies are considered to be independent sources of advice and information. Within limits, therefore, an advisory council can have an important impact on policy matters within its relevant area.

Marketing Boards

These agencies, few in number at the federal level, are hybrid structures that, within a particular economic sector, perform functions similar to the other agencies discussed above. They are at once commercial operations, advisory councils, adjudicative bodies and representative boards. They act in these several capacities to administer compulsory schemes for the production and marketing of natural products.[83] Their scope of activities is nevertheless constrained by provincial jurisdiction over the marketing of natural products produced and sold within a province. Federal jurisdiction pertains to interprovincial and export trade.[84] The two key economic sectors in which federal marketing boards operate are agriculture and fisheries.

Mandates

In the agricultural sector, the Agricultural Products Board (1949), the Canadian Wheat Board (1935), the Canadian Dairy Commission (1966), the Canadian Livestock Feed Board (1966) and the National Products

Marketing Council (1972) are the primary marketing agencies. The Wheat Board, for example, administers a marketing scheme for the sale of grains in Canada and in export markets and controls grain transportation systems within Canada.[85] Producers may, on application to the minister and subject to the approval of the Governor-in-Council, establish marketing plans. The Board is assisted by an Advisory Committee of producer representatives and acts as an advisory body to the minister on marketing activities and marketing strategies.[86]

The National Farm Products Marketing Council, in contrast, is an umbrella organization, the prime responsibilities of which are to advise the minister on matters relating to the establishment and operation of agencies created pursuant to the Act and to review and promote the efficient operations of those agencies within the objectives set out in the Act.[87] The Council is required to consult with provincial governments and agencies that exercise similar responsibilities as well as with producers and commodity boards. Two agencies have been established by proclamation under this Act: the Canadian Egg Marketing Board and the Canadian Turkey Marketing Board.

The Canadian Saltfish Corporation and the Freshwater Fish Marketing Corporation are responsible for the marketing of fish (salt or freshwater) and fish products in and out of Canada with a view to promoting efficiency and profit in the industry and to increasing interprovincial and international markets for fish.[88] Both corporations have advisory committees composed of representatives of fishermen.

Management Structure

The management structure of federal marketing boards varies with the agency. The Canadian Dairy Commission, the Canadian Livestock Feed Board and the Canadian Saltfish Corporation are listed in the Financial Administration Act as Schedule C (agency) corporations. The Freshwater Fish Marketing Corporation is listed as a Schedule D (proprietary) corporation. The Canadian Wheat Board is listed as an "other government corporation." The Agricultural Products Board and the National Farm Products Marketing Council constitute "other agencies"; that is, they are not agents of the crown.

Thus, the corporate structure is used in most instances, in that there is a board of directors or council headed by a chairman and vice-chairman. In the case of the Wheat Board and the Dairy Commission, the structure includes a Chief Commissioner, Assistant Chief Commissioner and three Commissioners. All appointments are made by the Governor-in-Council for fixed terms. As noted earlier, most agencies are served by advisory committees composed in whole or in part of producer representatives. Each agency is supported by expert staff. The minister is involved in the boards' operations to the extent that the approval of the minister or the

Governor-in-Council must be sought for all regulations passed and decisions taken by these agencies.

Controls

The provisions of the Financial Administration Act apply to those boards with corporation status. Operating budgets and estimates submissions are made to the Treasury Board through the designated ministers. Subsidy programs are supported by funds that in instances such as the case of the Wheat Board are included in departmental estimates. For those agencies that are not agents of the crown, provision is made in the enabling statute for operating funds to be made "out of moneys appropriated by Parliament."[89] The boards, however, have independent authority to hire staff. Annual reports are made to Parliament through the designated minister and annual audits are conducted by the Auditor General, except in the case of the Wheat Board and the Farm Products Marketing Council.

Consumer Interest

The essential purpose of the establishment of marketing boards is to assist the producer and to promote greater efficiency in the marketing of natural products. Price stabilization has therefore been a major objective. In recent years, however, consumer interest in marketing activities has been heightened by high rates of inflation and rising food costs. In some cases, the activities of federal marketing agencies have come under strong attack. For example, the charge has been made that, with the exception of the Canadian Wheat Board, national marketing boards provide few benefits in promoting orderly and efficient marketing but do add considerably to the cost of products.[90]

A consideration of the effects of regulation pursued by marketing boards, including direct and indirect costs, was included in the terms of the regulation reference to the Economic Council of Canada in 1978. The first studies released[91] indicate the pervasive nature of regulation of this kind and the general benefits and costs that accrue to society. In the case of marketing regulation at the federal level, the issues are complicated by the federal and provincial jurisdictional interests in the field. Responsibility is divided in certain respects and often leads to competition and counterproductive efforts by governments. The costs of these activities are borne mostly by the consumer.

Administrative Tribunals

It was noted earlier that regulatory commissions mainly perform legislative and adjudicative functions. In the exercise of the latter function, they are required to hold formal hearings and apply procedural safeguards in the hearing process on matters affecting individual rights. Nevertheless, a separate category of agencies serves in effect as subordinate courts and functions by and large as appellate bodies for individuals challenging administrative actions of officials or agencies. These agencies are administrative tribunals. While they may perform certain legislative functions for their operations, the adjudicative function is primary. Some examples of this type of agency include the Tax Review Board (1946, 1971), the Immigration Appeal Board (1967, 1978), the Tariff Board (1970), and the Anti-Inflation Appeal Tribunal (1975).

Mandates

In general, administrative tribunals have been established to deal with issues arising out of the application and administration of particular legislative acts. Since no legislation can of itself be so detailed as to provide for all eventualities of its application, Parliament must delegate discretionary authority to officials and agencies. Administrative tribunals serve as adjudicative forums on all matters of dispute involving mainly the rights, interests and property of individuals. The chief advantages of tribunals over courts are cheapness, accessibility, freedom from technicality, expedition and expert knowledge of their particular subject.[92]

The mandate of the Tax Review Board, for example, is to provide an easily accessible appeal process for taxpayers who wish to challenge rulings of the Department of National Revenue (Taxation). Specifically, it hears appeals on matters arising from the Income Tax Act, the Canada Pension Plan Act and the Estate Tax Act.[93] The Immigration Appeal Board hears appeals on matters arising out of the administration of the Immigration Act, including orders of deportation.[94] The Anti-Inflation Appeal Board was empowered to hear appeals from rulings and orders made by the Anti-Inflation Administrator.[95]

In addition to appellate jurisdiction, administrative tribunals are also vested with legislative authority for their operations and procedures. They may, for example, make regulations and rules pertaining to their activities, subject to the approval of the minister or Governor-in-Council. Since the policy objectives are set in the acts from which appeals are made, the issue of policy objects being set out in enabling acts of tribunals does not pertain.

Management Structure

The management structure of administrative tribunals normally consists of a chairman, a vice- or assistant chairman and a small number of board members. Members are appointed by the Governor-in-Council during good behaviour, subject to removal for cause. The terms of appointment are fixed and will usually be set for seven to ten years. The nature of appointments provides the high degree of independence required for the operation of agencies of this type.

Because these agencies function as courts, members appointed to them are often drawn and are sometimes required to be drawn from the legal profession. For example, the Tax Review Board Act requires that no member may serve as Chairman or Assistant Chairman of the Board unless he is "a judge of a superior court of Canada or a superior, county or district court of a province" or "a barrister or advocate of not less than ten years' standing."[96] The Immigration Appeal Board Act requires that the Chairman and at least two other members be barristers or advocates with ten years' experience in a province.[97] Given the degree of independence accorded by the nature of the appointments, the minister's responsibility and indeed involvement in such cases is minimal.

Controls

To complement the independence accorded these tribunals through the appointment of members, tribunals also enjoy substantial management autonomy from the provisions of the Financial Administration Act and the Public Service Employment Act. They are listed in the Financial Administration Act as "branches designated," but their constituent acts provide for the financial and personnel procedures to be applied in their operations. They are nevertheless required to report annually to Parliament through the designated minister and are subject to audit by the Auditor General.

The controls exercised over these agencies are therefore not so much ministerial or administrative as they are judicial. Perhaps the more salient control pertains to the legal aspect of their work. The decisions of these bodies are subject, with few exceptions, to judicial review by the higher courts on questions of law and jurisdiction.[98] Judicial review differs from appeal in that the former involves assessing the legality of a procedure or ruling a matter *ultra vires* the jurisdiction of the agency. It does not involve the substitution of the higher court's decision for that of the body being reviewed. Thus, judicial review acts as a control on these tribunals to the extent that it will provide the legal parameters within which they may operate.

Procedural Safeguards

Despite the statement on judicial review above, a recurring issue concerning the operation of administrative tribunals has been the question of adequate procedural safeguards. The essential problem here is the potential conflict between legal and administrative objectives. Administration must not only be efficient in the sense that the objectives of policy are securely obtained without delay, it must also satisfy the general body of citizens that it is proceeding with reasonable regard to the balance between the public interest it promotes and the private interests it disturbs. Adjudications must be acceptable as having been properly made.

The stated advantages of administrative tribunals may not be fully realized and rights of individuals may be lost if Parliament fails to see that tribunals are properly constituted to attain the real purposes of the legislation by a proper discharge of their powers and functions. The objectives of administration must be reconciled with the requirements of 'natural justice' being fulfilled. It is important, therefore, that Parliament be explicit when granting powers to a subordinate board or tribunal. Minimum procedural rules must be included in the legislation, with the provision for more detailed rules to be determined after a tribunal's essential functions have been ascertained. Regular reviews of the operations of tribunals may be desirable to ensure that there is continuing collaboration and rationalization of judicial and administrative processes to meet the needs of both public and private interests.

Independence or Integration?

It was noted at the outset that the several different types of nondepartmental bodies serve in differing capacities and contexts as instruments of government policy. While primarily administrative mechanisms, in differing ways they do support government objectives. However, given the nature of their operations, some degree of independence from direct government control is considered to be necessary. For example, agencies such as regulatory commissions and administrative tribunals require a high degree of independence to perform their quasi-judicial functions effectively. Advisory councils need some degree of independence to ensure they can serve as alternative and even critical sources of advice to government. Crown corporations and marketing boards endeavour to achieve government objectives by means of private-sector practices. Hence, some degree of independence is necessary to ensure that economic efficiency in their operations is appropriately obtained.

A problem arises, nevertheless, in reconciling the "policy function," however defined and circumscribed, with the administrative purposes of their operations. In most cases, Parliament has delegated authority to these agencies in general terms and provided only a general policy framework. Agencies exercise discretion in the determination of the practical means by which government objectives will be served. Ministers may be involved in approving regulations passed by the agencies or budgets proposed by them, for example, but direct intervention will be limited.

Determining how and for what a minister should accept responsibility in the operation of these agencies is a complex problem. If, as is commonly held, a minister and a government must be responsible for policy in its general and specific forms, then it follows that some mechanism is needed whereby that responsibility can be assumed. The inclusion of a directive power in agency statutes as proposed by the government and the Lambert Commission is one means of ensuring that responsibility is exercised and the accountability of the minister for policy is maintained. However, the use of directives could lead to something more than policy accountability.

If an agency is subject to regular direction by this means, it would lose its independence no matter how much autonomy it had been granted on administrative matters. Extensive use of policy directives could, over time, serve to integrate the nondepartmental body into a departmental structure. The critical question that ministers have to address in considering the adoption of directives is the purpose and extent to which they will be used. Directives should not provide a back-door means of redesigning nondepartmental agencies.

In the realm of administrative practices, recent proposals have emphasized the need for tighter controls to be exercised by government and more effective accountability to Parliament. In the first instance, any agency that spends public money should ensure that probity and prudence are passionately pursued in the expenditure of that money. Whether improved systems of financial administration, for example, are achieved by a more active involvement of the Treasury Board and its Secretariat or by external monitoring mechanisms must be examined closely. The imposition of standard practices applied in the public service proper could negate the initial rationale for the creation of a nondepartmental body in particular instances. Secondly, parliamentary scrutiny of the operations of nondepartmental agencies is an important element of accountability and control. The extent to which Parliament can in a dispassionate and nonpartisan fashion influence the performance of these agencies and their chief executive officers is tempered by the fact that boards of directors and ministers exercise the effective means of control.

In the final analysis, if controls—policy and administrative—become too pervasive the advantages of the nondepartmental form may be lost. These bodies have been used as flexible managerial tools, in that they have allowed government to undertake activities expeditiously and effectively without unduly burdening ministers with additional responsibilities. As their numbers have increased, however, they have added to the complexity of government operations and on occasion raised substantive questions about the extent of state intervention. Better means of control and coordination may serve to address the first problem; a reexamination of the purposes of these agencies is needed to deal with the second. In particular, the need to establish a balance between the independence accorded an agency and the integration of its activities with other government undertakings is critical for the effective performance of these agencies, whatever their particular purpose. Changes can be made in enabling legislation that can facilitate this process, but the practical integration of policy objectives and the separation of administrative operations is not a facile task. Given the large number of agencies of these different kinds, the magnitude of the problem is considerable. The following chapter considers some measures by which coordination of agency and departmental activities have been pursued.

Notes

1. J.E. Hodgetts, *The Canadian Public Service*, pp. 138-56; Royal Commission on Government Organization, *Report*, vol. V, pp. 54-77; Royal Commission on Financial Management and Accountability, *Report*, Part IV, "Crown Agencies," pp. 269-366.

2. Hodgetts, *The Canadian Public Service*, p. 138.

3. Ibid., pp. 138-39.

4. See also T. Hockin, *Government in Canada*, especially ch. 1.

5. Government of Canada, Privy Council Office, *Crown Corporations: Direction, Control, Accountability* (Ottawa: Supply and Services, 1977), p. 17.

6. Financial Administration Act, schedules B to D. A schedule B or departmental corporation is defined as "any Crown corporation that is a servant or agent of Her Majesty in right of Canada and is responsible for administrative, supervisory or regulatory services of a governmental nature," Section 66(3)(a) of the Act; a schedule C or agency corporation is defined as "an agent of Her Majesty in right of Canada and is responsible for the management of trading or service operations on a quasi-commercial basis, or for the management of procurement, construction or disposal activities on behalf of Her Majesty," Section 66(3)(b) of the Act; and a schedule D or proprietary corporation is one that "is responsible for the management of lending or financial operations, or for the management of commercial and industrial operations involving the production of or dealing in goods and the supplying of services to the public," section 66(3)(c)(i) of the Act. Reproduced by permission of the Minister of Supply and Services.

7. Royal Commission on Government Organization, *Report*, vol. V, p. 58.

8. Ibid., p. 59.

9. Canada, House of Commons, Public Accounts Committee, *Minutes and Proceedings of Evidence* (May 17, 1977). Subsequent amendments to this list were tabled. The Report of the Royal Commission on Financial Management and Accountability indicated that the count as of January 1979 was 426. See *Report*, p. 277. It should be noted that this later figure also included subsidiaries of parent crown agencies.

10. Royal Commission on Financial Management and Accountability, *Report*, p. 277.

11. Privy Council Office, *Crown Corporations: Direction, Control, Accountability, op. cit.* See also Privy Council Office, *Submissions to the Royal Commission on Financial Management and Accountability*, "Responsibility in the Constitution Part II: Non-departmental Bodies," pp. 2-1 to 2-198, for a detailed review of these agencies.

12. Royal Commission on Financial Management and Accountability, *Report*, pp. 285-89.

13. The classic references which address this issue include: C.A. Ashley, R.G.H. Smails, *Canadian Crown Corporations: Some Aspects of their Administration and Control* (Toronto: Macmillan of Canada, 1965); and Lloyd Musolf, *Public Ownership and Accountability: The Canadian Experience* (Cambridge, Mass.: Harvard University Press, 1959).

14. Some recent studies in this regard include: André Gélinas (ed.), *Public Enterprise and the Public Interest* (Toronto: Institute of Public Administration of Canada, 1978); G.B. Doern (ed.), *The Regulatory Process in Canada* (Toronto: Macmillan of Canada, 1978); A.R. Lucas, T. Bell, *The National Energy Board: Policy, Procedure and Practice*, prepared for the Law Reform Commission (Ottawa: Supply and Services, 1977); and J.W. Langford, "Crown Corporations as Instruments of Policy," in G.B. Doern and P. Aucoin (eds.), *Public Policy in Canada* (Toronto: Macmillan of Canada, 1979), pp. 239-74.

15. Five main types of agencies are discussed below: crown corporations, regulatory commissions, advisory councils, marketing boards and administrative tribunals. Although similar criteria were applied in dealing with each type as that outlined in the Lambert Report, the categories were different. For example, the Report identified independent deciding and advisory bodies, crown corporations and shared enterprises of the primary categories. In this discussion, crown corporations and shared enterprises are treated together and the other four types are distinguished rather than treated as a separate category.

16. This definition includes in part that offered in section 66(1) of the Financial Administration Act and the distinction on ownership provided in the Green Paper on Crown Corporations. See the latter document for discussion, p. 37.

17. See Ashley and Smails, *Canadian Crown Corporations*, pp. 3-5; and Hodgetts, *Canadian Public Service*, pp. 138-56.

18. Ibid. Only the New Democratic Party is politically committed to public ownership as party policy.

19. *Crown Corporations: Direction, Control, Accountability*, p. 14.

20. Corporations have also been created pursuant to the Canada Business Corporations Act or by letters patent. See *Crown Corporations: Direction, Control, Accountability*, p. 29.

21. *Revised Statutes of Canada*, 1970, Broadcasting Act, 1967-68, section 3(g). Reproduced by permission of the Minister of Supply and Services Canada.

22. See National Housing Act, Office Consolidation, *Revised Statutes*, 1970, ch. N-10, amended 1973-74, ch. 18, and 1974-75, ch. 38.

23. *Statutes of Canada*, 1974-75-76, 23-24-25 Eliz. II, vol. II, ch. 61 Petro-Canada Act, section 3.

24. The debates of the House of Commons and its committees contain many colourful exchanges on the question of CBC programming activities. One of the more interesting cases in this regard took place in 1964. The famous "This Hour Has Seven Days" dispute has been documented as a case study. See K. Kernaghan and A. Willms (eds.), *Public Administration in Canada: Selected Readings*, 2nd ed. (Toronto: Methuen, 1971), pp. 462-68.

25. Housing starts are used as a key indicator of economic growth.

26. Royal Commission on Financial Management and Accountability, *Report*, p. 283.

27. "During good behaviour," as opposed to "during pleasure," connotes tenure of office and hence greater independence from political control.

28. As Langford points out, this practice may enhance "responsiveness" of crown corporations, but it reduces their independence or separation from government administration. See Langford, "Crown Corporations as Instruments of Policy," p. 257.

29. Petro-Canada is an example. Section 5 of the Act provides for $500 million to be divided into one hundred common shares of the par value of $5 million each. Moneys come from the Consolidated Revenue Fund.

30. See note 6 above.

31. *Revised Statutes of Canada*, 1970, ch. F-10, Financial Administration Act, section 70(1).

32. Ibid., section 70(2).

33. Ibid., section 70(3).

34. Ibid., section 75(3). See Kroeker, *Accountability and Control, op. cit.*, pp. 26-28, for a discussion of the budgetary process for crown corporations.

35. Royal Commission on Financial Management and Accountability, *Report*, pp. 336, 350-54; and *Crown Corporations: Direction, Control, Accountability*, pp. 34-35.

36. Ibid.

37. *Crown Corporations: Direction, Control, Accountability*, p. 40.

38. *Revised Statutes of Canada*, 1970, Central Mortgage and Housing Corporation Act, ch. C-16, section 5(5).

39. Ibid., Canadian Commercial Corporation Act, ch. C-6, section 4(2).

40. *Statutes of Canada*, 1974-75-76, 23-24-25 Eliz. II, vol.II, ch. 61, Petro-Canada Act, section 7(2).

41. For example, during the debate on the Petro-Canada bill, the sponsoring minister, the Hon. Donald MacDonald stated: "Also within what might be regarded in part as a 'social function', the company will be expected to pay special attention to the education and training of native peoples in the petroleum sector." See House of Commons, *Debates* (Wednesday, March 12, 1975), p. 4037.

42. *Crown Corporations: Direction, Control, Accountability*, p. 51.

43. Ibid., pp. 22-24.

44. Ibid. A draft "Crown Corporations Act" was set out on pages 49-69.

45. Royal Commission on Financial Management and Accountability, *Report*, p. 585.

46. House of Commons, *Debates* (Wednesday, October 11, 1978), p. 2.

47. See G.B. Doern, "The Regulatory Process in Canada," in G.B. Doern (ed.), *The Regulatory Process in Canada* (Toronto: Macmillan of Canada, 1978), pp. 1-34.

48. See Canada, Economic Council of Canada, *Regulation Reference: a preliminary report to First Ministers* (Ottawa: Supply and Services, 1978), pp. 2-12.

49. An essential feature, therefore, is compulsion. See Doern, "The Regulatory Process in Canada," pp. 16-18.

50. Ibid., pp. 6-11 and Economic Council of Canada, *Regulation Reference* (November 1978), pp. 17-25.

51. That is, decisions of a quasi-judicial or adjudicative nature.

52. R. Schultz, "The Development of Regulation in Canada," a paper presented to Seminar on Regulatory Purpose and Policy, McGill University (Montreal: April 20-22, 1978).

53. Schultz, "The Development of Regulation in Canada," p. 3. It can also be pointed out that "social regulation," by and large, has been administered by traditional departmental forms rather than independent agencies. See Doern, "The Regulatory Process in Canada," pp. 16-17.

54. C. Lloyd Brown-John, "Defining regulatory agencies for analytic purposes," *Canadian Public Administration* (Spring 1976), vol. 19, no. 1, p. 142.

55. *Revised Statutes of Canada*, 1970, ch. N-6, National Energy Board Act, section 11(b).

56. Some of the problems and conflicts that can occur are identified in Lucas's study of the National Energy Board. See, in particular, pp. 21-42 of Lucas and Bell, *The National Energy Board*, 1977; and A.R. Lucas, "The National Energy Board," in Doern (ed.), *The Regulatory Process in Canada*, pp. 259-313.

57. *Revised Statutes of Canada*, 1970, ch. N-17, The National Transportation Act, 1966-67, section 27.

58. "Responsibility in the Constitution. Part II: Non-departmental Bodies," pp. 2-13 to 2-18.

59. A Telecommunications Act which revised and updated the broadcasting legislation was introduced in the House in November 1978. The bill died on the order paper of that session of Parliament and has not been reintroduced.

60. Royal Commission on Financial Management and Accountability, *Report*, pp. 309-25.

61. Ibid., p. 325.

62. Lucas, "The National Energy Board," pp. 282-96.

63. Broadcasting Act, 1966-67, section 20(2).

64. Lucas, "The National Energy Board", pp. 296-99.

65. M.J. Trebilcock, "The Consumer Interest and Regulatory Reform," in G.B. Doern, *The Regulatory Process in Canada*, pp. 94-127. The Berger Commission inquiry into the planned construction of the Mackenzie Valley Pipeline in 1976-77 set a precedent by providing funds to groups to allow them to make a presentation to the Commission. This practice has not been adopted by any regulatory commission to date.

66. National Transportation Act, 1966-67, section 25.

67. Broadcasting Act, 1966-67, section 23.

68. *Statutes of Canada*, 1974-75-76, 23-24-25 Eliz. II, ch. 75, Anti-Inflation Act. Section 24 provided for the Governor-in-Council to rescind an order made by the Administrator. This, in effect, provided an intermediary appeal route between the Administrator and the Tribunal.

69. See Lucas and Bell, *The National Energy Board*, pp. 43-49.

70. Royal Commission on Financial Management and Accountability, *Report*, p. 319.

71. C. Lloyd Brown-John, "Defining regulatory agencies for analytic purposes," p. 24.

72. See Economic Council of Canada, *Regulation Reference: A Preliminary Report*, for a discussion of the terms of the reference on pp. 1-2.

73. See G.B. Reschenthaler, "Regulatory Failure and Competition," *Canadian Public Administration* (Fall 1976), vol. 19, no. 3, pp. 466-86. For a broader consideration of the costs, benefits and issues in regulatory reform, see Economic Council of Canada, *Responsible Regulation: An Interim Report* (Ottawa: Supply and Services, 1979).

74. See P. Aucoin, "The Role of Functional Advisory Councils," in Doern and Aucoin, *The Structures of Policy Making in Canada*, pp. 154-78; and C. Lloyd Brown-John, "Advisory Agencies in Canada: an introduction," *Canadian Public Administration* (Spring 1979), vol. 22, no. 1, pp. 72-91.

75. *Revised Statutes of Canada*, 1970, ch. E-1, Economic Council of Canada Act, section 9.

76. Canada, *Estimates* for the fiscal year ending March 31, 1978, pp. 16-62.

77. Richard Phidd has written extensively on the subject of the role and functions of the Economic Council. See in particular Phidd, "The Role of Central Advisory Councils: The Economic Council of Canada," in Doern and Aucoin, *The Structures of Policy Making in Canada*; and R.W. Phidd and G.B. Doern, *The Politics and Management of Canadian Economic Policy*, pp. 53-67. The observation, nevertheless, is my own.

78. A key example here was the creation of the Science Council in 1966 as a new agency to perform functions which its predecessor, the National Research Council, was deemed unable to incorporate into its operations. See G.B. Doern, "The Role of Central Advisory Councils:

The Science Council of Canada," in Doern and Aucoin, *The Structures of Policy Making in Canada*, pp. 246-66; and G.B. Doern, *Science and Politics in Canada* (Montreal: McGill-Queen's University Press, 1972), pp. 1-100.

79. Royal Commission on Financial Management and Accountability, *Report*, p. 318.

80. Frank Milligan, "The Canada Council as a public body," *Canadian Public Administration* (Summer 1979), vol. 22, no. 2, pp. 269-89.

81. Royal Commission on Financial Management and Accountability, *Report*, pp. 314-15.

82. C.L. Brown-John, "Advisory Agencies in Canada: an introduction," especially pp. 86-91.

83. J.M. Sullivan, *A Statistical Summary of Marketing Boards in Canada, 1976-77* (Ottawa: Supply and Services, 1978), Agriculture Canada publication no. 78/6, p. 1.

84. Provincial jurisdiction obtains from the British North America Act, section 92(13), "property and civil rights in a Province"; federal jurisdiction obtains from section 91(2), "Trade and commerce."

85. *Revised Statutes of Canada*, 1970, ch. C-12, Canadian Wheat Board Act, section 4 and Part II, section 16-23.

86. Ibid., section 10.

87. *Statutes of Canada*, 1970-71-72, 19-20-21 Eliz. II, ch. 65, Farm Products Marketing Agencies Act, section 6.

88. *Revised Statutes of Canada*, 1970, ch. 37 (1st supp.), Canadian Saltfish Act, section 7.

89. Farm Products Marketing Agencies Act, section 15.

90. Elizabeth Bond, "Marketing Boards and the Consumer: An Expensive Affair," *Canadian Consumer* (December 1973), vol. 3, no. 6, pp. 26-29; and V.W. Yorgason, "But Who Reviews the Reviewers? The Case of Eggs," *Canadian Public Policy* (Summer 1976), vol. II, no. 3, pp. 511-19.

91. See in particular, *Responsible Regulation: An Interim Report* (1979), *op. cit.*

92. John Willis, "The Administrator as Judge: The Citizen's Right to an Impartial Tribunal," in J.E. Hodgetts and D.C. Corbett, *Canadian Public Administration* (Toronto: Macmillan of Canada, 1960), pp. 514-23.

93. *Statutes of Canada*, 1970-71-72, 19-20-21 Eliz. II, ch. 11, Tax Review Board Act, section 7.

94. *Revised Statutes of Canada*, 1970, ch. I-3, Immigration Appeal Board Act, sections 10 and 11.

95. Anti-Inflation Act, section 30.

96. Tax Review Board Act, section 4(2).

97. Immigration Appeal Board Act, section 3(7).

98. The Immigration Appeal Board Act contains a privative clause (section 22) which gives the Board exclusive jurisdiction over appeals from deportation orders and applications for admission of relatives to Canada pursuant to section 22 of the Immigration Act.

6
Mechanisms for Coordination, Consultation and Consensus Building

Given the scope and variety of structures that constitute the administrative machinery of government, the techniques and devices employed by the executive in effecting action and coordinating the different parts of the system are important tools of government. The discussion in earlier chapters demonstrated how the principles of individual and collective ministerial responsibility provide the framework for public-service management and policy development within the public service. The relationships between the central-policy and central-management agencies on the one hand and the departments on the other provide practical examples of the operational implications of those principles. The relationships between ministers and nondepartmental bodies demonstrate how the doctrine of ministerial responsibility is maintained in cases in which a measure of independence from direct political and administrative control has been delegated to an organization.

The implementation of the policy and administrative reforms undertaken by the Trudeau administrations during the 1960s and 1970s emphasized the structures and processes by which these reforms could be realized. Coordination and collaboration between and among the different parts of the administrative machinery were important dimensions of these activities. Furthermore, the emphasis placed on policy making defined in broad terms as policy and program design and development necessitated the development of appropriate mechanisms for coordination within the public service and for consultation and dialogue with external interests. The basic activities of policy making—the generation of ideas, the selection of ideas best suited and acceptable to the needs of the decision makers as well as the mobilization of support from the relevant constituency or constituencies—were pursued through the use of traditional and innovative techniques and interactions.[1]

In considering the basic activities of policy making, the choice of mechanisms and techniques for effecting coordination and collaboration within and outside the machinery of government is important, for there is a reciprocal relationship between what governments do and how they do it.[2] How policy is made can determine what kind of policy is made. For example, how an issue is defined can determine the pattern of organizational interests that will be involved. As governmental activities have expanded and many new structures have emerged, the patterning of interests has become more complex as the number of participants has increased. Phidd and Doern have cogently demonstrated evolution of this kind in the area of economic policy.[3] In 1939, for example, the Department of Finance was *the* economic portfolio. Forty years later, Finance is only one—albeit a key—department responsible for economic policy activities. Many others have appeared: Treasury Board Secretariat; Consumer and Corporate Affairs; Industry, Trade and Commerce; Manpower and Immigration, now Employment and Immigration; and the Ministry of State for Economic Development—not to mention other agencies such as the Economic Council of Canada and the Foreign Investment Review Agency. As the issues have been defined in more complex terms, there has been a greater differentiation in the structural forms responsible for the several aspects of the issues. In turn, more elaborate coordinative measures have been required.

Second, in those instances in which direct public participation is solicited, the forum of consultation or debate as well as the individuals and groups to be involved are important. The purpose of consultation of this kind is also a relevant consideration. The age of participatory democracy in the 1960s raised citizens' expectations of their role in policy making. A hard lesson was learned by public groups that participation did not mean decision taking; being consulted did not mean that government would do what interest groups or individuals suggested that it should do. For its part, the government shifted its attention to educating the public on government policy and soliciting views more formally and selectively. Participatory democracy had encouraged confrontation; the new frontier of consultation which emerged in the late 1970s reflected a renewed search for consensus between government and the different publics.

As discussed earlier, policy making within the administrative machinery is a top-down and bottom-up exercise. Coordination within and between departments and agencies that support ministerial decision making is effected by and large through the use of interdepartmental committees. In addition, experiments have been made to improve communications and coordinate activities within portfolios through the use of ministry or portfolio committees. The internal mobilization of support for government action is mainly directed to achieving consensus among the different actors in a particular policy-making network.

Outside the public service, the executive has employed a variety of techniques in its policy-making activities. Mechanisms such as royal commissions and task forces and techniques such as white and green papers have been employed as means of soliciting views and obtaining advice or demonstrating concern for public issues. Selective and informal consultations with interest groups and individual lobbyists have remained a regular part of policy making. The emphasis on direct government-public interaction during the last decade, nevertheless, has been perceived by many to shift attention away from Parliament as the primary forum for consultation and debate and as a channel for the expression of public views on policy issues. The role Parliament has played vis-à-vis the executive in policy making has been a limited one, although the institution provides important mechanisms that the executive can use as part of its policy-making activities.

The examination of coordinative and collaborative techniques will begin with the processes internal to the public service. Interdepartmental committees, task forces and portfolio committees will be considered with a view to identifying how internal interests are coordinated and mobilized. In considering how public input is solicited and obtained, formal and informal techniques and mechanisms of consultation and debate will be considered.

Coordination within the Administrative Machinery

The complex networks of interrelationships that influence the activities of policy making are integral to an understanding of government decision making. What decisions are taken and the kinds of interactions that lead to those decisions are pertinent considerations in analyzing public policy. The key activities of policy making within the public service are structured in large measure by the political decision-making process. Senior inter-departmental committees, for example, are the natural complements of cabinet committees; they can and do serve the purpose of resolving conflict as well as initiating and coordinating activities across government de-partments. Portfolio committees, on the other hand, seek to coordinate effectively the policy responsibilities of ministers for agencies reporting directly or indirectly to them. The support they provide to ministerial decision making is an integral part of the processes of coordination and collaboration within a policy sector. Thus, individual and collective ministerial responsibility is enhanced through committee processes within the administrative machinery.

Interdepartmental Committees

Interdepartmental committees exist at most levels in the public service, from the deputy-minister to the program-official levels. The actual number of interdepartmental committees is unknown, but one could estimate that there are several hundred at the senior-executive level alone.[4] Their status and influence are largely a function of the rank and number of representatives from the departments and central agencies. Senior-level committees are usually established by cabinet, which sets formal terms of reference for them.

Interdepartmental committees are used to serve a wide variety of functions. As mechanisms that support policy-making activities, they provide useful means whereby policy development and implementation can be effected. They are important means for central agencies to initiate or coordinate new undertakings. They support departmental policy making by bringing together a number of interested parties and resolving conflicts before recommendations are made to ministers. In each instance, consensus and support are sought through coordination. In the process, compromise may constitute the operating norm of committee proceedings. While it is difficult to classify interdepartmental committees precisely on the basis of functions performed, a number of common committee functions have been set out below as a means of examining some of the different interdepartmental committees.[5]

Committees to Initiate

Central agencies and departments will often propose an interdepartmental committee as a vehicle to initiate policy. If the establishment of such a committee is proposed in a memorandum to cabinet, the designation of the lead agency (or chair) as well as the constituent members will be identified formally and the terms of reference of the committee set out. For example, if the government receives an independently commissioned report such as a royal-commission report, the cabinet may establish a senior interdepartmental committee to review the study with instructions to recommend a government position of the report and its recommendations. If the study were on the subject of immigration, for example, it would be expected that the lead agency in this case would be the Department of Employment and Immigration and the report would be made to cabinet through the Minister of Employment and Immigration. In its review, the committee might see fit to recommend a continuing role for itself in monitoring the implementation of the policy recommendations that the lead agency puts forward.

On the other hand, in areas in which departmental jurisdiction is not readily identifiable or in which a major impetus is required, a central agency such as the Privy Council Office or the Treasury Board Secretariat may assume lead-agency responsibility. Once an initial report has been made, however, it is normal practice that any continuing responsibility for interdepartmental coordination be spun off to a lead department.

Committees to initiate are useful means of mobilizing departmental interest and support at an early stage in the policy process. They are normally short-term undertakings unless their mandates are changed to provide for a continuing role. Committees serve to bring together the relevant parties that may make a contribution to the development and formulation of policy initiatives or actions.

Committees to Negotiate or Arbitrate

In committees established to negotiate or arbitrate interests, the focus of attention is placed generally on "territorial" claims of the departments and agencies represented on the committee. In this sense, any committee that becomes involved in determining departmental responsibilities for a joint or multidepartmental undertaking may be considered to be a negotiating forum. An example of such a committee would be the Interdepartmental Committee on Harbours.[6] Its terms of reference included the examination of and recommendations for the rationalization of harbours' administration structure; the possible transfer of marine-program responsibilities from the Department of Public Works to Transport; and the rationalization of marine-engineering responsibilities between these two departments. In this case, the Treasury Board Secretariat chaired the committee, with the Privy Council Office, the Departments of Public Works, Transport and Environment as members. Another example of a committee of this nature would be the Ad Hoc Senior Officials Committee on Food Policy established in 1974 to review food policies throughout the government and to identify respective departmental responsibilities for the same. This committee was chaired by the Privy Council Office and was supported by a subordinate Co-ordinating Committee of officials.

Committees to negotiate assist in promoting effective implementation of policy and programs. The determination of appropriate departmental roles and the arbitration of conflicts arising from departmental claims can be important means of ensuring support for and the performance of policy decisions. Compromise may be necessary to achieve coordination of activities, but the responsibilities on an individual basis must be discharged.

Committees to Advise

In one sense, all interdepartmental committees advise, in that they report to a senior departmental official or minister and, as the case may be, through the minister to cabinet. Interdepartmental advisory committees may function on a continuing basis or for a specified period. An example of a committee of this nature was the Senior Interdepartmental Committee on Labour Relations set up in 1975 to develop a plan to improve labour relations within federal jurisdiction and to address problems arising from labour disruptions. This committee was chaired by the Privy Council Office and supported by a number of interdepartmental subcommittees.

Departments may seek to establish interdepartmental committees for purposes of coordinating the development of policy in a particular area and for advising ministers on developments. In cases such as the Departments of Transport and Industry, Trade and Commerce, for example, the scope of the departmental mandates requires extensive interdepartmental coordination in the preparation of policy and program advice. Some committees such as the Interdepartmental Highway Committee on Highway Policy have a long-established history. This committee, which is chaired by Transport, was set up in 1974 to replace the Highway and Road Co-ordinating Committee established in 1965. The committee reports annually to cabinet through the Minister of Transport on current and future highway activity of all federal departments. In general, committees to advise are primarily concerned with providing information and commentary or recommendations on developments in a policy area.

Committees to Evaluate

Interdepartmental committees may be established to evaluate policy and programs and to recommend appropriate courses of action. A noteworthy example of a committee that performs this function is the Committee of Senior Officials (COSO). It was noted earlier that this Committee was established in 1969 on a recommendation by the Advisory Group on Executive Compensation in the Public Service. In addition to its role as a senior interdepartmental body to evaluate performance of senior officials, it also sits as the senior interdepartmental forum for review of proposals for major government and departmental reorganizations. Subordinate committees and task forces may be established to undertake special assignments in relation to COSO's work on organization or particular departments may be responsible for preparing proposals and providing background material. The Privy Council Office chairs this Committee and it reports to the prime minister.

Another example of this type of committee is the Co-ordinating Committee of Officials, also referred to earlier. This interdepartmental body, which is chaired by a Treasury Board Secretariat official, reviews and recommends departmental requests for SX positions and considers macroorganizational issues of departments. It reports to the Treasury Board through the Secretary to the Board.

Committees to evaluate will normally consider a proposal or request and alternative courses of action. Central-agency concerns may dominate these types of forums, for these concerns are often directed to ensuring a consistent application of policy and program guidelines across the public service as a whole. An interdepartmental forum, however, provides an opportunity for a representation of interests to be brought to bear in considering a particular issue.

Committees to Monitor

These types of committees maintain a "watching brief" on departmental activities in a particular policy or program area. For example, the Interdepartmental Committee on External Relations established in 1970 was directed to coordinate all aspects of Canadian foreign policy and operations. The Department of External Affairs, which has policy responsibility, chairs the committee. Other members include: Industry, Trade and Commerce; Employment and Immigration; Treasury Board Secretariat; Canadian International Development Agency; and the Department of Public Works. A recent analysis of the work of this committee, however, has raised questions about its effectiveness as a coordinative monitoring body. Its ability to influence member departments, according to the review, has been limited.[7]

The work of the DM-10 Committee—so named because it is composed of ten deputy ministers—warrants special attention. It was established in 1975 following the introduction of wage and price controls and was extant until the controls program ended in 1978. It performed several functions, in that it initiated and it advised but, in particular, it monitored the whole range of economic and social policies of the government with respect to the controls program.[8] The Committee was chaired by the Secretary to the Cabinet and reported directly to the Cabinet Committee on Priorities and Planning through appropriate ministers. Policy papers were prepared by affected departments under the direction of appropriate ministers and were presented to and considered by the DM-10 committee before going to Cabinet Committee. Ministers then made decisions on subjects reported to it.[9]

Thus, committees to monitor are also concerned with coordinating activities and advising on matters considered by them as a result of their monitoring activities. They may be special-purpose and *ad hoc* or permanent bodies with a continuing role.

Interdepartmental Task Forces

Interdepartmental task forces perform many of the same functions as interdepartmental committees, but they normally operate as special-purpose bodies of a temporary nature. They consist generally of groups of officials at the middle-management or program level who have been seconded from departments and central agencies for the duration of the task force. Occasionally senior-level officials are involved in the work of these bodies. The assignments will usually take the form of a special study. For example, the Task Force on Decentralization in the Federal Public Service, which was set up in 1974, conducted a study on the feasibility of decentralizing the public service to the regions and reported to cabinet on proposals and opportunities for the same. The Task Force was chaired by the Treasury Board Secretariat and included membership from the Privy Council Office, Urban Affairs, Regional Economic Expansion and Public Works. The Interdepartmental Task Force on Direct Job Creation, which was set up in the same year, had a mandate—as its title implies—to design and coordinate employment programs. This Task Force was chaired by the Department of Manpower and Immigration (the name of the department was changed in 1977) and included members from ten other departments and agencies in the public service. An example of an interdepartmental task force set up to advise a department on internal matters was the task force established in 1969 by the Department of Transport. The use of "inside" consultants, although drawn from other departments and agencies, was a novel application of the task-force mechanism. The work of the task force, however, was not communicated effectively within the department. Greater attention was focused by the task force on establishing liaison with (and seeking approval of its plans from) senior officials in other parts of the public service. Not surprisingly, when its report was approved by cabinet, subsequent efforts at implementation were initially resisted within the Department of Transport.[10]

Interdepartmental committees and task forces are complementary forums to cabinet and its committees. In essence, they support the collective and individual responsibilities of ministers. The increasing interdependence of policy issues and the extensive initiation of new policy and program proposals have served to expand their use. As a result, the importance of "process" expertise has been emphasized. In a committee setting, process knowledge is a key attribute for participating officials. Substantive expertise may be secondary to an ability for making ideas acceptable to colleagues. Thus, the interplay between process and substance can be an important determinant of the outcome of committee proceedings.

The effectiveness of interdepartmental committees as instruments of policy making would be difficult to measure in qualitative terms. They can serve as effective forums for generating ideas, policy negotiation and advice. In cases in which territorial claims are predominant, they can act as mechanisms to resolve conflict. In difficult cases in which consensus or compromise may not be forthcoming, the committees may be disbanded or become dormant. There is no guarantee that interdepartmental committees will be effective in all circumstances, but they act as primary vehicles to coordinate activities through the representation of affected interests.

The representative nature of interdepartmental bodies nevertheless can be a hindrance to effective performance. A.W. Johnson, a former deputy minister and Secretary of the Treasury Board, has criticized harshly the "representative" approach to policy making and policy execution for stifling initiative and creativity by forcing consensus at the lowest common denominator of agreement.[11] He has argued that a bargaining situation inevitably results in a committee setting and the constraints imposed by the differing interests prevents clearcut decisions. Bargaining skills and effective coordination become more important than ideas or substantive reform. Finally, a large amount of energy is expended in these processes. Despite these objections, however, Johnson admits that the nature of collective decision making requires some degree of coordination and concludes that, while a single department or "individual" approach is preferable to the representative approach from the point of view of creativity and innovation, in practice some mix of the two approaches is necessary.[12]

What Johnson has argued against, it seems, is not the interdepartmental or representative approach *per se*, but rather the primary role that central agencies have played in the interdepartmental coordinative exercises. The emphasis placed on interdepartmental coordination during this period was supported by the several management reforms and policy innovations that were instituted. Interdepartmental committees and task forces were the primary vehicles by which central agencies and departments could communicate and coordinate their activities.

Given the nature of the decision-making process, however, interdepartmental committees will always be needed to provide coordination, to serve as bodies to generate ideas and to mobilize support internally for decisions that cabinet ministers must take collectively. The relative emphasis given to them and, in particular, to the activities of central agencies in these processes can be tempered by judicious intervention from the political level. Senior interdepartmental committees can be disbanded and alternative means employed to ensure appropriate coordination and collaboration between and among departments and agencies.

The Ministry System

A ministerial portfolio, as noted in an earlier chapter, may be considered as one in which a minister who is in charge of a department is also responsible for one or more agencies which operate with an arm's length relationship to him. In other words, a ministerial portfolio may include a department that reports directly to the minister on policy and administrative matters and several nondepartmental bodies that enjoy varying degrees of independence from political and administrative control. In the latter case, policy objectives are to be contained in the enabling legislation of these bodies. In both kinds of agencies, the appointment of senior officials is made by the Governor-in-Council.

No serious efforts were made to consider the problems arising from the need to coordinate the activities of agencies within a single portfolio until the mid-1960s. The increase in the number and kind of nondepartmental bodies highlighted the organizational problems created by the haphazard grouping of several entities around a minister; as well, the desire to create a policy focus for different government activities provided an impetus for reform. In 1964, the Bureau of Management Consulting Services examined department-agency relationships in several departments and considered several means by which coordination could be improved.[13] As new departments emerged through government reorganization legislation, efforts were made to group nondepartmental agencies with related activities around the "central policy" department in the portfolio. Beyond this, experiments in developing "ministry systems" were undertaken.[14]

The basic objectives of the "ministry system" in the several contexts in which it was considered were to clarify the roles and relationships between and among the minister, deputy minister and agency heads on the one hand and to rationalize and regularize the relationships of those agencies with central management on the other.[15] The heart of the issue, therefore, was to determine the appropriate lines of responsibility on policy and administrative matters as well as to develop means whereby appropriate coordination could be achieved. The necessary first step in delineating responsibilities and in improving coordination was to ensure that those agencies with related policy objectives would be grouped within a single ministry. The second step in improving coordination and facilitating communication was the establishment of a portfolio committee. Further institutionalization of the system was possible but was pursued, as will be discussed, in rather discrete cases.

The lines of policy and administrative responsibility for departments and nondepartmental bodies have already been discussed. Accepting that the department had primary responsibility for policy initiation and development, it followed that, in setting out the ministry system, the deputy minister would play a lead role in coordinating the several activities of the nondepartmental agencies to ensure effective policy implementation. Thus, the "portfolio committee" would be chaired by the deputy minister who, on behalf of his minister, would communicate the policy objectives of the department and work to relate the objectives and activities of the agencies to portfolio policy objectives.[16] The lines of communication would run downward from the minister to the department and outward to the several agencies. In this way, a global or comprehensive portfolio policy framework could be developed. The department would be the lead agency in the process. The role of the deputy minister in policy within the portfolio would thus be elevated and the administrative responsibilities of nondepartmental bodies would be defined more clearly. Formal support for the operation of the portfolio committee could be provided by the creation of a secretariat of officials seconded from the department and agencies in the portfolio.[17]

One of the first ministerial portfolios in which the ministry system was considered was the Solicitor General's Department. The 1966 Act that created the department identified several areas of responsibility of the minister, which in practical terms means that the National Parole Board, the Royal Canadian Mounted Police and the Canadian Penitentiary Service would report to him.[18] In 1973, following several studies and attempts of coordination within the portfolio, a Ministry Secretariat was established for the purpose of developing and coordinating policy across the portfolio.[19] Operational responsibilities of the nondepartmental agencies were untouched. However, the establishment of this Secretariat did not create a ministry system in which agencies were subordinated to the department on policy matters. In particular, the Commissioner of the

Royal Canadian Mounted Police ensured that direct liaison with the minister was maintained.[20] Thus, the ministry system may be said to have been only partially implemented in this case.

Steps were also taken to improve coordination in the Secretary of State's portfolio. The Department of State Act was amended in 1968 to include ministerial responsibilities for cultural agencies, libraries, museums, and the like.[21] Thus, the grouping of agencies was achieved. The second step—the creation of a portfolio committee—was less successful. Basically, the department lacked the policy capability to perform a coordinating role and could not command sufficient support from the several constituent bodies. In particular, it was faced with the predominance of the Canadian Broadcasting Corporation as the key cultural agency in the federal government. The legislation on the CBC includes policy objectives and the CBC for its part has relied on its own resources for policy support. Moreover, the President of the CBC has always enjoyed an independent yet direct relationship with the minister on matters of the CBC's policy and operations. The creation of an indirect relationship on policy matters would therefore likely be met with resistance. Finally, the President of the CBC has enjoyed a higher profile (and higher salary as a corporate executive in the public sector) giving him equal if not more status than that of the deputy minister of a department. These circumstances contributed to a short lifespan for the Council of Cultural Agency Heads, which was formed in the mid-1970s and operated briefly under the then Secretary of State. The department's role was quickly relegated and, while the minister met informally with the Council, the latter did not function as, or even pretend to approximate, a ministry portfolio committee.

The most concerted effort to fully implement a ministry system was undertaken in the Minister of Transport's portfolio in 1969. John Langford's analysis of the attempt at organizational reform and innovation reveals all of the basic problems of implementing a ministry system.[22] The creation of a ministry council responsible for coordinating and monitoring policy development and implementation in the portfolio resulted in several problems. Effective communications were lacking in the various steps and stages of implementing the system and resistance developed in several quarters of the portfolio. As in the Secretary of State example, one of the agencies in the portfolio was in certain respects a competitor with the department as a policy adviser to the minister. The legislation providing for the establishment of the Canadian Transport Commission had included a policy advisory role for the Commission which it was reluctant to relinquish. In the case of the other agencies, such as Air Canada and the Canadian National Railways, the relationships between the heads of these agencies and the deputy minister of the department were ones of imbalance. Establishing compatible objectives between corporate executives and public servants was not easily pursued.

A final variation of the ministry system might be exemplified by the integrated management models that were applied in two portfolios. The first involves the portfolio relations in urban affairs, which included the Ministry of State for Urban Affairs, the Central Mortgage and Housing Corporation and the National Capital Commission. The Ministry of State (created in 1971) was an experiment in policy initiation and coordination, in that the Ministry was not given any program responsibilities but rather was charged with policy development and intra- and intergovernmental coordination. However, line departments were not prepared to be co-ordinated on the basis that knowledge was power, particularly when they controlled the program funds. The provinces did not accept the legitimacy of a federal ministry in an area of provincial jurisdiction. Finally, the Central Mortgage and Housing Corporation did not accept the Ministry as the lead policy agency, particularly in the area of housing policy.

Following a review of the relationships between and among the agencies in this portfolio, an outside consulting firm recommended that the activities of the agencies be coordinated through the establishment of a portfolio-management committee. In December 1975, an amendment was made to the Central Mortgage and Housing Corporation Act to allow the position of Chairman of the Board of Directors of the Corporation (CMHC) to be held by the Secretary of the Ministry.[23] In addition, a portfolio committee was established which included the Secretary (as chairman) and the President of the Corporation and the Chairman of the National Capital Commission. The responsibilities of the chairman of the portfolio committee extended to the Ministry *and* to those activities in the CMHC (and to a lesser extent in the Commission) that pertained to urban policy. Since the appointment of the Secretary of the Ministry to be responsible for effecting these reforms was the former President of the CMHC the scheme was implemented with little difficulty. The attempt to integrate the Ministry's and the CMHC's policy functions, however, did little to change previous arrangements. The CMHC clung tenaciously to its responsibility. Gradually, the activities of the Ministry were wound down or integrated with CMHC, resulting finally in the disbandment of the Ministry in 1979.

Another example of an integrated portfolio-management model established by statute was the reorganization of the Manpower and Immigration portfolio in 1977.[24] The Act establishing the Department of Employment and Immigration and the Canada Employment and Immigration Commission provided that the deputy minister of the department would also be the Chairman of the Commission and its chief executive officer.[25] The Vice-Chairman would be an Associate Deputy Minister whose duties would be specified by the Chairman.[26] Thus, the department and the Commission are coordinated through an integrated management structure.

The relative lack of success of portfolio committees as effective instruments of policy coordination points up the problems of delegating authority to departments and nondepartmental bodies in such a way that policy and administrative parameters are clearly delineated. On the basis of the experiences noted above, it is clear that agencies have guarded their policy functions jealously and have not been prepared to take instruction from the minister through the deputy minister unless the deputy has the appropriate statutory authority. It was stated earlier that an agency with semi-autonomous status should not have active policy responsibilities. Nevertheless, these bodies are instruments of government policy and will develop and refine policy during the course of their normal operations.

The apparent means available for rationalizing policy responsibilities between and among the different bodies in a portfolio and coordinating the efforts of each unit in this regard are to modify the status of nondepartmental bodies to subordinate them to the department on policy matters and/or to establish more specific policy objectives for agencies in the enabling legislation. In the latter case, the application of policy directives, discussed in the last chapter, could be used to complement coordination within a portfolio if the department assumed responsibility for advising the minister on the directives to be issued to the agencies. Thus, not only would better ministerial accountability for policy be achieved, but improved coordination within the portfolio might also result.

The problems of internal coordination across government departments and agencies increase in direct relation to the number and kinds of organizations. For action to be taken in any one policy area, a number of different agencies must be mobilized to develop and support the activity. Interdepartmental committees provide a means whereby activities between departments may be coordinated to serve these ends. Within a particular ministerial portfolio, portfolio committees and integrated senior-management structures may be tried. A major effort was made during the Trudeau administrations in the 1960s and 1970s to rationalize relationships and structure processes in such a way that the interdependence of policy issues would be reflected in the processes by which policy was made. The coordinative mechanisms were therefore often elaborate and complex. One might say that these extraorganizational structures mostly represented shifting coalitions of interests within and between ministerial portfolios. In those cases in which central direction was required, central agencies would provide the impetus. In other cases in which departmental or portfolio leadership was needed, measures would be taken to structure the relationships to provide support for the minister. Above all, the processes of coordination, collaboration and consensus building within the machinery of government served to demonstrate its flexible and malleable nature.

Interaction with the Environment

The internal coordination of departmental and agency activities, however, is only one side of the activities that constitute policy making. The use of executive mechanisms and techniques for consultation and collaboration with individuals and groups is also important for generating support and building consensus on policy matters. Although in theory Parliament through its elected members is expected to represent the interests of individual citizens and groups in society, governments have also consulted directly with the public and have employed a wide variety of techniques in the process. In recent decades, public participation has been a vital element of policy making. Not only have people become more aware of government activities, but people have also taken more interest in participating in policy debates and discussions. For its part, the Trudeau government both initiated and responded to participative processes.

Consultation and collaboration can be pursued in a number of ways. On the one hand, formal techniques and mechanisms of consultation and investigation provide means of structuring the process within particular time frames. On the other hand, there is a high degree of interaction between the executive and outside interests that is relatively unstructured. The informal relationships of representatives of interest groups, professional lobbyists and consultants with politicians and public servants have expanded in scope and number as government activity has reached out to all societal functions. Maintaining balance between direct executive-public interaction and parliamentary-public interaction has not been easy. In recent years, the common perception has been that direct consultation has been emphasized over consultation through Parliament. Let us begin with an examination of several executive mechanisms of consultation, then consider the activities of interested groups and individuals.

Executive Mechanisms and Techniques

There are several formal means whereby the executive can initiate a process of consultation, investigation and/or debate on policy issues and proposals. In obtaining information and testing public opinion, these devices often help to generate support for government action. While their use may vary from administration to administration, they contribute to all stages and activities of the policy-making process.

Royal Commissions

Royal commissions are an ancient and venerable executive technique for fact finding, information gathering, public-opinion sampling, policy initiation and policy delay. In Canada, they are established pursuant to the Inquiries Act. Thus, they have the power to conduct public hearings, call for papers and call witnesses. Royal commissions in recent years have been either investigatory or policy oriented. Royal commissions of a strictly investigatory nature may be chaired by a single commissioner and constitute a formal inquiry into some wrongdoing. Examples include the Estey Commission on Air Canada set up in 1975 and the McDonald Commission on the Royal Canadian Mounted Police set up in 1977. Royal commissions that have dealt with policy questions have been more elaborate undertakings. The usual number of commissioners for a policy commission is three, although on occasion and largely for representative reasons there have been as many as seven commissioners, as in the case of the Royal Commission on the Status of Women set up in 1966. In addition, royal commissions can hire their own research staff—the size of which will be a function of the scope of the issue, the terms of the mandate and the length of the inquiry.

The golden age of royal commissions was the period 1958-68.[27] Both the Diefenbaker and the Pearson administrations used royal commissions extensively as means *and* ends of the policy process. In other words, royal commissions were established in response to policy concerns and as policy responses.[28] Royal commissions were not a primary vehicle used by the Trudeau administrations. Although the government inherited a large number of royal-commission reports from the Pearson period on taking office in 1968—including those of the Royal Commission on Taxation and the Royal Commission on Bilingualism and Biculturalism—it did not create many royal commissions of its own.

A number of investigatory commissions, as noted earlier, were established to inquire into particular cases. In addition to these, two policy-oriented royal commissions were established during the 1970s. The first was the Royal Commission on Corporate Concentration set up in 1975, which was headed by Mr. Robert Bryce, a former Secretary to the Cabinet and Deputy Minister of Finance. It was established as a policy response by the government to a takeover bid by Paul Desmarais of Power Corporation for control of Argus Corporation.[29] Ironically, within months of the release of the Commission report in 1978, another consortium headed by Conrad Black accomplished what the Commission had been established to investigate. In sum, this Commission had no further policy impact; rather, it was in itself a policy decision.

The second Royal Commission on Financial Management and Accountability set up in 1976 was also a policy response by the executive—in this case to harsh criticisms made by the Auditor General of financial-management practices in the federal government. The government recognized that improvements were needed but delayed action by establishing a royal commission to study the problems. Ironically, its report was released during the general-election campaign in the spring of 1979 and served to provide critical commentary on the government's performance.

A main value of royal commissions is the hearing process: it provides opportunities for individuals and groups to make submissions to a body that in turn will report to the executive. Second, as independent sources of advice, royal commissions can have significant impact on government policy. In particular, the use of expert research staff on the commissions can make important contributions in generating ideas and developing alternatives for government action. The limited use of royal commissions in recent years, however, might be attributed to a main disadvantage of this mechanism, the delay created by the length of the inquiry or study.

Task Forces

For gathering information, generating ideas and sampling public opinion, the task force is an attractive mechanism.[30] Task forces, in comparison with royal commissions, place more emphasis on the public-hearing process than on formal research. They will usually conduct their reviews within a shorter time than commissions but will be constituted formally in much the same way as royal commissions. For example, appointments are made by the Governor-in-Council and powers under the Inquiries Act can be granted. Thus, they serve as an alternative source of advice to the government as well as a means of mobilizing support on an issue.

An exceptional use of the task force was undertaken in 1968 when the minister responsible for housing created a task force on housing which he chaired.[31] By heading the inquiry, Mr. Hellyer identified himself with the report and its recommendations and subsequently found it necessary to resign when his cabinet colleagues would not support him. Collegiality in decision making was a hard lesson learned by this contender to the Liberal leadership in 1968.

Task forces can also be considered as means and ends in the policy process. For example, in 1977 the government established the Task Force on Canadian Unity as a policy response to the election of the Parti Québécois government in the province of Québec. The Task Force was cochaired by the Hon. Jean-Luc Pépin (a former federal cabinet minister) and the Hon. John Robarts (a former Progressive Conservative premier of Ontario) and comprised six other members representing the different regions in Canada.[32] The research staff was small and was assembled only for a short time. The major portion of the task-force activities were the public hearings conducted across the country. In this case, the result of the public-hearing process may well have served to refuel antagonisms between the two language groups rather than to generate consensus on issues. The report of the Task Force was released in February 1979. It offered no new findings on the state of the Canadian nation but it did contain a fresh expression of the extent and depth of the continuing crisis in Canadian federalism initially set out in the preliminary report of the Royal Commission on Bilingualism and Biculturalism some fourteen years earlier. For its part, the government released its own position paper on constitutional reform in July 1978 and thus in some respects preempted the Task Force's role as an alternative source of advice.[33]

A main value of the task-force technique is that it provides an expeditious means of testing public opinion and soliciting ideas on policy matters. As in the case of internal task forces, they serve to bring a small group of people together for a limited time to consider an issue and report on it. Given the importance of the hearing process to the deliberations of the task force, it might be said, however, that they provide an expression of opinion rather than a comprehensive analysis of issues in their final reports.

White Papers

The age of participation which was opened by the Trudeau Administration in 1968[34] led to a search for new techniques to test public support for policy proposals and to solicit views on proposed government policy. The elevation of a traditional parliamentary paper to the status of a participative technique was one of the new means that emerged.[35] Blue books and white papers have a long history in British parliamentary practice. They were used originally as means of informing parliamentarians and the interested public of government policy or action. Green papers appeared later and represented an attempt to test opinion at an earlier stage in the policy process before the government had decided on a policy approach. In Canada, white papers were used sparingly before 1968; green papers were not issued before that time.

From 1968 to 1972, eight white papers were released by the federal government for public debate.[36] Each was the result of internal policy reviews based on considerations of the recommendations and findings of investigatory bodies such as royal commissions, task forces or inter-departmental committees. Thus, each was an attempt to represent a government position on a policy matter. The fact that a paper was presented indicated that the government was either not satisfied with the results of the report or that it was necessary to refine the proposals it wanted to endorse. Because several of these papers were promoted for widespread public and parliamentary debate, they were considered as primary participative techniques.

The experience of the government with the debates that unfolded in several of the policy areas was not altogether a happy one. Conflict rather than consensus emerged in particular cases and led to a more cautious approach in the use of these documents.[37] From 1972, "discussion papers"—white, green, orange and blue—were issued on a highly selective basis and primarily for strategic reasons. For example, the government released a Green Paper on Communications Policy in 1973 primarily as a position paper to counter the policy of a provincial government (Québec) in the federal-provincial dialogue that was underway at that time. The Green Paper on Immigration of 1975 was released for public debate, even though the legislation which the government intended to introduce had already been drafted. It was unlikely, therefore, that the government had intentions of changing the proposals put forward as a result of the "debate." The release in 1977 of the blue paper on crown corporations— referred to in this book as a green paper—was used primarily for the purpose of testing parliamentary opinion in the dying days of a regime. The proposals nevertheless contained draft legislation for consideration.

The provision of policy information through the use of white and green papers can help to create an awareness of policy issues among parliamentarians and the public and to encourage an exchange of information and analysis. They can also serve as educational techniques. By providing information to Parliament and the public in the form of a white paper and by encouraging people to participate and feel involved in making decisions, the government hoped that individuals would understand problems better and be more receptive to change. In this way, consensus could be generated and support mobilized for government action.

Summary

Taken as a group of executive instruments to contribute to the processes of policy making, royal commissions, task forces, and white papers have particular advantages and disadvantages. If a major concern of contemporary governments is to develop a capacity to anticipate problems and gain lead time in their policy-making activities, these techniques will serve to create delay or lag rather than anticipation. By consulting the public, Parliament and other governments as the case may be, valuable time may be lost in making and implementing decisions. This may contribute to the appearance of indecisiveness on the part of the government, which in turn can affect its popularity. It is thus often difficult to determine when a study or debate is warranted or appropriate. For example, the Trudeau administration might have been better advised in 1976 to have undertaken major initiatives in improving financial-management practices in the public service than to have established a royal commission to look into problems that were already widely known and acknowledged. The review provided an opportunity for the problems to be publicized further. Even if the timing of the release of the report had been controlled and it had been released after—rather than during—the election campaign in the spring of 1979, the criticisms in the report would still have hurt that administration's political interests.

To a greater or lesser degree, these techniques are often perceived as bypassing Parliament and hence viewed as downgrading that institution. Consultation through the use of executive techniques such as these, while serving to provide alternative sources of advice to the government, can also be criticized as being too selective in their consultations. For example, groups that appear before royal commissions or task forces or make presentations in a white-paper debate may not represent a cross-section of public opinion, which presumably Members of Parliament are considered to represent. In the case of white papers, these processes do involve parliamentarians to a greater degree than in the case of royal-commission and task-force consultations, but may nevertheless be dominated by particular types of interests. Finally, the financial costs that accompany the operations and activities of these techniques are often criticized because such moneys could have been expended better on other purposes.

On the other hand, delay is sometimes a necessary condition in policy making. Opportunities for the public expression of views on a policy issue can serve as means of sampling opinion and determining how much or how quickly change or reform can be pursued. From the public's point of view, the solicitation of views and participation in public debate is essential in maintaining the vitality of the democratic process. If it is believed that every individual has the potential to develop a sense of political awareness and to participate in the affairs of government, then any effort to involve individuals in the process may be considered a positive action that will override undesirable consequences resulting from delay or financial costs. From the government's perspective, the strategic considerations of public participation must be analyzed carefully or conflict rather than consensus may be generated from such processes.

Interaction with Interest Groups

The current literature on interest and pressure groups testifies to the highly pragmatic nature of these organizations.[38] Given the nature of the cabinet-parliamentary system and the process of policy making in this context, most pressure-group activity is focused at the ministerial-official level.[39] Informed interest groups appreciate the importance of intervening at the point where the most impact can be made. The predominant types of interest groups have been the formally constituted institutional representatives of key agricultural, economic and cultural interests.[40] The era of participatory democracy of the 1960s witnessed the emergence of a large number of previously inarticulate interest groups, such as women and native peoples, and a number of issue-oriented groups, such as environmentalists and conservationists. The funding of "voluntary organizations" became a high priority of the Secretary of State's department in the early 1970s. The core-funding grants provided to the National Indian Brotherhood and the provincial Indian associations were a case in point.[41] Over time these organizations became institutionalized and gained recognition as legitimate interest-group representatives. While many of the new groups of this kind may not be considered in the same league as the

Canadian Manufacturers' Association, for example, their development and evolution resulted in characteristics and modes of operation similar to those of the institutional representatives.[42]

The forms of interest-group activity have evolved in recent years, sometimes in response to government initiatives. For the most part, the basic level of activity is for interest-group representatives to establish contacts with politicians and officials to exchange ideas and information and sometimes to make direct demands. A wide range of meetings takes place in private in ministers' and officials' offices: these meetings are sought by the small and the mighty. Recognition and hence legitimacy are the operative motives. The establishment of a permanent lobby with an office and funds is a key means of enhancing the stature of a group. The barter system of information exchange can be the lifeblood of the official and even ministers. Ministers' aides, for example, may consider this kind of network of contacts as important and potentially fruitful as the information network in the bureaucracy. Thus, it is in the interests of ministers and officials to establish and maintain contacts with groups that can provide information. In exchange, ideas or information may be offered.

This type of activity is an entrenched part of the policy-making process and constitutes the major portion of time spent by interest-group representatives. Informal channels may be the most effective means of obtaining response. If additional pressure is needed, some publicity may be generated to focus attention and ensure that appropriate audiences are obtained. In large measure, the process may be said to be manipulative but operates from the basis of establishing common interests for all affected parties.

There is also a traditional ritual which some groups observe—the annual public submission to cabinet. Groups such as the Federation of Canadian Municipalities make an annual pilgrimage to the Railway Committee Room in Centre Block to set out their demands or concerns. The case of the Federation is a good example of the emptiness of this formal process. Traditionally the Federation has demanded greater federal financial assistance and/or constitutional recognition. Short of a rewritten constitution in which recognition can be given to municipalities as a third level of government, there are severe limits to what the federal government can do to improve the financial position of the municipalities in Canada. Neither is there a ready political acceptance by the provinces to allow the federal government to deal directly with municipalities.

Other groups, such as the Canadian Manufacturers' Association and the Canadian Labour Congress, present formal briefs or submissions to cabinet on an annual basis in the same fashion. As the number of groups claiming an audience of this kind increased, measures were taken to facilitate the process. In 1977, for example, a selection of groups was slotted into a two-week period of meetings and roundtable discussions with ministers in an endeavour to economize on their time allotted to this activity.

The pattern of broad-based and rather unstructured participation which might be said to have typified the late 1960s and early 1970s was gradually replaced by more selective and structured forums. For example, greater emphasis was given to channelling interest-group participation into departmental advisory committees. Many nondepartmental bodies also created these types of forums.[43] In contrast to advisory councils that maintain a degree of independence and initiate research and provide policy advice in addition to serving as consultative bodies, departmental advisory committees are primarily mechanisms by which ministers and their officials can consult with clientele groups.

During the mid-1970s, the government became especially concerned with developing forums for discussion and consensus building with business and labour on economic issues. This concern was prompted in large part by the negative public reaction to the controls program of 1975.[44] In 1976, "The Way Ahead" document emphasized the needs for consultative forums of all kinds, but in particular it advocated the development of tripartite forums for consensus building.[45]

The consultative structure created by the Department of Industry, Trade and Commerce in 1978 was an interesting variation of this theme. Early in that year, the Department established a number of committees or task forces that consisted of representatives from industry and labour. The task forces considered issues in twenty-three different sectors or areas relating to industrial and economic development. Six months later, a Second Tier Committee was established to extend the work of the task forces or First Tier committees.[46] After the establishment of the Board of Economic Development in November 1978, the work of the Second Tier Committee was directed to this group of ministers.

In addition to mechanisms of this nature, private and public conferences have become increasingly popular as forums for discussion with representatives of government, business and labour. Conferences sponsored by departments of government and organizations and institutes such as the Economic Council, the Science Council, The Institute for Research on Public Policy and the Conference Board, for example, now compete with and in some cases have replaced the traditional public forums before which interest groups would make presentations. Consultation has become big business. While the clustering of interests and individuals ebbs and flows with shifts in public-policy concerns, the activity level of interest groups on the whole is high.

It is interesting to note in considering new forms of collaboration and consultation that many consultants and their firms have emerged in intermediary roles in serving interest groups and elected and appointed public officials. There have even been some outstanding examples of conflict of interest resulting from firms set up by former senior officials of government.[47] By and large, consultant firms serve corporate interests who wish to gain access to cabinet ministers or senior public officials. The fact that there is a considerable lack of awareness in the corporate sector about government operations opens the door for consulting services. Beyond establishing contacts between client and public official and undertaking research for corporate clients, consultants perform a useful function in conveying an understanding of the processes of government decision making to private-sector interests. Initiatives have also been taken in recent years by consultants who wish to provide services to the less sophisticated and less financially independent voluntary-sector organizations.[48]

In summary, interest groups look for points of access to decision-making processes. They may create access through the establishment of contacts and private meetings with ministers and officials or through requests or proposals for public meetings. The established, self-financing organizations tend to have an advantage over groups which are dependent on government funding for their operations in attempting to exercise influence, but accessibility is generally available to all who try. Furthermore, the creation of advisory committees or some other form of consultative forum by a government department or agency provides additional opportunities for interaction.

From the government's point of view, direct consultation between government and outside interests is an essential means of obtaining information and/or generating support for government proposals for action. The information generated by interest groups can be extremely useful to ministers and officials in developing policy. Second, consultations can also provide a basis for disseminating information and testing clientele opinion. For example, departmental advisory committees and advisory councils can serve as useful vehicles for these purposes through the clientele representatives that sit on these bodies. Thus, the public-relations aspect is an important feature of their operations.

Parliamentary Forums

The preceding discussion has focused on mechanisms and techniques employed by the executive to effect coordination and consultation among related structures and interests within the public service and with the affected clientele and interest groups outside. The involvement of Parliament in consultation and debate on policy matters normally occurs at a later stage in the process. Its role, as Van Loon and Whittington point out, is one of policy refinement.[49] Parliamentarians consider the products of the policy process in the form of legislation or expenditure plans and exercise limited influence in making changes at this stage. The dominance of the executive in determining the business of the House and in controlling the support of the government members ensures that most government proposals will be passed unchanged.

The pace and complexity of policy-making activities of recent decades has served to accentuate the imbalance between executive and parliamentary forums for consultation and collaboration. Efforts for parliamentary reform have not kept pace with the reforms and initiatives undertaken by the executive. Nevertheless, there has been fairly extensive use made of parliamentary committees as mechanisms for improved consultation and for the mobilization of consensus on issues before government policy is determined. For example, the use of parliamentary committees as forums for debate on white- and green-paper proposals was an important innovation of the Trudeau administration in the late 1960s and early 1970s. The papers were referred to standing committees of the House and, in some cases, of the Senate. The committees invited submissions from interested groups and individuals for formal presentation and discussion. In the case of the white-paper debate on taxation in 1969-70, the House and Senate committees hired expert staff and travelled across the country to conduct their hearings. Although some members—particularly those on the House committee—had difficulty in adjusting to the types of demands that these debates placed on them, the experiment in nonpartisan review had a beneficial impact in demonstrating the potential for parliamentary committees.[50]

There is also evidence that parliamentary committee scrutiny of government legislation has been increasingly effective.[51] While opinions differ on the degree of influence committee reports have had on amending legislative bills, the activities of committees in this area have been considerable.[52] Committee experience is an important element of a member's responsibility and experience.

A major handicap of parliamentary committees, however, is their partisan nature. The chairmen of House committees, with the exception of the Public Accounts Committee, is a member of the government caucus. Committee membership reflects party standings in the House. Government members will normally be in a majority and committee reports therefore will tend to support government proposals. A further difficulty of committee operations is created by the small number of members purported to carry the workload of committees. In 1978, John Reid, a Liberal Member of Parliament, estimated that about sixty-five members bear the brunt of committee work.[53] In the House then of 264 members, this figure represents only a quarter of the total.[54]

Recommendations for changes in committee procedures have stressed the need to develop some degree of independence and nonpartisanship in committee operations.[55] Proposals to expand research staff and facilities to assist members in the processing of materials and submissions have also been put forward. In an effort to provide for the renewal of Parliament, the Clark administration made several commitments in the Speech from the Throne in October 1979 to strengthen committee operations and to enhance their importance.[56] The Lambert Commission's recommendations for revitalizing House committees as forums for maintaining the accountability of ministers and officials could provide a further impetus for reform in the years ahead.

There have also been other changes in House procedure that may be considered to strengthen Parliament's role as a public forum. The televising of Question Period has given the Commons a higher public profile than in the past. The release of the Green Paper on Freedom of Information in 1977 by the Trudeau government and the subsequent introduction of freedom of information legislation are indications that greater access to government information will be available to members. Increased access to information would be of considerable importance to members for committee work.

Thus, the potential for further development of parliamentary forums for consultation and debate has not gone unrecognized. Committee hearings provide opportunities for interest-group representatives to be channelled through parliamentary as well as executive forums and provide a more balanced approach to consultation with outside groups. While the use of committees as mechanisms for consultation cannot be expected to entirely replace the use of executive techniques for direct interaction with interest groups, they can serve as vital alternative arenas of discussion. In broader terms, measures to enhance the capability of parliamentarians to scrutinize and review government proposals and legislation should reinforce the essential institutional role of Parliament in the governing process.

Summary

In an age of big government, the problems of coordination, collaboration and consensus building require continuing efforts to develop structures and processes that will provide effective and responsive government. The diversity of structures and interests that must be served has resulted in highly complex processes of policy making. Within the machinery of government, the grouping and regrouping of organizational interests in recent decades led to an expanded use of traditional coordinative mechanisms and to experimentation with new coordinative designs. As public participation increased, broader-based consultation was pursued with interest groups and individuals. New techniques and mechanisms emerged. For their part, parliamentarians were also engaged in discussions and debate on a wider range of issues. The potential of parliamentary committee was perhaps not fully exploited, but new developments and experiments did occur.

Figure 6-1
Mechanisms of Coordination and Consultation

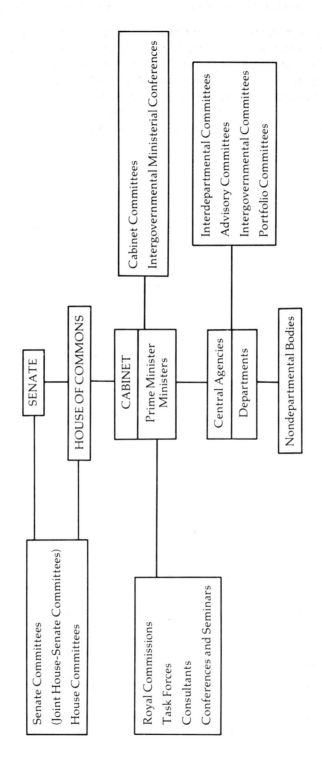

Thus, the diversity of interests and the range of consultative techniques and forums has made policy making a highly complicated exercise. The layers of formal and informal structures that can emerge around any issue create a complex and often constrained environment for decision making. That complexity, however, has another fundamental dimension. Let us turn to an examination of the mechanisms and techniques of federal-provincial collaboration and coordination.

Notes

1. In broad terms, policy making is aptly described as an "appreciative system" developed between the governors and the governed. The basic activities of any policy-making system are pursued over time as a continuing process of adjustment and adaptation in the relations between government and different groups in society. See Sir Geoffrey Vickers, *Value Systems and Social Process* (New York: Basic Books, 1968), especially pp. 83-95.

2. See T. Lowi, "Four Systems of Policy, Politics and Choice," *Public Administration Review* (July-August 1972), pp. 298-309.

3. R.W. Phidd and G. Bruce Doern, *The Politics and Management of Canadian Economic Policy* (Toronto: Macmillan of Canada, 1979), pp. 158-95.

4. An internal computer listing of interdepartmental committees made in the Privy Council Office in 1975 listed about two hundred committees. However, in his study of the transport portfolio, Langford identified eighty-five interdepartmental committees on which the Department of Transport had representatives. Not all were senior-level committees, but this case demonstrates the large number of bodies in existence in this one area. See J. Langford, *Transport in Transition: The Reorganization of the Federal Transport Portfolio* (Montreal: McGill-Queen's University Press, 1976), pp. 190-94.

5. Some of the committee functions listed here have been drawn from among those used by K.C. Wheare, *Government by Committee* (London: Oxford University Press, 1955). In his study, Wheare included royal commissions, parliamentary committees and other external bodies in his committee classification.

6. This committee prepared the basis for legislative amendments to harbour commissions legislation in 1976-77.

7. W.M. Dobell, "Interdepartmental Management in External Affairs," *Canadian Public Administration* (Spring 1978), vol. 21. no. 1, pp. 100-02.

8. P.M. Pitfield, "Toward a Post Control Economy," a paper presented to the Annual Conference of the Institute of Public Administration of Canada (Halifax: September 9, 1976), pp. 14-18.

9. Ibid., p. 15.

10. J. Langford, *Transport in Transition*, pp. 104-09.

11. A.W. Johnson, "Public Policy: creativity and bureaucracy," *Canadian Public Administration* (Spring 1978), vol. 21, no. 1, pp. 1-15.

12. Ibid., p. 15.

13. H.L. Laframboise, "The Portfolio Structure and a Ministry System: Model for the Canadian Federal Service," *Optimum* (Winter 1970), vol. 1, no. 1, p. 29.

14. See P. Aucoin, "Portfolio Structures and Policy Coordination," in Doern and Aucoin, *Public Policy in Canada*, pp. 213-38. Aucoin considers ministries of state and ministry systems as two models for policy coordination in his analysis.

15. Laframboise, "The Portfolio Structure and a Ministry System," p. 30.

16. Ibid., pp. 37-38, and discussion by Langford about the Transport experience in *Transport in Transition*, pp. 15-22.

17. Ibid.

18. See *Revised Statutes of Canada*, 1970, ch. S-12, Department of Solicitor General, section 4. The minister's responsibilities included all matters relating to reformatories, prisons or penitentiaries, parole and the Royal Canadian Mounted Police.

19. Solicitor General Canada, *Annual Report 1972-73* (Ottawa: Information Canada, 1973), p. 3.

20. See R. French and A. Béliveau, *The RCMP and the Management of National Security* (Toronto: Butterworth, for the Institute for Research on Public Policy, 1979), pp. 14-17.

21. *Revised Statutes of Canada*, 1970, ch. S-15, Department of State Act, section 4.

22. Langford, *Transport in Transition*, pp. 201-15.

23. *Statutes of Canada*, 1974-75-76, 23-24 Eliz. II, ch. 82, Central Mortgage and Housing Corporation Act, sections 15 and 16.

24. *Statutes of Canada*, 1976-77, 25-26 Eliz. II, ch. 54, Employment and Immigration Reorganization Act.

25. Ibid., section 8(1).

26. Ibid., section 8(2).

27. V.S. Wilson, "The Role of Royal Commissions and Task Forces," in G.B. Doern and P. Aucoin, *The Structures of Policy Making in Canada*, p. 115.

28. Ibid., p. 113.

29. Canada, *Report of the Royal Commission on Corporate Concentration* (Ottawa: Supply and Services, 1978), pp. xix-xxi.

30. Wilson, "The Role of Royal Commissions and Task Forces," pp. 121-26; and Fred Schindeler and C. Michael Lanphier, "Social Science Research and Participatory Democracy in Canada," *Canadian Public Administration* (Winter 1969), vol. 12, no. 4, p. 486.

31. See Lloyd Axworthy, "The Housing Task Force: A Case Study," in Doern and Aucoin, *The Structures of Policy Making in Canada*, pp. 130-53.

32. See Canada, The Task Force on Canadian Unity, *A Future Together: Observations and Recommendations* (Ottawa: Supply and Services, 1979) pp. 135-36.

33. Government of Canada, *The Constitutional Amendment Bill*, Text and Explanatory Notes (Ottawa: Supply and Services, 1978). The proposals were released in June 1978.

34. During the 1968 election campaign, the Liberal Party released a paper on the "Just Society," in which emphasis was placed on measures to increase participation of groups and individuals in the affairs of government. See "Statement by the Prime Minister on the 'Just Society'," (mimeo, May 1968).

35. See A.D. Doerr, "The Role of White Papers in the Policy Making Process: The Experience of the Government of Canada," unpublished Ph.D. dissertation (Ottawa: Carleton University, 1973).

36. Ibid., pp. 76-77 and 341.

37. In the case of tax reform, for example, major changes to the proposals were made in the final legislation introduced in 1971 in the face of strong opposition from certain interests. In particular, see M.W. Bucovetsky, "The Mining Industry and the Great Tax Reform Debate," in A. Paul Pross (ed.), *Pressure Group Behaviour in Canadian Politics* (Toronto: McGraw-Hill Ryerson, 1976), pp. 89-114, and Doerr, "The Role of White Papers in the Policy Making Process," pp. 299-317.

38. A. Paul Pross, "Pressure Groups: Adaptive Instruments of Political Communication," in Pross, *Pressure Group Behaviour in Canadian Politics*, pp. 1-26.

39. H.J. Dawson, "National Pressure Groups and the Federal Government," ibid., p. 50.

40. Dawson, ibid.

41. Doerr, "The Role of White Papers in the Policy Making Process," pp. 259-66.

42. For example, the marketing agencies established in the early 1970s had advisory committees that included producer representatives. See Chapter 5.

43. More specifically, the withdrawal of the Canadian Labour Congress from the board of the Economic Council of Canada at that time generated considerable concern in government circles.

44. "The Way Ahead: A Framework for Discussion" (Ottawa: Supply and Services, 1976), pp. 31-32. See also Phidd and Doern, *The Politics and Management of Canadian Economic Policy*, pp. 542-65.

45. See G.B. Doern and R.W. Phidd, "Economic Management in the Government of Canada: Some Implications of the Board of Economic Development Ministers and the Lambert Report," a paper prepared for the annual meeting of the Canadian Political Science Association (Saskatoon: mimeo, May 30, 1979), pp. 17-18.

46. At the time the creation of the Board of Economic Development Ministers was announced, one of the stated functions of the Board secretariat was the consideration of the economic-development recommendations of the Second Tier Committee.

47. Perhaps the most noteworthy example was the firm established by Mr. Simon Reisman and Mr. Jim Grandy after their resignations as deputy minister of Finance and deputy minister of Industry, Trade and Commerce, respectively, in 1974.

48. One Ottawa consulting firm prepared a cartoon-illustrated booklet, "Decision Making in the Government of Canada," which it used as instructional material for briefing sessions with voluntary associations.

49. Van Loon and Whittington, *The Canadian Political System*, pp. 416-55.

50. Doerr, "The Role of White Papers in the Policy Making Process," pp. 351-58.

51. See John M. Reid, "The Backbencher and the Discharge of Legislative Responsibilities," in W.A.W. Neilson and J.C. MacPherson (eds.), *The Legislative Process in Canada: The Need for Reform* (Toronto: Butterworth, for the Institute for Research on Public Policy, 1978), pp. 139-45.

52. Ibid., comments by John Fraser and Paul Thomas, pp. 146-63.

53. John Reid, "The Backbencher and the Discharge of Legislative Responsibilities," p. 140.

54. The increase in the number of seats in the House of Commons from 264 to 282 came into effect for the general election of 1979.

55. C.E.S. Franks, "Procedural Reform in the Legislative Process," in Neilson and Mac-Pherson, *The Legislative Process in Canada*, p. 256.

56. Canada, House of Commons, *Report of Debates* (October 9, 1979), p. 6. Proposals included reforms to provide greater assistance to parliamentary committees in the form of staff and other resources and the creation of four small select committees to examine a number of policy issues.

7
Perspectives On Responsive Government: The Federal-Provincial Interface

As governmental responsibilities and hence governmental activities have been defined in more complex and more differentiated terms and as governments have created new structural entities to assume those responsibilities and to conduct those activities, the need for coordination between and among government departments and agencies has increased accordingly. At the same time, expansion and specialization have also increased the need for direct consultation with affected groups and individuals. Thus, the mechanisms and techniques that have been developed and used have attempted to support responsive as well as responsible government.

Beyond the range of interactions and relationships established within the machinery of government and between government and clientele interests, another level of interaction is fundamental in the operation of a federal government within a national context. Intergovernmental relations, especially federal-provincial relations, constitute a primary component of policy-making processes at the federal level. The degree of interdependence between the activities of the two senior orders of government in Canada has been fostered by, and has resulted in, yet another level of complex and elaborate structures and mechanisms.

The literature testifies to the importance of federalism to the study and practice of government in Canada. The constitutional, legal, political, economic, social and cultural dimensions of the relationships between the centre and the regions have been exhaustively explored.[1] In the process, both the practice and study of those relations have evolved. Judicial interpretations of the areas of federal and provincial legislative competence as set out in particular in sections 91 and 92 of the British North America Act provided a primary focus of attention for many decades.[2] The shift from juridical to political and administrative means of accommodating federal-provincial conflict and of effecting intergovernmental cooperation occurred ostensibly after World War II. The effect of the Depression on provincial economies and the exigencies of mobilizing a national war effort necessitated pragmatic and often expedient measures in dealing with regional and national issues. Reconstruction and the introduction of the welfare state after the war were also pursued with the object of finding acceptable formulae for the political interests in the period. The development of techniques of "joint" and "co-operative" federalism for purposes of designing and implementing national programs moved the federal and provincial governments into collaborative, rather than isolated, modes of activity, and resulted in new approaches to the practice of federalism during the 1950s and 1960s.

The dimension of cultural duality gained new importance in the early 1960s with the election in 1962 of an assertive provincial government in Québec which was committed to linking a "positive state" role with nationalistic aspirations in the province. For its part, the federal government responded with the establishment in 1963 of a Royal Commission on Bilingualism and Biculturalism to examine and assess the impact of a changing cultural environment in Canada. By the end of the decade, governments in Canada became committed to a constitutional-review process intended to redesign and to modernize the constitutional framework of Canadian federalism. Combined political, economic and cultural forces provided the impetus for the search for a new balance in the relationships between provincial and federal governments.[3]

However, the constitutional review process of 1968-71 ended in disagreement. The federal initiative in 1975 to revive the process was unsuccessful, as changing economic circumstances in the nation as a whole and in the regions served to modify the agenda and, indeed, the approach to federal-provincial relations. Economic issues—particularly those related to energy and resources—were a major preoccupation for most governments, although cultural aspirations also took on a new force in Québec. The election in November 1976 of the Parti Québécois government in that province and the referendum on the sovereignty-association question have kept the issue of federal-provincial relations very much to the fore in the political *and* administrative arenas in this country. Events have moved so quickly and have been changing so rapidly in recent years and months that writers' commentaries are often obsolete before the printers' ink is dry. While there has been no dearth of proposals for change, there has been an absence of consensus on what the changes should be.

Thus, the concept of federalism in Canada continues to evolve in light of changing circumstances. While the traditional classical model of federalism—the watertight-compartment concept[4]—has not been operative in any formal sense for many years, the approach of governments has been to focus on the division of powers as the basis for determining relationships. In practical terms, it has been the model of collaborative federalism in its many forms—joint federalism, cooperative federalism, consultative federalism, administrative federalism, executive federalism—that has prevailed in the last several decades.[5] As governments at both levels have adopted a positive role and have come to expand the scope and nature of their activities, it has been recognized that cooperation and/or coordination in the undertaking of these activities are often required to achieve their respective objectives. Collaboration nevertheless has been pursued through a bargaining process in which the several dimensions of federal-provincial relations have served as levers of influence.[6]

Within the realm of collaborative models of federalism, therefore, there have been and are differing views of the nature of the relationship between provincial and federal governments. At the federal level, the expression of that relationship has evolved significantly in the last two decades. During the Pearson administrations, the notion of partnership was stressed. It would not be far-fetched to suggest that the philosophy of cooperative federalism in the 1960s incorporated economic and cultural elements of a contract theory of Confederation. Cooperative federalism of this era was characterized as a decentralizing force, in that the central government would withdraw gradually from areas of jurisdiction that were essentially provincial.[7] Although some authors have argued that the 1960s represented a period in which federal power was eroded by the provinces who, through the means of federal-provincial forums, were able to become involved in federal decision-making processes, it should be acknowledged that on balance the areas in which the provinces pressured for greater control were primarily ones on provincial jurisdiction.[8]

The first Trudeau administration expressed the need for strong central government and strong provincial governments. The decade from 1968, however, was a period in which the federal government adopted an increasingly aggressive role in federal-provincial relations. The phenomenon of "side-door federalism" prevailed.[9] The process followed these lines: the federal posture, in the first instance, would be to initiate an action in *support* of provincial interests and in the *national* interest.[10] As soon as a basis of cooperation was established, the federal government would subtly shift its role to one of *leadership* in these areas and the national interest would be displaced by the *federal* interest in the activity. On the part of the provincial governments, there was considerable resistance to these measures, particularly by the province of Québec. Nevertheless, with the election of the Parti Québécois in 1976, the federal government reinforced its efforts to provide strong central government to maintain national unity. The election campaigns of 1979 and 1980 were fought, in part at least, on this issue. In the political rhetoric of the campaigns, one could hear echoes of the organic theory of Confederation—"the nation is larger than the sum of its parts."

At the provincial level, expressions of the relationship between the federal and provincial governments have included equal status (Alberta) and special status (Québec's sovereignty-association proposal) as dominant themes. Traditionally, the province of Québec has demanded greater political autonomy on cultural and linguistic grounds.[11] Other provinces have demanded greater control over policies, programs and tax sources but have argued their cases from positions of varying economic and political strength. Until recently, the province of Ontario occupied the position of greatest opposition as well as support for federal action among the English-speaking provinces. With the strengthening of the economic power base in the West, Western provinces (especially Alberta and Saskatchewan) have made articulate claims to greater power sharing with the central government. In addition to resisting federal "intrusions" into areas of provincial jurisdiction, provincial governments have also come to claim an involvement in areas of jurisdiction previously accepted as ones exclusively federal—communications, international trade and foreign policy. Thus, the "intrusions process" has been pursued by both parties; as a consequence, the overlapping and duplication of government activities and services have surfaced as a concern equal in importance in some quarters to formal constitutional reform.[12]

An understanding of the relations between and among the federal and provincial governments is therefore fundamental to an understanding of Canadian public administration. Federalism reinforces the institutional focus of policy and program activity at the federal level. One might contend that the collaborative process in its varying forms has been a primary determinant of the nature of the substance of intergovernmental interaction and that policy actors have often considered changes in the rules of the consultative game as the key strategic means of modifying agreements and decisions.

The impact of federal-provincial relations on policy processes and policy outcomes must therefore be underscored. In the first instance, federal-provincial relations add several layers of structures and processes to the operation of the machinery of government in Canada. There are myriads of intergovernmental conferences and committees, from the ministerial level to the working level of officials. This network of forums and working groups has become highly developed in many areas of government activity. If coordinative and consultative processes *within* the federal public service nurtured the development of the interdepartmental process expert, federal-provincial consultation has produced its own type of process expert within the federal public service. At the provincial level, the emergence of central coordinating agencies to deal with federal and intergovernmental matters has also contributed to increased sophistication and specialization in this area of activity. Second, these consultative processes have resulted in a new set of problems for federal-provincial collaboration and liaison. As governments have expanded their activities, competition rather than cooperation has characterized the relations between them. As a consequence, the effectiveness of the mechanisms has been increasingly questioned.

The dynamic nature of Canadian federalism generates strains for the decision-making and operational activities of government at both levels. The means chosen to alleviate those strains and to accommodate conflicting interests are important components of government strategy. The question that decision makers must consider in developing responses is whether the mechanisms used are the most appropriate ones available.

The Mechanisms and Processes of Intergovernmental Liaison

The evolution and structure of intergovernmental consultative machinery has been well documented.[13] In particular, the work of Gérard Veilleux has provided a comprehensive, yet succinct, commentary on the nature and form of intergovernmental liaison.[14] In his analysis, Veilleux identifies the decade of the 1960s as the period in which there was a veritable explosion in the development of consultative machinery. The changing public-policy agenda, which, as noted earlier, impacted on the federal machinery of government, also supported the growth and development of intergovernmental mechanisms.

Prior to the 1960s, governments had consulted primarily on matters of financial arrangements between them. The determination of tax-rental, tax-sharing and equalization arrangements, for example, had been made through negotiation between federal and provincial politicians and officials. As the scope of policy issues in which both levels of government claimed an interest broadened, the range of matters on which ministers and officials consulted increased. For example, social policies and programs, economic-development measures and issues of environmental and cultural concern constituted some of the key foci of federal-provincial forums. Consultation led to collaboration in many areas and resulted in joint political and administrative agreements of different kinds.

Thus, the features of "executive federalism" were established. Intergovernmental ministerial forums were used as means of negotiating agreements and/or discussing policy concerns that in turn could lead to joint action. Intergovernmental committees of officials would be assigned to develop proposals for joint undertakings to be considered by ministers and would be responsible for working out and implementing agreements or accords at the political level. For example, the major shared-cost programs of the 1960s for health and welfare and post-secondary education were developed by groups of federal and provincial technical experts. The work of officials was instrumental in fostering cooperation between government levels. The final stage—the introduction of legislation to provide an authoritative base for these programs—would complete the process. In practice, the federal government has used the legislative process to establish joint programs, but the provinces have seldom responded with complementary legislative commitments.[15] In total, these activities tended to create the appearance of a supragovernmental level of decision making.

In considering the structures of intergovernmental liaison, one is struck by the degree of formality and sophistication that has been achieved. The mechanisms are fragile, however, in that they depend on self-generated impetus and support from the respective governments. Let us consider the essential elements of the structures that have developed in recent decades.

The Political Level

The First Ministers' Conference of prime ministers and premiers constitutes the apex of intergovernmental ministerial meetings. It represents
the forum in which the heads of government meet to discuss, debate and
negotiate issues of common concern. This forum has a high profile by
virtue of its participants and the agenda it considers. As heads of
governments, first ministers represent the interests of their respective
cabinets and seek to promote issues and proposals that best serve those
interests. Several factors determine the degree of influence that a particular first minister may exert in these forums. For example, the political
and economic significance of the activities of his government and the size
of the majority of the government he represents will affect the influence
he is (or is not) capable of exerting. However, the actors in these forums
change with changes in government. Since a government and hence a
prime minister or premier is not bound by the decisions or commitments
of its predecessor at a federal-provincial meeting, consensus may be
difficult to achieve and/or sustain.

The initiation of a process of constitutional review by the province of
Ontario in 1967 and by the federal government in 1968 served to
accentuate the importance of first ministers' meetings.[16] The formalization
and regularization of these meetings were assisted greatly by the constitutional review. The frequency of the meetings provided a high profile for
the proceedings and constitutional reform became a key centre of policy
action within public services for several years. Furthermore, the constitutional review enhanced other forums of intergovernmental consultation
to the extent that consultation activities were related to the constitutional-review process in substantive terms.

The collapse of the constitutional discussions in Victoria in 1971 was
not accompanied by a phasing out or reduction in the number of meetings
of first ministers. Instead, economic issues—especially the energy issue
from 1973—replaced constitutional reform as agenda items. One could
contrast the first ministers' meetings of the 1970s with those of the
1960s. Whereas the meetings of the 1960s aimed at establishing joint
programs, the meetings of the 1970s focused on the development of
policy approaches to different issues that would be compatible with the
concerns of the several governments. In addition, funding arrangements
for joint programs were reexamined, particularly those of social security
and of tax arrangements between the two levels of government.[17]
Furthermore, constitutional reform reemerged by the late 1970s as an
agenda item for first ministers.

At the ministerial level, a labyrinth of federal-provincial meetings has
developed over the years. As the record shows, there are few areas of
government activities in which regular federal provincial meetings have

not been held.[18] An interesting feature of these meetings has been the complementarity of ministerial portfolios at each level of government. For every federal portfolio, a provincial counterpart has been created, or vice versa. For example, meetings of ministers have included traditional government functions served at both levels, such as finance, agriculture and justice as well as recently developed policy sectors such as industry, economic development, resources and consumer affairs. The frequency of these meetings has varied. The more active forums have convened annually.

While intergovernmental consultation has tended to be conducted within particular sectors of policy interests and government activity, relationships have been established between the several forums. On occasion, the first ministers' conference has acted as an arbiter of contentious issues arising from other intergovernmental forums. In addition, the deliberations of finance ministers and provincial treasurers on joint tax and spending arrangements have related to the work of other ministerial forums in some instances. At the risk of imposing a comparison, it would not be far-fetched to apply a cabinet committee model to these different political level meetings. For example, a meeting of agriculture ministers might result in an "agreement" to extend services provided under a subsidy or stabilization program. The "agreement" would have financial implications that would require amendment to federal-provincial financing arrangements. Finance ministers and provincial treasurers would consider the matter but would refer it to first ministers for commitment in principle to the agreement before considering its financial implications in detail. Assuming that first ministers would agree that the program extension was acceptable, the matter would then be worked back through the federal-provincial ministerial forums. Obviously, this is a hypothetical case that in practice would occur only in exceptional circumstances. Nevertheless, it should be recognized that linkages have been established between the different ministerial forums that might be considered to approximate cabinet-committee processes writ large, despite the absence of formal decision-making authority by these meetings.

An interesting variation of the intergovernmental ministerial consultative mechanisms was seen in the trilevel conferences on urban affairs held in November 1972 and October 1973.[19] The establishment of the federal Ministry of State for Urban Affairs in 1971 was controversial. The provinces considered urban affairs to be a matter of exclusive provincial jurisdiction. Although the federal government had justified its entry into the field on the grounds of serving the national interest, the question of the legitimacy of its involvement had to be established. The federal government intended to establish that legitimacy by fostering intergovernmental consultation.[20] In strategic terms, if the provincial governments agreed to meet in a forum with the federal government and representatives of the municipal governments, *de facto* recognition of a federal role could be obtained.

In the first instance, the question of municipal participation was a major issue. Since municipalities constitutionally are creations of the provinces, the provinces wished to determine the nature and form of municipal participation within provincial delegations. The federal government, on the other hand, saw its interests best supported by a separate municipal delegation. It would be difficult for the provinces to obstruct proceedings if a federal-municipal alliance could be formed. For their part, the municipalities considered that a separate delegation was an essential step to recognition as the third level of government. However, the problem of status beleaguered municipal leaders. The national municipal organization, the then Canadian Federation of Mayors and Municipalities, was a voluntary federation of provincial urban and rural municipal associations. At the time, no special representative role was played by the large cities and not all municipal associations or large cities were members. Nevertheless, the municipalities chose the vehicle of their national pressure group to represent them. Through skilful bargaining and negotiation in the federal-provincial-municipal steering committee which was set up to organize the first conference, the municipalities obtained recognition as a separate delegation.

The first conference (held in Toronto in 1972) was important for purposes of form. No substantive discussions took place, although governments set out their positions on their respective roles and responsibilities in the area of urban affairs. The second conference (in Edmonton in 1973) witnessed a different approach by each delegation. This time, the agenda included substantive policy items: management of growth, housing, transportation and local government finance. The federal government offered program support to provincial governments in exchange for an involvement in provincial-planning exercises. The municipal delegation was preoccupied with the question of finance. A radical wing wanted an enhanced financial base guaranteed by the senior levels of government and was reluctant to accept the majority view to pursue a gradual approach in this area. For their part, the provinces viewed the federal initiatives with ambivalence. If there was something to be gained from the federal proposals, they would consider them but, if the proposals appeared to represent a federal intrusion, their participation would not be forthcoming.[21] The consensus that emerged from the conference included, *inter alia*, an agreement to establish a trilevel task force on public finance. The task force was established and ultimately issued a report, but a third conference was not held to consider it.[22] The provincial governments were not prepared to support further consultation at the national level on urban matters.

The example of national trilevel consultation points out several characteristics and difficulties of intergovernmental political liaison. As noted earlier, the basic operating norms of these forums support a bargaining process. Participants attend as representatives of their respective governments. They act, therefore, as spokesmen for particular interests and concerns of their jurisdiction. An element of brokerage will be involved in achieving consensus, but where differences are irreconcilable there are no means available to force agreements.

The federal government usually takes the initiative for convening intergovernmental meetings since it is the national government. To breathe life into these processes, however, incentives must be created to encourage the participation of the several actors and commit them to ongoing activity. In this respect, the federal government has used its financial resources and control of agenda setting for these conferences as strategic means of encouraging participation. For example, the federal spending power has been used as a means of inducing provinces to create or participate in shared-cost programs;[23] agendas have been designed to ensure that items included would relate to particular provincial interests. Provinces have also negotiated with the federal government on agenda items as a means of developing their own incentives to participate.

From the provincial perspective, the main incentive for participation is provided by the national forum at which they can articulate regional and provincial concerns. In addition to using these conferences as means of obtaining a national audience for their particular grievances, it has been argued that the provinces have also used these meetings as a means of claiming involvement in federal policy matters.[24] In the latter respect, it is difficult to determine which level of government has made the greatest advances in involving itself in the affairs of the other. However, a steady progression of mutual involvement is apparent. In the process, governments have moved from exchanging information as a basic function of these forums to harmonizing programs and activities and jointly determining policies.[25] There have been many pressures which have supported this interdependence, but perhaps the most significant one has been the expansion of government activities at both levels.

The structures and processes of executive federalism have been criticized as being overdeveloped on the one hand and as requiring further sophistication and formal institutionalization on the other.[26] In both perspectives, a major problem pertains to the displacement of the accountability of governments to their respective legislative bodies. For example, executive agreements negotiated in public or private intergovernmental forums preempt the involvement of the legislatures. If the legislature is involved, it is asked to ratify decisions that have been taken elsewhere and that are often presented as *faits accomplis*. As extra parliamentary forums of debate, federal-provincial conferences create the impression of governing entities responsible only to themselves.

Second, the format of federal-provincial ministerial meetings has been criticized for adding to the strains within the federal system. Instead of serving to accommodate conflicting interests, these forums accentuate them. Provincial representatives are expected to express regional or provincial concerns and bargain as necessary for arrangements that best serve those interests. The federal government is not a neutral arbiter or coordinator of diverse interests. It too has interests that it seeks to promote and that may conflict with those of the provinces. The extent to which the federal government may claim to speak for national interests, however, has increasingly been modified by provincial claims to represent part of the national perspective.[27]

The problems of accountability and regionalism generated by the processes of executive federalism raise questions about the role of federal legislative institutions. Parliament was designed to provide a *national* forum for the representation of regional interests and views. In the House of Commons, regional interests would be represented and accommodated within party caucuses. In practical terms, regional representation has been a cornerstone of cabinet building, although problems arise when the governing party does not include elected representatives from all regions. The Senate, an appointed rather than an elected body, was intended to provide directly for the representation of regional interests.[28] However, the development of mechanisms of federal-provincial liaison have only involved the executive. For their part, parliamentarians have made few concerted efforts to become involved. For example, neither the House of Commons nor the Senate has pressured the government for the estab-lishment of a standing committee on federal-provincial relations as a minimum response to these extraparliamentary processes.

Proposals for constitutional reform have been put forward—particu-larly in recent years—by federal and provincial governments, the Task Force on Canadian Unity and others. They have proposed, *inter alia*, a reconstituted upper chamber, such as House or Council of the Federation or House of the Provinces, that would not only represent regional interests more directly but also monitor federal-provincial agreements. This type of proposal constitutes only one aspect of a package of reform proposals in each case and to comment on it out of context runs the risk of distorting or oversimplifying the complex and sophisticated nature of the several reform proposals. Within a limited context of the mechanisms and processes of executive federalism, however, two observations may be made. In the first instance, a restructuring of the federal upper house to represent the regional interests and to provide a legislative forum for scrutiny and review of federal-provincial executive accords would support the formal institutionalization of the machinery of intergovernmental liaison. It would enhance rather than streamline the processes of executive federalism. To the extent that this would reinforce the pattern of power

brokerage between governments, regional cleavages would be accentu-
ated. Second, the use of a federal upper chamber as the legislative body
for reviewing intergovernmental accords and agreements could affect the
procedures and functions of the House of Commons. If, for example, the
upper chamber had veto authority over Commons' proposals it considered
to be detrimental to provincial interests, the legislative authority of the
federal government could be regularly challenged.[29] No constitutional
division of powers can be so precise as to preclude questions of jurisdictional authority. If disputes were to be negotiated and arbitrated through
a federal upper chamber, the implications for federal legislative authority
could be severe. In addition, the implications of such a process for
ministerial responsibility at the federal level could mean the displacement
of that responsibility and accountability to the elected chamber. In other
words, some caution is advised in looking for solutions and alternatives to
the current problems and practices of executive federalism. Unintended
consequences may exacerbate the problems.

It seems apparent, nevertheless, that major efforts are required to
establish a better equilibrium between mechanisms designed for executive
consultation between governments and the role of legislatures in relation
to federal-provincial activities. Ministerial meetings can assist and facilitate
collaborative efforts between and among governments, but they should
be viewed as flexible political mechanisms. In view of the dynamics and
inherent weaknesses of these processes, there seems to be a limited utility
in using these forums as vehicles for molding consensus on major issues.
For example, it is highly questionable, on the basis of past experience, that
the use of first ministers' conferences alone can provide the means for
effecting constitutional reform. Techniques other than intergovernmental
executive meetings may be needed to determine what changes can and
will be made.[30]

The Administrative Level

The structure of federal-provincial administrative meetings and working
groups supports and expands on the activities at the political level. Some
of this machinery is highly developed and sophisticated in form and
operation. On the whole, it has served to foster cooperation rather than
generate conflict and to facilitate the decision-making process at the
political level. The structures have developed and evolved in concert with
the changing policy agendas of governments.

Federal-provincial administrative forums may be grouped in order of
their development into three main categories. The first pertains to those
committees and working groups that have grown up around and have
supported the development of federal-provincial financial arrangements
from the period of World War II to the present. The second group consists
of those federal-provincial meetings and committees of officials engaged

in joint policy and program development and implementation in the various substantive policy sectors such as transportation, environment, health and welfare, which emerged in large numbers during the 1960s and early 1970s. The third and more recent category includes the meetings and committees of officials whose functions are largely parapolitical. This group includes the intergovernmental process experts who seek not only to coordinate the joint efforts of federal and provincial technical experts in policy and program areas but also to develop strategy and obtain information for their political masters for federal-provincial political consultations. Generally speaking, the structures and networks created by these different types of mechanisms interrelate in a complementary manner, although problems of coordination can arise.[31]

In the first group, special mention must be made of the Federal-Provincial Continuing Committee on Fiscal and Economic Matters composed of finance officials.[32] The Committee was created in 1955 to prepare for the ministerial conferences that negotiated and decided the 1957-62 tax-sharing arrangements. Its general purpose was to discuss and exchange information on fiscal and economic matters as well as to examine questions that might be referred to it by the federal-provincial first ministers' conference. It has also supported the meetings of federal and provincial finance ministers and treasurers. For example, in 1964 the Tax Structure Committee, a committee of the Conference of Ministers of Finance and Provincial Treasurers, was established to study and report on the general policy to be expected and followed in the period 1967-72 for tax-sharing, shared-cost programs and government spending. The Committee was charged with conducting a joint review of the nature and extent of federal and provincial taxes in relation to the respective financial responsibilities of governments. It was also asked to analyze the federal-provincial aspects of the Carter Royal Commission report on taxation which was released in 1967. The Continuing Committee provided the staff support for the Tax Structure Committee in these undertakings and contributed substantially to the development of the fiscal arrangements for 1967-72 and the federal-provincial considerations of the federal tax-reform measures through to 1971. The Continuing Committee participated in the negotiations for the 1972-77 and 1977-82 fiscal arrangements. For all intents and purposes, the Committee constitutes a permanent feature of federal-provincial administration in this area. The degree of professional expertise and intergovernmental cooperation achieved by the work of this body is particularly noteworthy.[33]

In the second category, a large number of substantive program committees operate at the senior-official and working-group levels. The lists of these committees and meetings are long ones. For example, in the single area of transportation, Langford identified thirty-six federal-provincial committees.[34] Veilleux's thirteen-page list of federal-provincial committees is dominated by official-level bodies.[35] An interesting aspect of this list is the number of committees that are intergovernmental regional forums. This might be interpreted as a recognition by governments that some issues may be more appropriately dealt with regionally or bilaterally in particular program areas.

The work of these committees covers a wide range of activities. They are at once policy and program coordinators. They may engage in program design, development and implementation. The inventory of federal-provincial programs compiled by the Federal-Provincial Relations Office in Ottawa bears witness to the scope and variety of the programs that have been developed through joint means.[36] Secondly, these committees function as monitoring agents. Once a program is in place, there may be a need for federal monitoring of provincial activity or vice versa. On the other hand, this form of activity may simply be directed to effecting information exchange on a continuing basis. Because administrative improvements result from this type of activity, this type of committee work can be beneficial.

For the most part, federal-provincial collaboration at the administrative level provides a strong support base for intergovernmental cooperation. Officials working in these areas share common professional values with their counterparts in other governments and work easily together. On the other hand, studies have demonstrated that this is not always the case.[37] Professional perspectives can and do differ among officials working in federal and provincial governments. When professional differences are linked to political differences between governments, the likelihood of resolving conflict is minimal. The outcome may be a separate set of programs operated by each of the governments.

These committees may be considered the intergovernmental equivalent of the interdepartmental technical committees primarily concerned with efficient and effective program coordination within a public service. While the main aim of intergovernmental committees is to resolve problems and to develop the administrative means to make federalism work effectively, their work can generate conflict on an intergovernmental plane. If matters cannot be resolved at the official level, they are passed on to the political forums for resolution. Thus, increased professionalism in public services, while providing a basis for better rapport and understanding of technical issues, does not necessarily reduce conflict when the interests of governments differ.

A third category of intergovernmental administrative machinery that has emerged in recent years includes those offices in federal and provincial governments that support high-level intergovernmental consultation. The Federal-Provincial Relations Office in Ottawa and its provincial counterparts are the primary administrative units in this category.[38] As noted earlier, the federal Office of the Secretary for Federal-Provincial Relations was established in 1975, although a federal-provincial relations division had been created in the Privy Council Office as early as 1968. At the provincial level, the province of Québec was the first to create a separate ministry of federal-provincial relations in 1961. The provinces of Ontario, Alberta, Newfoundland and, in 1979, Saskatchewan and British Columbia have also established separate ministries for this purpose. In other cases, intergovernmental coordination is handled within the premier's office, as indeed it was in each of the provinces cited above before separate ministries were established.

The primary functions of these units do not fall into any specialized technical category. They support and sometimes intervene in the activities of intergovernmental technical committees and participate in committees and meetings with their counterparts in other governments to lay the groundwork for intergovernmental consultation at the political level. Knowledge is power in the sense that the information that an official obtains about other governments' positions on issues and planned actions can be used to develop strategies to recommend to his minister. In this way, influence can be exercised by the public official in the political arena. The fact that their activities are so closely tied to political negotiations and are conducted from departments and offices that play a central coordinative role within the particular government emphasizes the importance of process expertise. Moreover, the official becomes involved in the intricate networks of information exchange within and between the political and administrative levels and, while he may be working to foster consultation, he may have difficulty in maintaining a politically neutral stance. The development of strategies and positions for ministers requires a high degree of sensitivity and understanding of political objectives and concerns. Representing and protecting the minister's and the government's interests become an integral part of the consultative exercises he supports and promotes.

The interjection of intergovernmental coordinative mechanisms between the political level of consultation and the administrative level of technical cooperation thus elaborates and expands the formal and informal network of contacts and complicates further the processes of bargaining and negotiation in any particular situation. The fact that this category of intergovernmental coordinators has emerged in recent years reflects the expansion of intergovernmental activities generally and the recognition that additional administrative support for intergovernmental policy consultations has been required.

The array of administrative bodies, committees and meetings established since the 1960s has added to the complexity of federal-provincial liaison. As a result, effective coordination has often been difficult to achieve not just between public services and agencies of different governments but also within public services of particular governments.[39] For example, at the federal level, the Federal-Provincial Relations Office provides a central coordinating capability for all federal-provincial matters. Its influence on federal-provincial activities throughout the federal public service has not been pervasive, but it has played a primary coordinative role in key activities such as preparations for first ministers' conferences. Moreover, most departments in the federal public service have created special divisions for federal-provincial coordination and liaison in their organizations. These units may support or supplement the intergovernmental activities in which a department is involved. Thus, they may coordinate activities within the department as well as establish an independent network of contacts with provincial departments and agencies. Perhaps ironically, however, the staff of federal-provincial relations divisions in federal departments are located in Ottawa.

Furthermore, the federal public service is highly decentralized. Nearly three-quarters of its departmental operations are conducted through regional offices. As noted in Chapter 3, decentralization measures were implemented in the 1970s to improve sensitivity and responsiveness in the provision of federal services. However, these measures served to relocate jobs but did not result in the delegation of decision-making authority to regional centres. Deconcentration rather than decentralization has been the pattern. Since policy directions come from Ottawa, regional-office operations are often not well integrated with the activities of provincial government offices in those areas. Despite the extent of federal-provincial administrative liaison, the deconcentration has not always fostered coordinated policy and program development. Lack of communication between different government jurisdictions at the regional level has created friction and deterred cooperative working relationships on many occasions.[40]

Administrative interdependence can also create problems of accountability. While information exchange between governments has seldom caused problems, joint-program development and administration have. The administration of shared-cost programs demonstrates the type of problem involved. For example, agreement to establish a shared-cost program would normally be obtained at a meeting of federal and provincial ministers following preliminary discussions at the official level. The federal minister, on behalf of his government, would then introduce legislation in the House of Commons to provide an authoritative base for the expenditure of federal moneys for a joint program. A main feature of such a bill would be the terms and conditions under which federal contributions would be made. In other words, the federal government would agree to support and/or help establish a provincial program, provided the program met certain standards.

Provincial commitments to participate would be established by letters of agreement or contracts. The provinces would normally contribute half the cost of the program and assume responsibility for its administration. In addition to the budget distortions that these programs have created at the provincial level, there have been problems of accountability relating to the auditing of federal moneys spent by the provinces.[41] Although provisions would be included in the enabling legislation to require provinces to comply with audit reports, in some cases provinces, most notably Québec, have refused to do so. In such cases, it is difficult for the federal government to determine if federal moneys have been spent for authorized purposes. Recent block-funding arrangements, that is, lump sum payments, particularly in the health and welfare fields, have attempted to overcome this type of problem.

Another type of difficulty pertains to the processes of policy determination. For example, in the preparation for a ministerial meeting, a federal deputy might commit himself during consultations with his provincial counterparts to a policy or program proposal in order to obtain agreement on other matters under consideration. Although it would be expected that no official would make an unqualified commitment and would indicate that his minister's approval would be needed before he could confirm the proposals, the influence exercised by the official would serve to shift the onus of responsibility from the minister who, when advised of the situation, might be reluctant to endorse the proposal but would feel obliged if it was presented as a necessary condition for agreement on other matters. In this kind of context, it is difficult to determine who is responsible for what and to whom.[42]

If administrative collaboration has made federalism work, it has also contributed to accentuating conflict. As the processes have become more elaborate, the number of structures and actors involved in the different activities have created a complicated web of interrelationships within and between governments. In areas in which difficulties arise, the problems raise fundamental questions that beg resolution at the political level. Let us consider some of the broader issues.

The Implications: A Touch of Constitutional Heresy?

A simple scenario of the evolution of the machinery of executive federalism could be represented in the following way. The initial motivations for formalized federal-provincial consultations were primarily financial. Ministers and officials met during the 1950s and 1960s to work out tax arrangements and shared-cost program agreements that would provide a better balance between the responsibilities and financial resources of each level of government. As the revenue bases of both levels of government expanded, services and programs were extended jointly and independently. During the 1960s in particular, the federal government applied its spending power to a wide range of activities. Because many of these activities came under provincial jurisdiction, appropriate administrative mechanisms had to be developed. The sharing of responsibilities in most areas of government activity created a high degree of inter-dependence between governments. On another plane, the constitutional review processes of the 1960s and 1970s helped to enhance political consultations on a broad range of policy issues. The emergence of the intergovernmental process coordinators represented a further stage of development of intergovernmental collaboration as the specialization of the nature and function of activities increased. As the structures and processes have become more elaborate, however, the effectiveness of their operation has been increasingly called into question.

A major contention put forward in this book is that the rate and scope of change in federal government activities have contributed to the development of a highly complex system of structures and processes by which government responsibilities are discharged and activities undertaken. While the principles of ministerial responsibility have provided the essential framework within which the changes have occurred, strains in the management and accountability systems have often resulted. On the federal-provincial plane, the expansion of federal and provincial activities has threatened to make the constitutional division of powers obsolete. The actions of initiating executives have often represented a competitive struggle for power and resources between and among governments. The spending jungle of the 1960s and 1970s, like the tax jungle of the 1930s, has tended to weaken the operation of cabinet-parliamentary systems in a federal state. As resources have become scarcer and as governments have shifted from spending to regulatory measures, the competitive urge has not receded. Determining responsibility and maintaining accountability of government action are continuing problems.

In a pungent and perceptive article, Alan Cairns has characterized the impact of big governments at both levels relating in a competitive way as the "other crisis in Canadian federalism."[43] National unity in terms of Québec-Canada relations has so preoccupied political leaders, he argues, that other problems have not been given due consideration. In his analysis, the growth of big government in the last two decades has led to a decline in the effectiveness of the constitutional division of powers to act as a constraint on the activities of government. The "federal-provincial game" of policy and program development has been pursued to extremes. Instead of representing flexibility in the division of powers, political and admini-strative arrangements seem to ignore the constitutional parameters respecting division of powers.[44]

Examples can be readily found to demonstrate the diminishing influence of the constitutional division of powers in determining the activities of governments. Generally speaking, the development of federal and provincial programs has reflected a horizontal rather than a vertical division of powers. In the social-policy field, for example, both the federal and provincial governments have established departments and programs in the areas of health and welfare, manpower, consumer and corporate affairs, labour and native peoples. Most of these areas are ones of provincial jurisdiction, but responsibility is shared in others. In the renewable-resource policy field, jurisdiction is shared in the case of agriculture, primarily federal in the case of fisheries, and primarily provincial in environmental matters. Both levels of government have promoted program expansion in each case. In the nonrenewable-resource policy field, Section 109 of the British North America Act assigns responsibility to the provinces for "all lands, mines, minerals and royalties." Nevertheless, the federal department of Energy, Mines and Resources uses the federal trade and commerce power, Section 91(2) and the "peace, order and good government" clause in the preamble of Section 91 as the constitutional basis for its activities. Currently, the resource field, particularly energy, is an area of intense competition between provincial and federal governments for control and regulation. In the communications policy field, the provinces have extended their authority in the absence of clear constitutional division. Federal authority has been based on a number of judicial decisions that dealt with specific cases. No comprehensive ruling has been made, but the federal government has assumed responsibility for regulating radiocommunications including broadcasting. In the mid-1970s several provinces, in particular Québec, challenged the federal government over the right to regulate cable broadcasting. Despite a Supreme Court ruling that upheld the federal government's authority, the dispute over cable broadcasting continues. Another example in which provincial involvement in an area of federal jurisdiction has been claimed is international affairs. Provincial involvement has been directed primarily to educational matters but has included trade and economic issues in some cases.

These examples provide only a partial list of the extent to which governments have pursued what have often become competing policy and program interests. Not surprisingly, these developments have resulted in concern about overlap and duplication of government functions. Provincial governments in particular have objected to the *chévauchements* or intrusions of the federal government into areas of provincial jurisdiction. In an effort to reconcile differences and reduce overlap, several exercises were undertaken in the middle and late 1970s. One of the followup activities of the Western Economic Opportunities Conference of 1973, for example, was a consideration by a committee of senior officials from Ottawa and the Western provinces of the areas in which duplication existed.

The federal-provincial task force on overlap and duplication established by the First Ministers' Conference in 1977 represented an effort to address this problem on a national scale. Moreover, the regulatory reference by the prime minister to the Economic Council in 1978 instructed a consideration of duplication and overlap in regulatory fields. In 1977, the Federal-Provincial Relations Office in Ottawa undertook a study of relations between the federal government and the province of Québec for the period 1967-77 with a view to determining the degree of interaction between these two governments. In each of these instances, preliminary findings suggested the need for constitutional clarity on the responsibilities of each level of government to provide a basis for the possible rationalization of services and regulations.

The search for solutions to the problems of big governments is taking place in a highly complicated political and economic environment. Attempts to restrain government expenditures, for example, treat only one facet of the problem. Restraint does not necessarily involve the rationalization of services or activities between governments. Neither does it address the jurisdictional questions respecting the appropriate spheres of government responsibilities. Comprehensive constitutional reform, however, may not be possible in the face of conflicting interests and proposals for change. The fact that there is no clear consensus—especially among federal and provincial political elites—about the nature of our federal system and the relationships between and among governments acts as a major deterrent to effecting reform. The range of options and the scope for change are broad, but achieving agreement on the method and the approach to change is difficult.

If lack of agreement on the redefinition of the constitutional division of powers creates a major obstacle to the rationalization and harmonization of administrative activities of federal and provincial governments, proposals that focus on developing intrastate rather than interstate solutions might be considered.[45] The intrastate approach could involve measures that strengthen provincial influence within the federal government particularly central institutions. Second, the approach could involve central initiatives to regional diversities that do not involve the provincial governments.[46] Within the realm of public administration, the two aspects of this approach might be pursued in the following ways. With respect to the first, the "provincialization" of central administrative bodies through the appointment of provincial representatives to the boards of federal regulatory commissions, crown corporations and advisory councils could be considered. Unlike the proposal to provincialize the federal upper chamber, the implications of this measure would not raise major problems of responsibility and accountability. The appropriate minister responsible for these bodies would assume responsibility and be held accountable for them. He would, however, have the benefit of regional views formally incorporated into the administrative structures.

The second aspect of this approach—the decentralization of the federal public service—could be reexamined. For example, the existing

Figure 7-1
Intergovernmental Structures

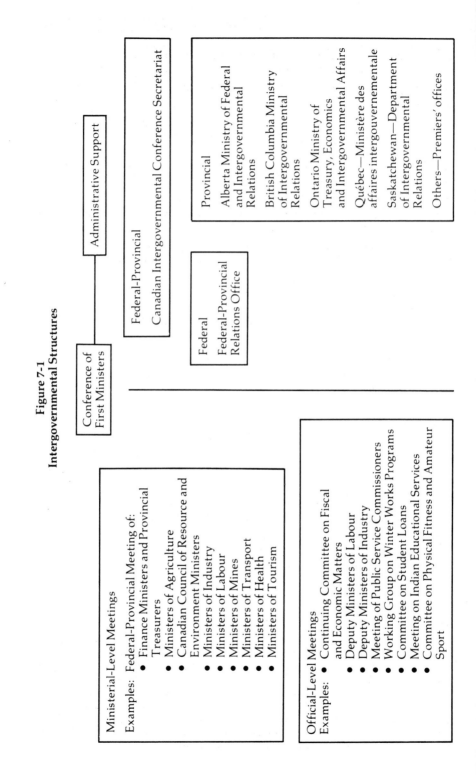

Administrative Support

Conference of First Ministers

Federal-Provincial
Canadian Intergovernmental Conference Secretariat

Federal
Federal-Provincial Relations Office

Provincial

Alberta Ministry of Federal and Intergovernmental Relations

British Columbia Ministry of Intergovernmental Relations

Ontario Ministry of Treasury, Economics and Intergovernmental Affairs

Québec—Ministère des affaires intergouvernementale

Saskatchewan—Department of Intergovernmental Relations

Others—Premiers' offices

Ministerial-Level Meetings

Examples: Federal-Provincial Meeting of:
- Finance Ministers and Provincial Treasurers
- Ministers of Agriculture
- Canadian Council of Resource and Environment Ministers
- Ministers of Industry
- Ministers of Labour
- Ministers of Mines
- Ministers of Transport
- Ministers of Health
- Ministers of Tourism

Official-Level Meetings

Examples:
- Continuing Committee on Fiscal and Economic Matters
- Deputy Ministers of Labour
- Deputy Ministers of Industry
- Meeting of Public Service Commissioners
- Working Group on Winter Works Programs
- Committee on Student Loans
- Meeting on Indian Educational Services
- Committee on Physical Fitness and Amateur Sport

policy to deconcentrate federal departmental operations could be extended to include the actual delegation of decision-making authority with the relocation of jobs to the regions. An organizational model could include a deputy minister and a small policy-coordination secretariat located in Ottawa with regional assistant deputy ministers located in the regions and responsible for departmental policy and program operations in the area. Greater regional contact by the minister and his deputy would be required to ensure effective coordination, but it would be expected that the development and administration of policies and programs would be more responsive to local needs. In this way, the rationalization of government activities and mechanisms of federal-provincial liaison within a region could also be promoted. Nevertheless, the implications of decentralization for the central decision-making processes of cabinet would have to be considered. An entirely different environment for decision making that would result could require new structures and processes of coordination. In addition, the questions of cost and feasibility of massive decentralization measures would have to be weighed carefully.

In the final analysis, federalism is both a frustration and a challenge to public administration. As objects and instruments of change, public services respond to political direction. While they may be used as active agents of reform and indeed contribute to the problems of growth and complexity, they are also passive participants in the broader political environment. For example, the bilingualization of the federal public service will not resolve the internal debate in the province of Québec and between Québec and Ottawa on the question of sovereignty-association. The decentralization of public services—such as the location of Petro-Canada offices in Calgary—will not diminish the tension between Ottawa and Alberta over natural resources. Nevertheless, these measures can act as counterweights, albeit in limited ways, in the process of adjustment and accommodation between the federal and provincial governments. Within the context of constitutional and political change, however, administrative reforms are secondary issues. They can support the achievement of political goals, but they cannot resolve major political issues.

Notes

1. Some of the classic governmental studies include: Canada, *Report of the Royal Commission on Dominion-Provincial Relations in Canada, 1937-1939* (Ottawa: King's Printer, 1940), and Province of Québec, *Report of the Royal Commission of Inquiry on Constitutional Problems* (Québec City: Queen's Printer, 1956). Among academic works, Professor Smiley has provided several incisive analyses, including: *The Canadian Political Nationality* (Toronto: Methuen, 1967); *Constitutional Adaptation and Canadian Federalism since 1945*, Documents of the Royal Commission on Bilingualism and Biculturalism, No. 4 (Ottawa: Queen's Printer, 1970); and *Canada in Question*, 2nd ed. (Toronto: McGraw-Hill Ryerson, 1976).

2. The collection of decisions compiled by R.A. Olmsted, *Decisions Relating to the British North America Act, 1867, and the Canadian Constitution, 1867-1954*, 3 vols. (Ottawa: Queen's Printer, 1954), has been a primary reference. For an excellent recent work see: Peter W. Hogg, *Constitutional Law of Canada* (Toronto: Carswell, 1978).

3. See Smiley, *Canada in Question*, especially pp. 40-52.

4. The definition offered by K.C. Wheare in his book, *Federal Government, op. cit.*, emphasized the independent yet coordinate status of each level of government. In *Attorney General for Canada* v. *Attorney General for Ontario and Others* (1937) A.C. 326, Lord Atkin of the Judicial Committee of the Privy Council in England coined the phrase that "the ship of state . . . still retains the watertight compartments which are an essential part of her original structure." As cited in Paul Fox, *Politics: Canada*, 2nd ed. (Toronto: McGraw-Hill, 1963), p. 64.

5. Smiley, *Constitutional Adaptation and Canadian Federalism since 1945.*

6. See Richard Simeon, *Federal-Provincial Diplomacy: The Making of Recent Policy in Canada* (Toronto: University of Toronto Press, 1972), for an elaboration of the bargaining model of federal-provincial relations. In William Riker, *Federalism: Origin, Operation and Significance* (Boston: Little, Brown, 1964), the concept of federalism as a bargain was applied as a model for a broad analysis of federal systems.

7. See Jean-Luc Pépin, "Co-operative Federalism," in J.P. Meekison (ed.), *Canadian Federalism: Myth or Reality*, 1st ed. (Toronto: Methuen, 1968), pp. 320-29.

8. Smiley, *Canada in Question*, p. 57. The arguments supporting an erosion of federal powers presume a recognition of a dominant role for the central government. The alternative concept—that the provinces are equal partners—is used to justify provincial involvement not only on matters of provincial jurisdiction but on federal matters as well.

9. See T.A. Hockin, *Government in Canada*, especially pp. 31-63; and Claude Morin, *Québec versus Ottawa: The Struggle for Self-Government, 1960-72*, English ed. (Toronto: University of Toronto Press, 1976).

10. Morin, ibid.

11. See Province of Québec, *Report of the Royal Commission Inquiry on Constitutional Problems*; and Statements by the Rt. Hon. Maurice Duplessis, Prime Minister of Québec, in *Proceedings of the Federal-Provincial Conferences* (Ottawa: Queen's Printer, 1950 and 1955).

12. See Richard Simeon (ed.), *Confrontation and Collaboration: Intergovernmental Relations in Canada Today* (Toronto: Institute of Public Administration of Canada, 1979). An initial statement by the Progressive Conservative Minister of Federal-Provincial Relations on the Clark government's approach to constitutional renewal emphasized gradualism and disengagement in relations with the provinces. See William Jarvis, "Poursuivre la rénovation du régime fédéral," *Le Devoir* (mardi, 30 octobre 1979), pp. 5 and 12.

13. For example, see E. Gallant, "The Machinery of Federal-Provincial Relations I," and R.M. Burns, "The Machinery of Federal-Provincial Relations II," in J.P. Meekison (ed.), *Canadian Federalism: Myth or Reality*, 1st ed., pp. 287-97 and 298-304, respectively; R.M. Burns, *Report on Intergovernmental Liaison on Fiscal and Economic Matters*, Institute of Intergovernmental Relations, Queen's University (Ottawa: Queen's Printer, 1969); G. Veilleux, *Les Relations Intergouvernementales au Canada, 1867-1967* (Montréal: Les Presses de l'Université du Québec, 1971), and "L'évolution des mécanismes de liaison intergouvernementale," in Simeon, *Confrontation and Collaboration*, pp. 35-77.

14. Veilleux, "L'évolution des mécanismes," ibid.

15. See Kenneth Wiltshire, "Working with Agreements—Comparing Canadian and Aus-

tralian Experience," a preliminary background paper presented to the Annual Conference of the Institute of Public Administration of Canada (Winnipeg: mimeo, August 1979).

16. See Smiley, *Canada in Question*, 2nd ed., pp. 40-41, for a discussion of events respecting the convening of these two conferences.

17. See G. Veilleux, "Intergovernmental Canada—Government by Conference? A Fiscal and Economic Perspective," a paper presented to the 1979 Annual Conference of the Institute of Public Administration of Canada (Winnipeg: mimeo, August 29, 1979), pp. 2-3.

18. Veilleux, "L'évolution des mécanismes," pp. 64-77.

19. The first conference was held *in camera*; the second was public. The papers and communiqués from both are in the public domain.

20. The proclamation establishing the Ministry contained several sections that specified the Ministry's intended intergovernmental role. In addition, the preamble stated that "the close co-operation of governments is required to ensure that the urban environment evolves in a manner beneficial to all Canadians," SOR/71-320 (July 28, 1971), pursuant to section 14 of the Government Organization Act, 1970, *Revised Statutes of Canada*, 1970, ch. 14, 2nd supplement. See also, David Cameron, "Urban Policy," in Doern and Wilson (eds.), *Issues in Canadian Public Policy*, pp. 244-50.

21. The province of Québec dramatically expressed its view on the second conference by sending a group of officials, but no provincial minister, to "observe" the proceedings.

22. The Chairman of the Task Force, John Deutsch, died before the report was completed. After some delay, two volumes of analyses and statistics were released in 1975.

23. The constitutional basis of the spending power claimed by the federal government has been section 91(3) of the British North America Act respecting the power of the Parliament of Canada to raise money by any mode of taxation and section 91(1A), the federal power to make laws respecting public debt and property. See Canada, *Federal-Provincial Grants and the Spending Power of Parliament* (Ottawa: Queen's Printer, 1969).

24. In particular, see comments by Gordon Robertson, "The Role of Interministerial Conferences in the Decision-Making Process," in Simeon (ed.), *Confrontation and Collaboration*, pp. 78-88.

25. A senior Ontario official has aptly identified the three major functions of intergovernmental conferences to be: information exchange, policy and program harmonization and policy determination. See Don Stevenson, "The Role of Intergovernmental Conferences in the Decision-Making Process," in Simeon (ed.), *Confrontation and Collaboration*, pp. 89-98.

26. Simeon, ibid., pp. 10-11.

27. At a federal-provincial first ministers' conference in 1978, Prime Minister Trudeau posed the question: Which government speaks for Canada? Mr. Lougheed, Premier of Alberta, was quick to reply "We all do."

28. Senate seats are allocated on a regional basis, recognizing the Maritimes, Ontario, Québec and the West as the key regions. Recently, the northern territories have been given representation as well. See British North America Act, section 22.

29. For example, the proposal for a reformed upper chamber (styled the Council of Federation) made by the Task Force on Canadian Unity included a suspensive veto for the Council for "proposed federal legislation deemed to belong to the category of powers described as concurrent with provincial paramountcy." See Canada, Task Force on Canadian Unity, *A Future Together* (Ottawa: Supply and Services, 1979), p. 128.

30. Ultimately change will evolve through the political process. The use of referenda, for example, may come to be applied by governments in addition to the province of Québec.

31. See Ken Kernaghan, "The Role of Intergovernmental Officials in Canada," a paper presented to the Annual Conference of the Institute of Public Administration of Canada (Winnipeg: mimeo, August 31, 1979). Professor Kernaghan sets out three complementary models to explain the role of officials in intergovernmental relations. The models include: cooperation, bargaining and bureaucratic politics. In particular, the paper focuses on the question of the responsibility of these officials for the power they exercise in the political system.

32. The work of this Committee has received considerable attention. In particular, see A.R. Kear, "Co-operative Federalism: A Study of the Federal-Provincial Continuing Committee on Fiscal and Economic Matters," in Meekison (ed.), *Canadian Federalism: Myth or Reality*, pp. 305-16, and three papers presented at a panel discussion on "Federal-Provincial Policy Co-ordination: The Work of the Federal-Provincial Continuing Committee on Fiscal and Economic Matters," at the Annual Conference of the Institute of Public Administration of Canada (Fredericton: September 1972). They included remarks by: Mr. R.B. Bryce, then constitutional adviser to the prime minister; Professor R.M. Burns, Director of the Institute of Intergovernmental Relations, Queen's University, Kingston; and, Michel Belanger, Secretary to the Treasury Board, Québec.

33. See A.S. Rubinoff, "Federal-Provincial Relations: Is Our Conduct Changing?" a paper presented to the Annual Conference of the Institute of Public Administration of Canada (Victoria: mimeo, September 1977).

34. Langford, *Transport in Transition*, pp. 194-95.

35. Veilleux, "L'évolution des mécanismes," pp. 64-77.

36. Canada, Federal-Provincial Relations Office, "A Descriptive Inventory of Federal-Provincial Programs and Activities" (Ottawa: Supply and Services, 1975).

37. In particular, see J.S. Dupré et al., *Federalism and Policy Development: the case of adult occupational training in Ontario* (Toronto: University of Toronto Press, 1973); and A.G.S. Careless, *Initiative and Response: The Adaptation of Canadian Federalism to Regional Economic Development* (Montreal: McGill-Queen's University Press, 1977).

38. Kernaghan, "The Role of Intergovernmental Officials," pp. 16-17.

39. For an excellent analysis of how federal-provincial relations have affected federal policy processes in key activity areas and have impacted on federal government organization, see V.S. Wilson, "Federal Provincial Relations and Federal Policy Processes," in Doern and Aucoin, *Public Policy in Canada*, pp. 190-222.

40. Several examples of this are provided in Careless, *Initiative and Response*. See especially pp. 166-175.

41. The administration of these programs has been fraught with controversy. By making funds available through its general spending power the federal government can influence provincial-government spending priorities. If the federal government decides to terminate a program or cut back on funds, as it has done on occasion, provincial governments are required to use additional provincial funds to maintain the level of program services or cut back on the program. In either circumstance, there may be political costs to the provincial government if the program affects an important clientele group. Detailed analyses of the effects of shared-cost programs on federal and provincial budgetary processes can be found in D.V. Smiley, "Conditional Grants and Canadian Federalism," Canadian Tax Papers no. 32 (Toronto: Canadian Tax Foundation, 1971). See also Wiltshire, "Working with Agreements," and Veilleux, "A Fiscal and Economic Perspective."

42. See Kernaghan, "The Role of Intergovernmental Officials," pp. 23-29, for a discussion of the responsibility of intergovernmental officials.

43. A.C. Cairns, "The other crisis of Canadian federalism," *Canadian Public Administration* (Summer 1979), vol. 22, no. 2, pp. 175-95.

44. Ibid., pp. 186-87.

45. In fact, many of the proposals for constitutional reform have included both interstate and intrastate solutions. For example, proposals for a redefinition of the division of powers are examples of the first; the restructuring of the federal upper chamber or the federal Supreme Court is an example of the second. One of the most comprehensive analyses of interstate and intrastate proposals for constitutional reform was conducted in 1978 by a group of scholars at the University of Guelph for the Task Force on Canadian Unity. The Guelph papers examined the entire range of constitutional and institutional issues as a total integrated package. In view of the interrelated nature of reform proposals, it is difficult to single out one or two aspects of change and comment in detail, for so many linkages can relate to reforms in other areas. However, a narrow context has been established in the discussion to exemplify some alternatives without reference to the full range of implications.

46. See A.C. Cairns, "From Interstate to Intrastate Federalism" (Kingston, Ontario: Institute of Intergovernmental Relations, Queen's University, 1979). Discussion Paper no. 5, p. 11.

8
Conclusions

The dimensions of influence and change in the federal executive machinery of government in past years have encompassed every facet of government organization and operation. Public-policy agendas have reflected a qualitative as well as a quantitative shift in the activities of government. Growth and specialization within the public service have helped to create a changing environment in which government functions are performed. Organizational and management initiatives have thus attempted to provide increasingly sophisticated mechanisms and techniques to foster effective performance. Although measures of restraint and conservation of public resources have slowed the rate of expansion in the federal government in recent years, it cannot be expected that the problems of size and complexity will recede substantially in the future. Retrenchment cannot take us back to simpler times but could support a period of consolidation in the management of government affairs.

The exercise of responsible government in our cabinet-parliamentary system is based on the principles of individual and collective responsibilities of ministers that require their personal accountability to Parliament and to each other. The management and structure of the public service supports the responsibilities of ministers and is influenced by the political environment in which public-service functions are performed. Thus, conditions and constraints on policy and administrative operations in the public sector differ from those in the private sector. The application of business practices and procedures and of "systems" techniques borrowed from the disciplines of science and technology for "rationally" organizing the flow of business and measuring productivity can contribute to improved administrative efficiency. Policy efficiency, however, is determined ultimately by ministerial requirements and institutional processes. Although political considerations can sometimes hinder the achievement of administrative efficiency, they ensure the provision of public policies and services that reflect political goals and objectives and that are sensitive to public needs.

In considering the operation and reform of the executive machinery of government in the past decade or more, the impact of collegial decision making on policy processes and administrative practices has been noteworthy. The exercise of collective responsibility during a period in which individual ministerial responsibilities were elaborated and realigned emphasized the interdependent nature of government activities and stressed the need for coordination of policies and programs between and among departments and agencies. Administrative reform and innovation were nurtured by central initiatives and direction. In turn, departmental responses to central initiatives expanded organizational capability and served to create inter- and intradepartmental mechanisms for coordination and collaboration. The search for consensus and support for government action contributed to several different kinds of consultation and inter-action at political and administrative levels. The government extended its direct contact with outside interests and consulted widely with groups and individuals. Furthermore, intergovernmental collaboration generated expansion at both levels of government, which has led to concerns about overlap and duplication of federal and provincial policies and programs. Internal and external influences have thus served to create a highly complex policy-making and management environment.

The achievements of the period, nevertheless, demonstrated the flexibility and adaptability of the executive apparatus. As governments played an active role in generating demands as well as responding to them, public-service organizations were shaped and formed to carry out and provide new functions and services. By and large, responsive gov-ernment became synonymous with growth and expansion. In the process, institutional and internal accountability systems were often challenged by external influences that demanded responsiveness without strict respon-sibility and accountability of government for its actions. With the introduction of a number of restraint measures and pressures from the Auditor General to improve financial management in the mid-1970s, the federal government began to shift its attention to ways and means to improve performance of and in government as well as to strengthen accountability. In addition to internal-management reforms, several studies of the problems were undertaken, particularly including the work of the Royal Commission on Financial Management and Accountability.

While the scope of administrative responsibility has grown with the increased delegation of authority to officials, the principles of ministerial responsibility provide the basis whereby accountability in the system is maintained. Thus, ministerial accountability begins with the exercise of political control over the public service. Moreover, political direction and control is supported by internal management systems that provide a struc-ture of checks and balances over administrative action. Furthermore, the answerability of ministers to Parliament—particularly in the House of Commons—for all actions undertaken by ministers or on their behalf is reinforced by the answerability of public officials to ministers for the efficient and effective management of the public service. While other controls (such as judicial controls) may be exercised over the public service, these three elements—political control, internal management controls and parliamentary scrutiny—are instrumental to maintaining political account-ability. The following discussion will focus on these three elements of control and reexamine some of the current measures of and concerns about them.

Political Control

Ministerial accountability to Parliament presumes the exercise of political control over the public service. The prime minister plays a preeminent role in the exercise of collective responsibility through his prerogative to appoint ministers and to assign responsibilities to them, to appoint senior officials and to organize cabinet business. Although ministers discharge individual responsibilities, the convention of collective responsibility requires them to account internally to each other for the exercise of their individual authority. Thus, ministers exercise control collectively through cabinet and cabinet committee processes as well as individually through personal direction of departmental operations.

The structure of the cabinet committee system influences the manner in which collective political control will be exercised. As discussed in Chapter 2, the cabinet committee system from 1968 included coordinating committees such as the Cabinet Committee on Priorities and Planning, Legislation and House Planning, Federal-Provincial Relations, Treasury Board and operational policy committees such as Economic Policy and Social Policy.

The deliberations of these two types of committees were intended to ensure collective consideration of ministerial proposals from a number of perspectives. For example, the setting of priorities by the Cabinet Committee on Priorities and Planning established a process whereby ministers were responsible for developing a broad framework of goals within which their departments and agencies would be required to respond. However imperfectly developed and implemented, the process of establishing priorities created a level of awareness among ministers of the general goals of the government program and their implications for individual ministerial initiatives. Second, departmental policy and program proposals were considered by the several operational committees. Detailed discussion of proposals in the context of government priorities was possible in these forums. Furthermore, departmental expenditure submissions were considered by Treasury Board. The expenditure guidelines applied by the Board were based on the review of the economic situation and expenditure forecasts conducted by the Cabinet Committee on Priorities and Planning. In all instances, proposals and recommendations would receive final approval by full cabinet. Thus, an additional opportunity existed for full discussion, if necessary, of matters considered by committees.

Despite efforts to relate committee activities, there was a lack of integration of the several committee decision streams, particularly in the area of expenditure management. The consideration of policy and program proposals by operational committees and resource requests by Treasury Board were conducted separately. In addition, the establishment of spending priorities by the Treasury Board based on the fiscal framework developed by the Cabinet Committee on Priorities and Planning occurred several months after the Board requested departments to prepare program-forecast submissions.[1]

The Lambert Commission's assessment of this problem resulted in the recommendation of the preparation of the five-year Fiscal Plan to provide the means whereby the processes of setting priorities, establishing a fiscal framework and setting expenditure guidelines could be integrated effectively and applied to departmental planning exercises. As discussed in Chapter 3, the preparation of the Fiscal Plan was intended to provide a single focus for the government's collective management responsibilities and to enhance planning capability at the ministerial level.

While the Lambert proposal was designed in the context of the cabinet-committee system of the Trudeau administration, the basic elements of the proposal were adapted by the Clark administration to fit the two-tiered cabinet committee system put into place in June 1979. The essential design of the "resource envelope" system introduced in the summer of 1979 was to place responsibility for the management of expenditures with the inner cabinet and the five policy sector committees of cabinet. The inner cabinet assumed responsibility for the large "envelope" expenditures such as public debt and fiscal transfers to the provinces. The policy sector committees managed the seven other envelopes: economic development, justice and legal affairs, social and native affairs, external affairs and aid, defence, services to government and Parliament. Committees were asked to prepare plans for their respective policy areas. The inner cabinet established the overall expenditure limits on the basis of government priorities and in conjunction with the assessment of the economic situation from the Minister of Finance and a review of the expenditure situation by the President of the Treasury Board. The inner cabinet would formulate recommendations on the allocation of funds to each envelope and transmit them to the policy committees to be used as a framework for committee consideration of departmental submissions. Decision making authority for the allocation of funds *within* an envelope was delegated to the committees; inner cabinet had final responsibility for approving the overall spending plans resulting from committee deliberation. Thus, ministers could through committee assert direct control over the structure of departmental expenditures. In particular, the system provided a means to apply expenditure ceilings in each policy sector and to link policy with resource allocation decisions.

The Treasury Board's role in arbitrating departmental program submissions was reduced although its responsibility for approving departmental requests in the areas of financial management, personnel policy and administrative policy was highlighted. The Treasury Board's role was to become more clearly identified with purely management concerns in government. Second, the staff of the Ministries of State for Economic Development and Social Development were nurtured as policy-sector coordinating agencies. In turn, the process-orientation of the Privy Council Office was emphasized.

The new committee processes were just taking hold, however, when the Clark government was defeated in December 1979. While no official statement on cabinet committee structure and operation under the current Trudeau administration has yet been issued, many innovations introduced in 1979 have remained and are continuing to evolve. It should be noted that the need to tighten expenditure control over government programs and to mesh government priorities and the general expenditure framework with departmental planning efforts was recognized well before 1979. One could say that the means and methods whereby those objects may be achieved have been systematically pursued with an impetus provided by a change of government in 1979.

A two-tiered cabinet structure could serve to strengthen the decision-making role of committees and integrate the policy and resource allocation decision streams. Nevertheless, inner cabinet operations exclude a large number of ministers from discussion on primary issues of the government program and policy directions. The elimination of full cabinet deliberations on committee decisions removes an essential forum in which collective views of ministers can be brought to bear on policy issues. Over time, collective responsibility as it has traditionally been exercised may be subject to significant modification.

The collective control by ministers is complemented and balanced by individual ministerial direction over departments and agencies. The personal accountability of ministers derives from the exercise of individual responsibility. As ministers' responsibilities have increased, deputies have assumed greater responsibility for policy and administration in their departments. Ministers rely heavily on their senior officials to provide support on a broad range of activities, including the preparation of cabinet submissions, the preparation and defence of departmental estimates before the Treasury Board and the preparation of material in response to questions in the House and for testimony before House committees.

Ministerial direction and control over departments is exercised on a day-to-day basis. The relationship between the minister and his deputy is a critical element of achieving departmental responsiveness to ministerial needs. The minister's involvement in the annual evaluation of his deputy minister's performance is another key means by which control is exercised. Ministers have the opportunity to provide individual assessments of their deputies to the Committee of Senior Officials on Executive Personnel and to make collective evaluations of senior personnel's performance through the Cabinet Committee on the Public Service.[2] Measures to strengthen ministerial involvement in the initial stages of the review would enhance accountability to ministers. The process as outlined in Chapter 4 continues to evolve as more comprehensive and rigorous evaluation systems are developed.

Efforts to extend political control and direction over nondepartmental bodies have provided a sharper focus for ministerial responsibility vis-à-vis these agencies. Attempts to harmonize portfolio relationships and to establish ministry systems and portfolio committees as mechanisms to enhance policy coordination and ministerial direction met with limited success. However, the potential of directive powers—as proposed in the government's Green Paper of 1977 and the Lambert Commission report and as contained in several enabling statutes of corporations—would serve to provide the basis for more effective control and accountability on policy matters. The number and scope of activities of these agencies, though, raises questions about the ability of ministers to exercise consistent and regular control. The power of appointment of chief executive officers and board directors by the prime minister may in reality constitute the most effective means of maintaining accountability.

A major problem in the political management of public-sector organizations, especially departments, relates to the discontinuity in individual ministerial leadership. Not only have ministerial workloads become more onerous in recent years, requiring a substantial delegation of responsibility to senior officials, but the rate of turnover of ministers in portfolios has also been high. While collegial decision-making processes can in part offset constant shifts in ministers, collective direction can never entirely compensate or replace individual ministerial leadership in maintaining control and accountability of departmental activities. Strong collective direction, if not balanced by strong individual leadership, may serve to diminish individual ministerial responsibility or at least circumscribe it. Senior officials and their subordinates are expected to provide continuity through a series of different ministers during the life of a particular government and/or through changes in government. The absence of strong political direction to a department, however, could enhance officials' influence on the one hand or weaken their ability to be effective on the other.

Internal Management Controls

Accountability within the public service is obtained primarily through a system of internal checks and balances of administrative control. The management structure not only supports the exercise of individual and collective ministerial responsibility, but also provides a network of counterweights to ensure that administrative authority is exercised responsibly. In addition, the Public Service Commission and the Auditor General act as monitors of administrative action independent of the framework of management under the authority of ministers. Thus, the countervailing influences between central agency and departmental responsibilities designed to achieve balance and control are assisted by external scrutineers of financial- and personnel-management practices.[3]

In addressing the problems of internal management and control in the early 1960s, the Glassco Commission proposed a package of reforms that would *let* the managers manage on the one hand and revitalize central administrative leadership on the other. The implementation of those reforms in the late 1960s was accompanied by other changes that expanded the role of the Privy Council Office as a central policy coordinator and the role of the Treasury Board and its Secretariat as central manager. Departments were required to respond to central-agency initiatives during a period when they were also promoting their own program expansion. With increased activity in all quarters, the internal checks and balances did not, at least in the opinion of the Auditor General, provide effective systems of management and accountability.

As noted in an earlier chapter, the Lambert Commission proposals, in seeking a "mutually compatible management system," favoured greater centralization of management responsibility. Despite the profound transformation and elaboration of central-agency functions—especially within the Treasury Board Secretariat—the Commission centred its proposals for structural reform on the Secretariat. The formula to be applied was to develop measures to *"require* the managers to manage" and strengthen planning and administrative leadership at the top. Improvement in the management *of* government would be achieved through the consolidation of financial- and personnel-management functions under the Treasury Board, restyled the Board of Management. In addition to a Financial Management Secretariat, a Personnel Management Secretariat would, *inter alia*, be responsible for the staffing and training functions currently discharged by the Public Service Commission. The creation of a new corporate personnel agency with staffing and training functions was also recommended by the Special Committee on the Review of Personnel Management and the Merit Principle, although the Committee's rationale for the proposal differed from that of the Commission.[4] Furthermore, both studies recommended that the role of the Public Service Commission be focused mainly on appeal and audit functions.

In a historical perspective, these proposals for the consolidation of central-management functions represent yet another stage in the continuing struggle between central agencies and departments on the one hand and the Treasury Board and the Public Service Commission on the other. As noted in the previous section, the proposal for the centralization of planning activities through the preparation of the proposed Fiscal Plan would enhance the role of the Minister of Finance over expenditure management and would reinforce the activities of Finance, Treasury Board

Secretariat and Privy Council officials in coordinating expenditure-planning efforts in support of ministerial decision making. With respect to internal management, the consolidation of the central-management functions would expand the range of central-management responsibilities requiring coordination with departments. For example, the responsibilities of the proposed Financial Management Secretariat would direct, coordinate and/or arbitrate departmental activities with respect to:

- program-resource requests
- assistance in preparing departmental work plans
- program evaluation
- selection and training of senior financial officers
- management audits
- accounting systems
- audit services

The responsibilities of the proposed Personnel Management Secretariat would relate to departmental activities in the following areas:

- personnel policy
- recruitment and staffing
- organization and classification
- management-development training
- official-languages policy
- employee-appraisal systems

The proposed relationship between the central-management agencies and the Public Service Commission is perhaps one of the more intriguing aspects of the current reform proposals. The Glassco Commission had recommended a decentralized structure for personnel management across the public service and a clarification of responsibilities between the Treasury Board and the Public Service Commission in areas of personnel policy. With the introduction of collective bargaining, the Commission also lost the responsibility for pay administration and classification to the Treasury Board. To fill the void created by these reforms, the Commission refurbished its mandate by developing language and management training programs and by undertaking special recruitment programs in support of Treasury Board personnel policies. The Lambert Commission and the D'Avignon Committee have recommended that the Public Service Commission lose again, this time by proposing the transfer of staffing as well as training functions from the Commission to the proposed central personnel-management secretariat. The D'Avignon Committee, however, also proposed a new dimension of activity for the Commission in the area of employer-employee relations, which in a limited way would allow the Commission to act as a check on the central personnel-management secretariat.[5] Thus, the wheel of expansion and specialization goes around.

The result of the implementation of these proposals could increase the current complexity of the system of checks and balances. The shift in responsibilities from one agency to another and the creation of new responsibility centres within central agencies and departments will not necessarily strengthen accountability systems. They will require the establishment of new lines of communication and reporting between central agencies and departments. A major restructuring of the Public Service Commission and reorientation of its responsibilities could create significant upheavals in systems of personnel management. Despite arguments to the contrary, there is a value in having an independent staffing agency, which is charged with protecting the merit principle, also administer recruitment and staffing programs designed to support corporate personnel policies. In particular, the implementation of policies designed to promote a "representative public service" may be suspect if the agency responsible for development and implementation reports directly to a minister.

In considering the departmental operations, one may question the assumption that an era of letting the managers manage has led to severe laxity in managerial accountability for administration action. During that period, departmental managers were caught up in responding to central-agency reform initiatives. The "saturation psychosis" of administrative reform left little time to focus on evaluating programs that by and large were being expanded. The current proposals seem directed to creating a new era of saturation psychosis that would focus reform on the development of new evaluation and appraisal systems. The reform momentum generated by the Auditor General's criticisms and expanded mandates could simply create larger central agency bureaucracies.

Furthermore, the proposed system of checks and balances would do little to untangle the complex environment in which departmental managers attempt to manage. The proposition that central management of the public service as a whole must support departmental needs presumes an active involvement of departmental management in the establishment of administrative practices and standards of administrative performance. The Glassco report recommended that departmental managers be responsible for implementing accountability systems. The Auditor General has claimed that these measures were never fully implemented. The Lambert and D'Avignon proposals reiterated the importance of a major involvement of departmental managers in developing standards of performance and systems of accountability, albeit with closer central agency supervision. Generating new demands on departments for administrative reform, however, might offset the potential for major departmental initiatives. A reactive rather than initiative approach could emerge, given the number of departmental responsibilities to be discharged. Departmental managers often have to balance demands from central agencies against demands from ministers. Performance standards will invariably be affected by particular circumstances.

In summary, sound management systems do not necessarily mean better government performance. Although the 1977 legislation on the Office of the Auditor General expanded his mandate to include value-for-money auditing and thus opened the door to more critical review of departmental operations, the measurement of effectiveness has a political as well as an administrative component. Efficiency and propriety are necessary requisites of departmental management, but answerability to ministers and responsiveness to political needs may, in the final analysis, determine administrative action.

Parliamentary Scrutiny

The primary element of ministerial accountability is parliamentary scrutiny of the conduct of ministers. Ministers are personally answerable to the House on a daily basis whether in debate or in Question Period. The extent to which Parliament holds ministers accountable depends on the will of the House to hold them answerable.[6] While ministerial resignation or government defeat may be exceptional outcomes of House measures to hold a minister or cabinet accountable, the fear of scandal or political embarrassment provides a strong incentive for ministers to act responsibly and account accordingly for their actions. Since deputy ministers support the individual responsibility of ministers directly and help maintain the collective responsibilities of ministers, their role in supporting the accountability of ministers is also pertinent.

In the main, the government seeks legislative approval for the passage of legislation and for measures on the levying of taxes and the expenditure of public funds. When the government has a majority and hence holds the confidence of the House, approval will be obtained following appropriate debate procedures. Question Period provides a key means of demanding accountability of specific day-to-day issues. For detailed review and examination of government measures, the House uses a system of committees.[7] Ministers appear before standing committees to respond to questions on departmental estimates. They are expected to defend departmental policy and administration and answer on all matters that pertain to departmental operations. Senior departmental officials assist them in this process through the provision of background material and personal appearances before the committees. The Public Accounts Committee that, unlike other House committees, is chaired by a member of the official opposition party, conducts the post-audit review of government spending. In this case, the Committee considers the report of the Auditor General in conjunction with the government's statement of Public Accounts.[8]

Despite the reforms in procedure and committee operations in 1965 and 1968, there has been a continuing concern that Parliament does not play an effective role in holding ministers and officials accountable. The revamping of the committee system to provide for more active scrutiny and review of government business did not keep pace with change and reform in executive processes. In the opinion of some, control of the public purse was lost by Parliament in 1968 when the House agreed to allow departmental estimates to pass without deletion or reduction in any items of expenditure.[9] In the interests of facilitating debate, members gave up their right to control directly government spending proposals.

As discussed in Chapter 6, current proposals for reform have focused on ways and means of improving the quality of committee performance. Nevertheless, problems of partisanship, poor committee attendance and members' lack of experience on committees remain as major stumbling blocks in effecting reforms. The Lambert Commission recognized the problems and offered a full-scale model of reform of committee operations to address these problems and help improve accountability. In the first instance, it recommended a reduction in the number of committees and in the number of members on the committees. Presumably members could enhance their expertise by concentrating their efforts on one or two committees. A reduced committee workload would provide more time to devote to committee responsibilities. Second, it was proposed that committee chairmen be elected for the life of a Parliament and receive remuneration for their work. In addition, it was recommended that committees have a budget and staff to support their activities. These reforms would strengthen the ability of committee members to conduct detailed scrutiny and analysis of departmental submissions.

The major innovative proposals made by the Commission included the establishment of a Standing Committee on Government Finance and the Economy, the structuring of the committee system to provide for "portfolio" reviews of departmental and nondepartmental bodies and the direct accountability of deputy ministers to the Public Accounts Committee. The purpose of the Standing Committee on Government Finance and the Economy would be to review the proposed Fiscal Plan and all tax legislation. Such a committee could serve as a useful forum for discussion of material on expenditure forecasts that the government might be prepared to submit to it and would serve as an initial step in improving committee deliberations of departmental spending plans.

The Commission was also preoccupied with ways and means of improving the form and content of the Estimates to provide members with a more detailed and meaningful description of government spending activities. It also proposed that House-committee recommendations for partial reductions in items in the Estimates be allowed. The automatic and regular referral of departmental and nondepartmental annual reports to standing committees represented another measure of ensuring regular review of government activities. Better-quality information on agency operations through reports and a redesign of departmental estimates would thus enhance members' ability to scrutinize and review.

The proposed portfolio committee structure—while providing a focus for review of related departmental and nondepartmental agency activities—could overburden members, given the variety of bodies to be examined. An alternative approach used in several provincial legislatures could be the creation of a separate standing committee on nondepartmental agencies to specialize in this area. In view of the large number of these kinds of agencies, however, there seems to be no easy solution for developing a scheme by which systematic review of these agencies might be feasible.

As noted in Chapter 4, the proposal for the direct accountability of deputy ministers to the Public Accounts Committee raises questions about ministerial responsibility for departmental operations. Unless deputies are accorded a positive duty to ensure propriety in expenditure, as are permanent heads in their role as Chief Accounting Officers in Great Britain, there is little likelihood that such a measure would enhance accountability. Instead, it could provide an opportunity for ministers to shift blame for program failures to officials by holding the latter accountable for the effectiveness of programs.[10] Under the proposal, cases of disagreement between the minister and the deputy minister would place the deputy in an awkward position, for his opinion would have to be subordinated to that of the minister, who would remain legally responsible for the administration of the department. Officials do appear before committees of the House in any event. A more active participation of senior officials could be called for without changing any rules or procedures.

Generally speaking, the main thrust of the Lambert proposals for parliamentary reform was directed to strengthening the accountability of ministers and of officials to Parliament for management of and in government. While many of the proposals may serve as a basis for future reform, problems of overloading members are a constant danger. As in the case of administrative reform, there are practical and human limits to effecting change. Moreover, unless members are willing to demand greater accountability of government, it is unlikely that major reform would be undertaken. Furthermore, the government would have to be willing to support any changes.

Nevertheless, the potential for reform—particularly as it pertains to parliamentary committees—is considerable, not just as means of strengthening accountability of the government to Parliament, but also as a means of involving members more actively in the affairs of government. The provision of information through Freedom of Information legislation and

Figure 8-1
A System of Accountability: Lambert-D'Avignon Proposals

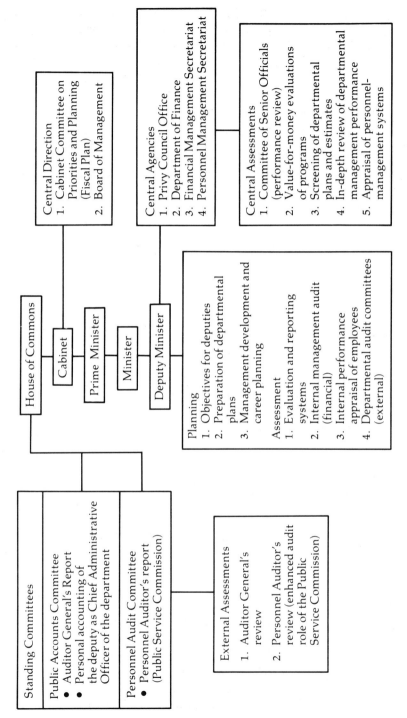

other sources and, perhaps equally important, the capacity to analyze information provided to members are fundamental. The extension of the use of scrutiny committees may also be an important future consideration. For example, the D'Avignon Committee recommended the creation of a parliamentary committee to review personnel audit reports of the Public Service Commission to complement the Public Accounts Committee review of the Auditor General's reports on financial-management practices.[11] Suggestions have also been made to have the reports of the Official Languages Commissioner referred to a standing committee of the House for similar review purposes.

As discussed earlier, committees may also serve to support broader parliamentary functions. For example, standing and special committees of the House and Senate could be used more extensively as forums for consultation and debate on proposed government measures. Furthermore, the establishment of a standing committee on federal-provincial relations to review federal-provincial agreements is another dimension of parliamentary activity that could be seriously explored. In other words, there are ways in which executive dominance of government may be counter-balanced by legislative processes.

In the final analysis, the executive is dependent on the support of Parliament. Majority governments are not necessarily less immune to questioning and criticism than minority governments, although the majority government's tenure of office is assured. Responsiveness to the will of the electorate encompasses many facets, not the least of which are to be found in parliamentary forums. Above all, responsible government is government that ensures that the exercise of power is constrained by the institutional limits placed on it. The public service functions within this environment and is subject to the constraints imposed by the political institutions. Thus, the kind and quality of government that citizens and their elected representatives are prepared to accept will influence how well the governing systems work.

Notes

1. See Royal Commission on Financial Management and Accountability, *Report*, p. 73; and J.R. Mallory, "The Lambert Report: Central Roles and Responsibilities," *Canadian Public Administration* (Winter 1979), vol. 22, no. 4, p. 521.

2. See Chapter 4 and "Senior Personnel in the Public Service of Canada: Deputy Ministers," pp. 3-32 to 3-41.

3. Royal Commission on Government Organization, *Report*, vol. I, pp. 61-63.

4. Canada, *Report of the Special Committee on the Review of Personnel Management and the Merit Principle* (Ottawa: Supply and Services, 1979), p. 158. The rationale of the Committee differed from that of the Lambert Commission. A main preoccupation of the Committee in determining roles and responsibilities was the problem of conflict of interest for the Public Service Commission as an independent agent of Parliament on the one hand and as an arm of management on the other.

5. In addition to auditing corporate and departmental personnel administrative practices, hearing appeals and investigating complaints, the Public Service Commission would arbitrate and review and, if necessary, veto agreements under the National Staffing Council. This body would be a new forum of collective bargaining that would consist of members of the Personnel Management Secretariat and representatives of the bargaining agents. Thus, the Commission would act as a tribunal for bargaining processes and, one might say, a check on the central personnel-management secretariat that represented the employer for purposes of bargaining. Ibid., pp. 131-35.

6. See "Responsibility in the Constitution. Part I: Departmental Structures," pp. 1-47.

7. The role of Senate committees has not been included in the discussion. Nevertheless, they do perform reviews and scrutiny of nonfinancial legislation that the House may send to them.

8. See Chapter 3.

9. See R.L. Stanfield, "The Present State of the Legislative Process in Canada: Myths and Realities," in W.A.W. Neilson and J.C. MacPherson (eds.), *The Legislative Process in Canada: The Need for Reform* (Toronto: Butterworth, 1978), pp. 44-45. Standing Order 58(2) of the House of Commons reads in part: ". . . the business of supply shall consist of motions to concur in interim supply, main estimates and supplementary or final estimates; motions to restore or reinstate any item in the estimates . . ." *Standing Orders of the House of Commons* (Ottawa: Supply and Services, 1978), p. 48.

10. See Paul Thomas, "The Lambert Report: Parliament and Accountability," *Canadian Public Administration* (Winter 1979), vol. 22, no. 4, pp. 561-62. The essential point that Thomas makes on this issue is that "Deputies are *answerable* before Parliament, but only ministers are *responsible*." Ibid., p. 560.

11. *Report of the Special Committee on the Review of Personnel Management and the Merit Principle*, pp. 71 and 93.

Bibliography

1. General References

Campbell, Colin. *Canadian Political Facts, 1945-76.* Toronto: Methuen, 1977.

Canada, Royal Commission on Financial Management and Accountability. *Progress Report.* Ottawa: Supply and Services, 1977.

_____. *Final Report.* Ottawa: Supply and Services, 1979.

Canada, Royal Commission on Government Organization. *Report.* 5 vols. Ottawa: Queen's Printer, 1962.

_____, Privy Council Office. *Submissions to the Royal Commission on Financial Management and Accountability.* Ottawa: Supply and Services, 1979.

_____, *Organization of the Government of Canada 1978/79,* 12th ed. Published by Macmillan of Canada in cooperation with Treasury Board Canada and the Canadian Publishing Centre. Ottawa: Supply and Services, 1978.

_____. *Revised Statutes,* 1970, 1st and 2nd supplements. 7 vols. Ottawa: Information Canada, 1970.

_____. *Statutes of Canada.* Ottawa: 1968-79.

Dawson, R.M. *The Government of Canada,* 5th ed. Edited by Norman Ward. Toronto: University of Toronto Press, 1970.

Doern, G.B., and Aucoin, Peter, eds. *The Structures of Policy Making in Canada.* Toronto: Macmillan of Canada, 1971.

_____, eds. *Public Policy in Canada.* Toronto: Macmillan of Canada, 1979.

Hockin, T.A. *Government in Canada.* Toronto: McGraw-Hill Ryerson, 1976.

Hodgetts, J.E. *The Canadian Public Service 1867-1967: A Physiology of Government.* Toronto: University of Toronto Press, 1973.

Hodgson, J.S. *Public Administration.* Toronto: McGraw-Hill, 1969.

Kernaghan, Kenneth, ed. *Public Administration in Canada: Selected Readings,* 3rd ed. Toronto: Methuen, 1977.

_____, ed. *Bureaucracy in Canadian Government,* 2nd ed. Toronto: Methuen, 1973.

_____. *Canadian Cases in Public Administration.* Toronto: Methuen, 1977.

Lindblom, C.E. *The Policy Making Process*. Englewood Cliffs, N.J.: Prentice Hall, 1968.

Mallory, J.R. *The Structure of Canadian Government*. Toronto: Macmillan of Canada, 1971.

Schultz, R., et al., eds. *The Canadian Political Process*, 3rd ed. Toronto: Holt, Rinehart and Winston, 1979.

Van Loon, R.J., and Whittington, M.S. *The Canadian Political System: Environment, Structure and Process*, 2nd ed. Toronto: McGraw-Hill Ryerson, 1976.

Vickers, Sir Geoffrey. *The Art of Judgment, A Study in Policy Making*. New York: Basic Books, 1965.

————. *Value Systems and Social Process*. New York: Basic Books, 1968.

2. Executive Roles and Structures

The Prime Minister and Cabinet

Hockin, T.A. *Apex of Power: The Prime Minister and Political Leadership in Canada*, 2nd ed. Toronto: Prentice-Hall, 1976.

Matheson, W.A. *The Prime Minister and the Cabinet*. Toronto: Methuen, 1976.

Punnett, R.M. *The Prime Minister in Canadian Government and Politics*. Toronto: Macmillan of Canada, 1977.

Radwanski, G. *Trudeau*. Toronto: Macmillan of Canada, 1978.

D'Aquino, T. "The Prime Minister's Office: Catalyst or Cabal?" *Canadian Public Administration* 1974, vol. 17, no. 1, pp. 54-79.

Doern, G.B., "Horizontal and Vertical Portfolios in Government." In Doern, G.B., and Wilson, V.S., eds. *Issues in Canadian Public Policy*. Toronto: Macmillan of Canada, 1974, pp. 310-36.

Johnson, A.W. "Management Theory and Cabinet Government." *Canadian Public Administration* 1971, vol. 14, no. 1, pp. 73-81.

Lalonde, Marc. "The Changing Role of the Prime Minister's Office." *Canadian Public Administration* 1971, vol. 14, no. 4, pp. 509-37.

Mallory, J.R. "Mackenzie King and the Origins of the Cabinet Secretariat." *Canadian Public Administration* 1976, vol. 19, no. 2, pp. 554-66.

Robertson, Gordon. "The Canadian Parliament and Cabinet in the Face of

Modern Demands." *Canadian Public Administration* 1968, vol. 11, no. 3, pp. 272-79.

Sharp, M. "Decision-Making in the Federal Cabinet." *Canadian Public Administration* 1976, vol. 19, no. 1, pp. 1-7.

Senior Officials

Campbell, C., and Szablowski, G. *The Superbureaucrats: Structure and Behaviour in Central Agencies.* Toronto: Macmillan of Canada, 1979.

Heeney, Arnold. *The Things That Are Caesar's.* Toronto: University of Toronto Press, 1972.

Balls, H.R. "Decision-Making: The Role of the Deputy Minister." *Canadian Public Administration* 1976 vol. 19, no. 3, pp. 417-31.

Bridges, The Rt. Hon. Lord. "The Relationships between Ministers and the Permanent Departmental Head." *Canadian Public Administration* 1964, vol. 7, no. 3, pp. 295-308.

Bryce, R.G. "Reflections on the Lambert Report." *Canadian Public Administration* 1979, vol. 22, no. 4, pp. 572-80.

Cameron, D.M. "Power and Responsibility in the Public Service: Summary of Discussions." *Canadian Public Administration* 1978, vol. 21, no. 3, pp. 358-72.

Cloutier, S. "Senior Public Officials in a Bicultural Society." *Canadian Public Administration* 1968, vol. 11, no. 4, pp. 395-406.

Hodgson, J.S. "The Impact of Minority Government on the Senior Civil Servant." *Canadian Public Administration* 1976, vol. 19, no. 2, pp. 227-37.

Johnson, A.W. "The Role of the Deputy Minister." *Canadian Public Administration* 1961, vol. 4, no. 4, pp. 363-73.

Kernaghan, K. "Responsible Public Bureaucracy: a rationale and a framework for analysis." *Canadian Public Administration* 1973, vol. 16, no. 4, pp. 527-603.

_____. "Politics, Policy and Public Servants: Political Neutrality Revisited." *Canadian Public Administration* 1976, vol. 19, no. 3, pp. 432-56.

_____. "Changing concepts of power and responsibility in the Canadian public service." *Canadian Public Administration* 1978, vol. 21, no. 3, pp. 389-406.

————. "Power, Parliament and Public Servants in Canada: Ministerial Responsibility Re-examined." *Canadian Public Policy* 1979, vol. V, no. 3, pp. 383-96.

Kirby, M.J.; Kroeker, H.V.; Teschke, W.R. "The Impact of Public Policy-Making Structures and Processes in Canada." *Canadian Public Administration* 1978, vol. 21, no. 3, pp. 407-17.

McKeough, W.D. "The Relations of Ministers and Civil Servants." *Canadian Public Administration* 1969, vol. XII, no. 1, pp. 1-8.

Pickersgill, J.W. "Bureaucrats and Politicians." *Canadian Public Administration* 1972, vol. 15, no. 3, pp. 418-27.

Robertson, R.G. "The Changing Role of the Privy Council Office." *Canadian Public Administration* 1971, vol. 14, no. 4, pp. 487-508.

Departmental and Nondepartmental Organizations

Ashley, C.A., and Smails, R.G.H. *Canadian Crown Corporations: Some Aspects of their Administration and Control.* Toronto: Macmillan of Canada, 1965.

Aucoin, P., and French, R. *Knowledge, Power and Public Policy.* Science Council of Canada, Special Study no. 31. Ottawa: Information Canada, 1974.

Baldwin, J.R. *The Regulatory Agency and the Public Corporation* Cambridge, Mass.: Ballinger, 1975.

Canada. *Annual Reports.* Various departments and agencies of the government of Canada.

————, Law Reform Commission. *The Immigration Appeal Board.* Ottawa: Supply and Services, 1977.

————, Privy Council Office. *Crown Corporations: Direction, Control and Accountability.* Ottawa: Supply and Services, 1977.

————, Treasury Board. *Departmental Planning and Evaluation Groups in the Federal Government,* revd. ed. Ottawa: Supply and Services, 1976.

Doern, G.B., ed. *The Regulatory Process in Canada.* Toronto: Macmillan of Canada, 1978.

French, R. and Béliveau, A. *The RCMP and the Management of National Security.* Toronto: Butterworth, 1979.

Gélinas, A., ed. *Public Enterprise and the Public Interest.* Toronto: Institute of Public Administration, 1978.

Hill, O. Mary. *Canada's Salesmen to the World: The Department of Trade and Commerce, 1892-1939.* Montreal: McGill-Queen's University Press, 1977.

Janisch, H.N. *The Regulatory Process of the Canadian Transport Commission.* The Law Reform Commission of Canada. Ottawa: Supply and Services, 1978.

Langford, J.W. *Transport in Transition: The Reorganization of the Federal Transport Portfolio.* Montreal: McGill-Queen's University Press, 1976.

Lucas, A.R., and Bell, T. *The National Energy Board.* Law Reform Commission. Ottawa: Supply and Services, 1977.

Musolf, L.D. *Public Ownership and Accountability: The Canadian Experience.* Cambridge, Mass.: Harvard University Press, 1959.

Phidd, R.W., and Doern, G.B. *The Politics and Management of Canadian Economic Policy.* Toronto: Macmillan of Canada, 1978.

Aucoin, P. and French, R. "The Ministry of State for Science and Technology." *Canadian Public Administration* 1974, vol. 17, no. 3, pp. 461-81.

Babe, R.E. "Regulation of Private Television Broadcasting by the Canadian Radio and Television Commission: A Critique of Ends and Means." *Canadian Public Administration* 1976, vol. 19, no. 4, pp. 552-86.

Brown-John, C.L. "Defining Regulatory Agencies for Analytic Purposes." *Canadian Public Administration* 1976, vol. 19, no. 1, pp. 140-57.

———. "Membership in Canadian Regulatory Agencies." *Canadian Public Administration* 1977, vol. 20, no. 3, pp. 513-35.

———. "Advisory Agencies in Canada: An Introduction," *Canadian Public Administration* 1979, vol. 22, no. 1, pp. 72-91.

Dobell, W.M. "Interdepartmental Management in External Affairs." *Canadian Public Administration* 1978, vol. 21, no. 1, pp. 82-102.

Doern, G.B. "The National Research Council: The Causes of Goal Displacement." *Canadian Public Administration* 1970, vol. 13, no. 2, pp. 140-84.

Doern, G.B.; Hunter, I.A.; Swartz, D.; Wilson, V.S. "The Structure and Behaviour of Canadian Regulatory Boards and Commissions: Multi-Disciplinary Perspectives." *Canadian Public Administration* 1975, vol. 18, no. 2, pp. 189-215.

Gélinas, A. "Le rapport Lambert: les organismes de la couronne." *Canadian Public Administration* 1979, vol. 22, no. 4, pp. 541-57.

Hamilton, R.E. "A Marketing Board to Regulate Exports of Natural Gas." *Canadian Public Administration* 1973, vol. 16, no. 1, pp. 83-95.

Irvine, A.G. "The Delegation of Authority to Crown Corporations." *Canadian Public Administration* 1971, vol. 14, no. 4, pp. 556-79.

Johnson, A.W. "Public Policy: Creativity and Bureaucracy." *Canadian Public Administration* 1978, vol. 21, no. 1, pp. 1-15.

Kristjanson, K. "Crown Corporations: Administrative Responsibility and Public Accountability." *Canadian Public Administration* 1968, vol. 11, no. 4, pp. 454-59.

Laframboise, H.L. "Portfolio Structure and a Ministry System: A Model for the Canadian Public Service." *Optimum* 1970, vol. 1, no. 1, pp. 29-46.

Mansbridge, S.H. "The Lambert Report: recommendations to departments." *Canadian Public Administration* 1979, vol. 22, no. 4, pp. 530-40.

Milligan, F. "The Canada Council as a Public Body." *Canadian Public Administration* 1979, vol. 22, no. 2, pp. 269-89.

Phidd, R.W. "The Economic Council of Canada: Its Establishment, Structure and Role in the Canadian Policy-Making System 1963-74." *Canadian Public Administration* 1976, vol. 19, no. 1.

Pitfield, M. "The Shape of Government in the 1980's: Techniques and Instruments for Policy Formulation at the Federal Level." *Canadian Public Administration* 1976, vol. 19, no. 1, pp. 8-20.

3. Management and Policy Processes

Expenditure Management

Bird, R.M. *The Growth of Government Spending in Canada.* Toronto: Canadian Tax Foundation, 1970.

Canada, Finance. *Estimates for the fiscal years ending March 31, 1968 to 1979.* Ottawa: Supply and Services.

——, Finance. *Attack on Inflation.* Ottawa: Supply and Services, 1975.

——, House of Commons. *Minutes and Proceedings of the Standing Committee on Miscellaneous Estimates.* Ottawa: 1975-77.

——, Privy Council Office. *The Way Ahead: A Framework for Discussion.* Ottawa: Supply and Services, 1976.

——, Supply and Services. *Public Accounts* for the years 1969 to 1978 inclusive. Ottawa: Supply and Services.

_____, Treasury Board. *Program Forecasts and Estimates Manual.* Ottawa: Queen's Printer, 1969; revised 1972.

_____, Treasury Board. *Planning, Programming and Budgeting Guide,* revd. ed. Ottawa: Queen's Printer, 1969.

_____, Treasury Board. *Guide on Financial Administration for Departments and Agencies of the Government of Canada.* Ottawa: Information Canada, 1973.

_____, Treasury Board. *Operational Performance Measurement,* Vols. I and II. Ottawa: Information Canada, 1974.

_____, Treasury Board. *Benefit-Cost Analysis Guide.* Ottawa: Information Canada, 1976.

_____, Treasury Board. *Performance Measurement.* Ottawa: Supply and Services, 1977.

_____, Treasury Board. *Federal Expenditure Plan: How Your Tax Dollar Is Spent, 1977/78.* Ottawa: Supply and Services, 1977.

_____, Urban Affairs. *The Federal Urban Domain,* Vol. I. "Overview of the Federal System." Ottawa: Information Canada, 1973.

Doern, G.B., and Maslove, A.M., eds. *The Public Evaluation of Government Spending.* Toronto: Butterworth, 1979.

Gow, D. *The Progress of Budgetary Reform in the Government of Canada.* Special Study no. 17 for the Economic Council of Canada. Ottawa: Information Canada, 1973.

Hartle, D.G. *A Theory of the Expenditure Budgetary Process.* Toronto: University of Toronto Press, 1976.

_____. *The Expenditure Budget Process in Canada.* Toronto: Canadian Tax Foundation, 1978.

Kroeker, H.V. *Accountability and Control: The Government Expenditure Process.* Montreal: C.D. Howe Institute, 1978.

National Finances. Toronto: Canadian Tax Foundation, 1968-78.

Strick, J.C. *Canadian Public Finance,* 2nd ed. Toronto: Holt, Rinehart and Winston, 1978.

Ward, N. *The Public Purse.* Toronto: University of Toronto Press, 1964.

White, W.L., and Strick, J.C. *Policy, Politics and the Treasury Board in Canadian Government.* Don Mills: Science Research Associates, 1970.

Balls, H.R. "Improving Performance of Public Enterprises through Financial Management and Control." *Canadian Public Administration* 1970, vol. 13, no. 1, pp. 100-23.

———. "Planning, Programming and Budgeting in Canada." *Public Administration* 1970, vol. 48, pp. 289-305.

Cutt, James. "Efficiency and Effectiveness in Public Sector Spending: The Programme Budgeting Approach." *Canadian Public Administration* 1970, vol. 13, no. 4, pp. 396-426.

Fowke, D.V. "Toward a General Theory of Public Administration for Canada." *Canadian Public Administration* 1976, vol. 19, no. 1, pp. 24-40.

Gow, D. "The Setting of Canadian Public Administration." *Public Administration Review* 1973, vol. 33, no. 1, pp. 5-13.

Hartle, D.G. "Techniques and Processes of Administration." *Canadian Public Administration* 1976, vol. 19, no. 1, pp. 21-33.

———. "Canadian Experience with New Budgetary Methods." *Public Finance* 1972, vol. 27, pp. 239-46.

Hicks, M. "The Treasury Board of Canada and its Clients: Five Years of Change and Administrative Reform: 1966-71." *Canadian Public Administration* 1973, vol. 16, no. 2, pp. 182-205.

Hodgson, J.S. "Management by Objectives—the experience of a federal department." *Canadian Public Administration* 1973, vol. 16, no. 3, pp. 422-31.

Jacques, J., and Ryan, E.J., Jr. "Does management by objectives stifle organizational innovation in the public sector?" *Canadian Public Administration* 1978, vol. 21, no. 1, pp. 16-25.

Johnson, A.W. "The Treasury Board of Canada and the Machinery of Government of the 1970's." *Canadian Journal of Political Science* 1971, vol. 4, pp. 346-66.

———. "Planning, Programming and Budgeting in Canada." *Public Administration Review* 1973, vol. 33, no. 1, pp. 23-31.

Jordan, J.M., and Sutherland, S.L. "Assessing the Results of Public Expenditure: Program Evaluation in the Canadian Federal Government." *Canadian Public Administration* 1979, vol. 22, no. 4, pp. 581-609.

Laframboise, H.L. "Administrative Reform in the Federal Public Service: Signs of a Saturation Psychosis." *Canadian Public Administration* 1971, vol. 14, no. 3, pp. 303-25.

Lemire, J.M. "Program Design Guidelines." *Canadian Public Administration* 1977, vol. 20, no. 4, pp. 666-78.

Mallory, J.R. "The Lambert Report: Central Roles and Responsibilities." *Canadian Public Administration* 1979, vol. 22, no. 4, pp. 517-29.

Osbaldeston, G.F. "Planning in Government." *The Canadian Business Review* Summer 1975, pp. 36-37.

Phidd, R.W. "The Economic Council Annual Review: Whither Economic Planning in Canada?" *Canadian Public Policy* 1976, vol. 3, no. 2, pp. 262-69.

Personnel

Bird, R.M. *Growth of Public Employment in Canada*. Toronto: Butterworth, 1979.

Canada, Advisory Group on Executive Compensation in the Public Service. Six Reports. Ottawa: Privy Council Office, 1968, 1971, 1973, 1975, 1977, 1978.

_____, Civil Service Commission. *Report of the Preparatory Committee on Collective Bargaining in the Public Service*. Ottawa: Queen's Printer, 1965.

_____. "Official Languages in the Public Service of Canada." Resolution adopted by Parliament in June 1973. Mimeo.

_____. *Report of the Special Committee on the Review of Personnel Management and the Merit Principle*. Ottawa: Supply and Services, 1979.

_____, Parliament. *Minutes of Proceedings and Evidence of the Special Joint Committee on Employer-Employee Relations in the Public Service*. 1st session, 30th Parliament, 1974-75-76. Report, February 1976.

_____, President of the Privy Council, Employer-Employee Relations in the Public Service of Canada. *Proposals for Legislative Change*. Parts I and II. Ottawa: Information Canada, 1974.

_____, Public Service Commission. *Annual Reports*. Ottawa: Supply and Services, 1968-78 inclusive.

_____, Public Service Commission. *Post Employment Guidelines*. Ottawa: Supply and Services, 1977.

_____, Public Service Commission. "Public Service and Public Interest." Ottawa: Supply and Services, 1978.

_____, Royal Commission on Bilingualism and Biculturalism. "The Federal Capital: Government Institutions." Study No. 1. Ottawa: Queen's Printer, 1969.

Dwivedi, O.P. *Public Service Ethics: Report of the Study Group on Ethics in the Public Service*. Brussels: International Association of Schools and Institutes of Administration, 1978.

Hodgetts, J.E., et al. *The Biography of an Institution*. Montreal: McGill-Queen's University Press, 1972.

Kernaghan, W.D.K. *Ethical Conduct: Guidelines for Government Employees*. Toronto: Institute of Public Administration, 1975.

————, ed. *Executive Manpower in the Public Service: Make or Buy?* Toronto: Institute of Public Administration, 1975.

Carson, J.J. "Bilingualism in the Public Service." *Canadian Public Administration* 1972, vol. 15, no. 2, pp. 190-93.

Crispo, J. "Collective Bargaining in the Public Service." *Canadian Public Administration* 1973, vol. 16, no. 1, pp. 1-3.

Kernaghan, K. "Representative Bureaucracy: the Canadian perspective." *Canadian Public Administration* 1978, vol. 21, no. 4, pp. 489-512.

Wilson, V.S., and Mullins, W.A. "Representative Bureaucracy: linguistic/ethnic aspects in Canadian public policy." *Canadian Public Administration* 1978, vol. 21, no. 4, pp. 513-38.

Policy Consultation

Canada, Economic Council of Canada. *Regulation Reference: A Preliminary Report to First Ministers*. Ottawa: Supply and Services, 1978.

————, Economic Council of Canada. *Responsible Regulation: An Interim Report*. Ottawa: Supply and Services, 1979.

————, Royal Commission on Corporate Concentration. *Report*. Ottawa: Supply and Services, 1978.

————, Science Council of Canada. *The Politics of an Industrial Strategy: A Seminar*. Ottawa: Supply and Services, 1979.

Dodge, W., ed. *Consultation and Consensus: A New Era in Policy Formulation?* Ottawa: Conference Board of Canada, 1978.

Gorecki, P.K., and Stanbury, W.T. *Perspectives on the Royal Commission on Corporate Concentration*. Toronto: Butterworth, 1979.

Pross, A.P., ed. *Pressure Group Behaviour in Canadian Politics*. Toronto, McGraw-Hill Ryerson, 1975.

Richardson, E. *Consumer Interest Representation: Three Case Studies*. Ottawa: Canadian Consumer Council, 1972.

Stanbury, W.T. *Business Interests and the Reform of Canadian Competition Policy, 1971-75.* Toronto: Methuen, 1977.

Wheare, K.C. *Government by Committee.* London: Oxford University Press, 1955.

4. Legislative Control

Canada. *Annual Report of the Auditor General* to the House of Commons for the fiscal years ended March 31, 1975-78. Ottawa: Supply and Services.

———. *Report of the Independent Committee for the Review of the Office of the Auditor General* (Wilson Committee). Ottawa: Information Canada, 1975.

———, House of Commons. *Minutes and Proceedings of the Standing Committee on Public Accounts.* Ottawa: Supply and Services, 1976, 1977, 1978.

Clarke, Harold D., Campbell, Colin, Quo, F.Q., and Goddard, Arthur, eds. *Parliament, Policy and Representation.* Toronto: Methuen, 1980.

Jackson, R.J., and Atkinson, M.M. *The Canadian Legislative System*, 2nd ed. Toronto: Macmillan of Canada, 1980.

Neilson, W.A.W., and MacPherson, J.C., eds. *The Legislative Process in Canada: The Need for Reform.* Toronto: Butterworth, 1978.

Stewart, J. *The Canadian House of Commons: Procedure and Reform.* Montreal: McGill-Queen's University Press, 1977.

Balls, H.R. "The Watchdog of Parliament: The centenary of the legislative audit." *Canadian Public Administration* 1978, vol. 21, no. 4, pp. 584-617.

Denham, R.A. "The Canadian Auditor-General—What is Their Role?" *Canadian Public Administration* 1974, vol. 17, no. 2, pp. 259-73.

———. "New Public-Sector Audit Legislation in Canada." *Canadian Public Policy* 1978, vol. IV, no. 4, pp. 474-88.

Franks, C.E.S. "The Dilemma of the Standing Committees of the Canadian House of Commons." *Canadian Journal of Political Science* 1971, vol. 4, no. 4, pp. 461-76.

Hartle, D.G. "The Role of the Auditor General of Canada." *Canadian Tax Journal* 1975, vol. 23, no. 3, pp. 193-204.

Henderson, M. "My War with the Government: The Confessions of the Auditor General of Canada." *MacLean's* July 1973, vol. 86, no. 7, pp. 26, 60-64.

MacGuigan, M. "Parliamentary Reform: Internal Impediments to Enlarging the Role of the Backbencher." Conference on Legislative Studies. Toronto: York University, 1977.

Thomas, P.G. "The Influence of Standing Committees of the Canadian House of Commons on Government Legislation." Conference on Legislative Studies. Toronto: York University, 1977.

_____ . "The Lambert Report: Parliament and Accountability." *Canadian Public Administration* 1979, vol. 22, no. 4, pp. 557-73.

5. Federal-Provincial Relations

Canada. *Federalism for the Future*. Ottawa: Queen's Printer, 1968.

_____ . *A National Understanding*. Ottawa: Supply and Services, 1977.

_____ . *A Time for Action: Toward the Renewal of the Canadian Federation*. Ottawa: Supply and Services, 1978.

_____ . *The Constitutional Amendment Bill, C-60, Text and Explanatory Notes*. Ottawa: Supply and Services, 1978.

_____ , Federal-Provincial Relations Office. *A Descriptive Inventory of Federal-Provincial Programs and Activities to December 1976*. Ottawa: Supply and Services, 1977.

_____ , Task Force on Canadian Unity. *A Future Together*. Ottawa: Supply and Services, 1979.

_____ , Treasury Board. *Decentralization to Benefit All Provinces*. Ottawa: Supply and Services, 1978.

_____ , Treasury Board. "Federal Government Decentralization Program Statement." Hon. Jean Chrétien, Minister responsible for federal government's decentralization program. Federal Task Force on Decentralization. Ottawa: Supply and Services, 1977.

Careless, A.G.S. *Initiative and Response: The Adaptation of Canadian Federalism to Regional Economic Development*. Montreal: McGill-Queen's University Press, 1977.

Dupré, J.S., et al. *Federalism and Policy Development: The Case of Adult Occupational Training in Ontario*. Toronto: University of Toronto Press, 1973.

Meekison, J.P., ed. *Canadian Federalism: Myth or Reality*, 3rd. ed. Toronto: Methuen, 1977.

Morin, Claude. *Québec versus Ottawa: The Struggle for Self Government 1960-72*, English ed. Toronto: University of Toronto Press, 1976.

Simeon, R. *Federal-Provincial Diplomacy: The Making of Recent Policy in Canada*. Toronto: University of Toronto Press, 1972.

_____, ed. *Must Canada Fail?* Montreal: McGill-Queen's University Press, 1977.

_____, ed. *Confrontation and Collaboration—Intergovernmental Relations in Canada Today*. Toronto: Institute of Public Administration, 1979.

Smiley, D.V. *Conditional Grants and Canadian Federalism*. Toronto: Canadian Tax Foundation, 1963.

_____. *Canada in Question: Federalism in the Seventies*, 2nd ed. Toronto: McGraw-Hill Ryerson, 1976.

Veilleux, G. *Les Relations Intergouvernementales au Canada 1867-1967*. Montréal: les Presses de l'Université du Québec, 1971.

Burns, R.M. "Intergovernmental Relations in Canada." *Public Administration Review* 1973, vol. 33, no. 1, pp. 14-22.

Cairns, A. "The Governments and Societies of Canadian Federalism." *Canadian Journal of Political Science* 1977, vol. X, no. 4, pp. 695-725.

_____. "The other crisis of Canadian Federalism." *Canadian Public Administration* 1979, vol. 22, no. 2, pp. 175-95.

_____. "From Interstate to Intrastate Federalism." Discussion Paper No. 5. Kingston: Institute of Intergovernmental Relations, Queen's University, 1979.

Davies, D.G. "Tri-Level Task Force on Public Finance in Canada: A Review." *Canadian Public Policy* 1977, vol. 3, no. 1, pp. 114-17.

Dyck, R. "The Canada Assistance Plan: The Ultimate in Cooperative Federalism." *Canadian Public Administration* 1976, vol. 19, no. 4, pp. 587-602.

Gélinas, A. "Le Cadre général des institutions administratives et la déconcentration territoriale." *Canadian Public Administration* 1975, vol. 18, no. 2, pp. 253-68.

Pratt, L. "The state and province-building: Alberta's development strategy." In Panitch, L., ed., *The Canadian State: Political Economy and Political Power*. Toronto: University of Toronto Press, 1977.

Simeon, R. "The Federal-Provincial Decision-Making Process." In *Intergovernmental Relations*. Toronto: Ontario Economic Council, 1977.

Smiley, D.V. "The Structural Problems of Canadian Federalism." *Canadian Public Administration* 1971, vol. 14, no. 3, pp. 326-43.

––––––. "Territorialism and Canadian Political Institutions." *Canadian Public Policy* 1977, vol. III, no. 4, pp. 449-57.

Stevenson, G. "Federalism and the Political Economy of the Canadian State." In Panitch, L., ed., *The Canadian State: Political Economy and Political Power*. Toronto: University of Toronto Press, 1977.

Thayer, F.C. "Regional Administration: the failure of traditional theory in the United States and Canada." *Canadian Public Administration* 1972, vol. 15, no. 3, pp. 449-64.

Usher, D. "How Should the Redistributive Power of the State Be Divided between Federal and Provincial Governments?" *Canadian Public Policy* 1980, vol. VI, no. 1, pp. 16-29.

West, E.G., and Winer, S.L. "The Individual, Political Tension, and Canada's Quest for a New Constitution." *Canadian Public Policy* 1980, vol. VI, no. 1, pp. 3-15.

Index

Accountability, 1, 5, 8, 9, 13, 14, 78, 83, 97-99, 101, 108, 113, 118, 129, 130, 148, 174, 181, 183, 190-191, 194-196, 198, 200-201

Accounts (see Public Accounts)

Administrative Tribunals, 126-129

Advisory Councils (see also Multiculturalism and Status of Women), 4, 107, 120, 121

Advisory Group on Executive Compensation in the Public Service of Canada, 87, 98, 141

Agricultural Products Board, 124

Agriculture, Minister of, 19; Deputy Minister of, 100

Air Canada, 109, 146; Estey Commission on, 150

Alberta, 167-168, 178, 185

Anti-Inflation, Appeal Tribunal, 127; Board, 116, 119

Atomic Energy Control Board, 115, 117

Atomic Energy of Canada Limited, 109

Auditor-General, 5, 55, 58-60, 78, 86, 97, 112, 118, 123, 126, 191, 195, 198-199

Bibeau, G., 67

Bilingualism and Biculturalism, Royal Commission on, 3, 66, 130, 151, 166

Black, C., 150

Board of Economic Development, 22, 23

Board of Management, 61, 196

British Columbia, 120, 178

British North America Act, 13, 165, 182

Brown-John, C.L., 124

Bryce, R., 150

Budget: expenditure budget, 54, 61, 95; "A" and "B", 54

Bureau of Management Consulting, 144

Cabinet, 7, 12, 13, 17, 23, 29, 33, 35, 192-193; committee secretariats, 30, 31; committees, 24-27, 29, 94, 192-193; composition, 15-19; coordinating function, 24-29; Secretary to, 30, 100, 142

Cabinet Memorandum, 93

Canada Council, 121, 123

Canadian Broadcasting Corporation, 109-110, 146

Canadian Dairy Commission, 124-125

Canadian Federation of Mayors and Municipalities, 155, 172

Canadian Labour Congress, 155

Canadina Livestock Feed Board, 124

Canadian Manufacturers' Association, 155

Canadian National Railway, 146

Canadian Radio-Television Telecommunications Commission, 115-119

Canadian Saltfish Corporation, 125

Canadian Transport Commission, 115-119, 146

Canadian Wheat Board, 124-126

Central Management, 7, 42, 43, 50-52, 71, 196, 198

Central Mortgage and Housing Corporation, 109-110, 112, 147

Chrétien, J., 15, 79

Clark, Prime Minister, 16, 29; administration of, 17, 22-23, 35, 159, 193

Collective Bargaining, 63; Preparatory Committee on, 3, 63

Committees, Interdepartmental, 62, 93, 137-142

Communications, Department of, 21; Deputy Minister of, 100; Minister of, 19

Competition Act, 19

Comptroller of the Treasury, 57
Comptroller-General, Office of, 59
Conference Board of Canada, 156
Consumer and Corporate Affairs, Department of, 19, 21, 137; Deputy Minister of, 100; Minister of, 19
Continuing Committee on Fiscal and Economic Matters, 176
Corporate Concentration, Royal Commission on, 150
Crossman, R., 82
Crown Corporations, 4, 107-114, directives to, 112-114

Decentralization, 183
de Cotret, R., 17
Departments (see also individual titles), 7, 20, 89-92
Deputy Ministers, 19, 62, 78; appointment of, 79, 80; career planning, 83, 87-88; performance assessment, 97-101; relationship with ministers, 81-82; responsibilities, 78-83, 85-88, 99
Deregulation, 120; Ministry of, 120
Desmarais, P., 150
Diefenbaker, J., 16
Doern, G.B., 24, 137

Economic Council of Canada, 120-123, 137, 156
Economic Development; Minister of State, 24; Ministry of State, 137, 194
Employment and Immigration, Department of (also refers to Manpower and Immigration), 21, 23, 137, 139, 142, 147; Deputy Minister of, 100; Minister of, 19

Energy, Mines and Resources, Department of, 21, 182; Deputy Minister of, 100; Minister of, 19
Environment, Department of, 21, 23, 140; Deputy Minister of, 100; Minister of, 19
Estimates, Preparation of, 54-56; main, 55, 85; supplementary, 55
External Affairs, Department of, 23, 141; Deputy Minister of, 100; Minister of, 19

Family Allowances, 45
Federal-Provincial Fiscal Arrangements, 176
Federal-Provincial Relations, 8; committees, 175-178; ministerial conferences 120, 170-175, 182; Office of, 30, 32-34, 177, 179, 183; Secretary to the Cabinet for, 33, 100, 177
Federalism, 8, 12, 30, 33, 165-168
Finance, Department of, 2, 21-24, 51, 57, 118, 137, 196; Deputy Minister of, 100; Minister of, 15, 16, 19, 51, 56, 57, 111
Financial Administration Act, 63, 79, 85, 107-108, 111-113, 126, 128
Financial Management and Accountability, Royal Commission on (Lambert Commission), 4, 43, 52, 58, 60, 69, 78, 80, 86, 97, 99, 101, 108, 112-113, 118-119, 123, 129, 150, 191, 193, 196-198, 200-201
Fiscal Plan, 56, 97, 196
Fisheries, Minister of, 15
Fisheries and Oceans, Department of, 23
Fisheries and Oceans Research Advisory Council, 121

Foreign Investment Review
    Agency, 116-117, 119, 137
French, R.D., 27
Freshwater Fish Marketing
    Corporation, 125
Fulton Committee on the Civil
    Service, 101

Government Acitivities, growth
    of expenditures in, 4, 44, 46
Government Organization Acts,
    1966, 21; 1969, 21; 1970, 21-
    22; 1976, 23;1979, 23
Government Organization,
    Royal Commission on (Glassco
    Commission), 2, 5, 21, 42, 51,
    57, 68, 77, 86, 95, 99, 107, 196
Governor-in-Council,
    appointments, 79, 111-113,
    117, 119, 123, 125, 127, 151
Green Papers, 152, 158, 159

Hodgetts, J.E., 51
House of Commons, 52; cabinet,
    relation to, 199; committees,
    99, 158-159, 200; question
    period, 159, 199; speech from
    the throne, 159
Howe Institute, C.D., 156

Immigration Appeal Board, 127-
    128
Indian Affairs and Northern
    Development, Department of,
    19, 21, 22; Deputy Minister of,
    100; Minister of, 19
Industry, Trade and Commerce,
    Department of, 21, 137, 156;
    Deputy Minister of, 100;
    Minister of, 16, 19, 21, 79
Inflation, 4, 45, 63
Inquiries Act, 149, 151
Institute for Research on Public
    Policy, 156
Interdepartmental Committees
    (see Committees)
Interpretation Act, 78

Johnson, A.W., 59, 69, 143
Judicial Review, 119, 128
Justice, Department of, 21, 23,
    24; Deputy Minister of, 100;
    Minister of, 19

Kroeker, H.V., 14

Labour, Deputy Minister of, 100;
    Minister of, 19
Langford, J., 146

Manpower and Immigration (see
    Employment and Immigration)
Marketing Boards, 107, 124
Medical Research Council, 121-
    122
Ministerial Responsibility, 1, 3, 5,
    7, 8, 13, 14, 35, 42-43, 50, 78,
    81, 181, 191
Ministers of State, 23; (see also
    Economic Development,
    Science and Technology and
    Urban Affairs)
Ministry of State, 22-23; (see also
    Economic Development,
    Science and Technology, Social
    Development and Urban
    Affairs)
Ministry System, 144-148
Multiculturalism, Advisory
    Council on, 121

National Capital Commission,
    154
National Defence, Deputy
    Minister of, 100; Minister of,
    19
National Energy Board, 107, 116-
    119
National Farm Products
    Marketing Council, 124-125
National Health and Welfare,
    Deputy Minister of, 100;
    Minister of, 19
National Housing Act, 110
National Indian Brotherhood,
    154

National Research Council, 121-122

National Revenue, Department of, 23, 127; Deputy Minister of, 100; Minister of, 19

National Transportation Act, 116

Natural Science and Engineering Research Council, 122

Newfoundland, 178

Non-departmental Bodies, 4, 7, 106-108, 195; directives, 129-130; (see also Crown corporations, regulatory commissions, advisory councils, adminstrative tribunals, marketing boards)

Occupational Categories and Groups, 64

Official Languages Act, 52, 79; Commissioner, 67, 79; Parliamentary resolution, 67; policy, 66-68

Ontario, 167, 170, 178

Orders-in-Council, 51

Osbaldeston, G., 79

Parliament, 12, 85, 106, 109, 118, 123, 126-129, 137, 153, 157, 203; Crown in Parliament, 13

Pay Research Bureau, 66

Pearson, Prime Minister, 16, 66; government of, 16, 18, 20, 24, 167

Pépin, J-L., 16, 151

Personnel Management, 60-61; Special Committee on Merit Principle and Personnel Management (D'Avignon Committee), 196-198, 203

Petro-Canada, 109-110, 114, 185

Phidd, R., 137

Planning, Programming, Budgeting Systems, 3, 52-53, 56, 95

Post Office, Department of, 19; Postmaster-General, 19; Deputy Postmaster-General, 100

President of the Privy Council, 19

Prime Minister, 7, 14, 27, 30, 35; Office of, 3, 30, 34

Priorities and Planning, Cabinet Committee on, 24, 29, 52-53, 55, 142-143

Privatization, 114

Privy Council Office, 3, 27, 30-32, 34, 57, 82, 94, 113, 139, 140, 142, 196

Provincial Governments, 2

Public Accounts, Committee on, 55, 99, 108, 113, 158, 199, 201

Public Service, composition of, 44, 48, 49; size, 43, 44, 47, 49

Public Service Commission, 61, 63-64, 67, 71, 79-82, 85, 87, 98, 195-198

Public Service Employment Act, 52, 63, 79, 112, 128

Public Service Staff Relations Act, 63, 65, 112; Board, 64

Public Service Superannuation Act, 112

Public Works, Department of, 23, 140-141; Deputy Minister of, 100; Minister of, 19

Quebec, 6, 151, 166-167, 180, 182, 185

Regional Economic Expansion, Department of, 21, 142; Deputy Minister of, 100; Minister of, 19

Regulatory Commissions, 4, 115-117

Reid, J., 158

Resource Allocation, 52-56, 96

Resource Envelope, 193

Responsible Government, 12, 190
Robarts, J., 151
Royal Canadian Mounted Police, 145; McDonald Commission on, 150
Royal Commissions, 137, 149; (see also Air Canada; Bilingualism and Biculturalism; Corporate Concentration; Financial Management and Accountability; Government Organization; Royal Canadian Mounted Police; Taxation)

Saskatchewan, 168, 178
Schultz, R., 115
Science Council of Canada, 123, 156
Science and Technology, Minister of State for, 19; Ministry of State, 21-22; Secretary of State for, 100
Secretary of State, 19; Department of, 22, 146, 154; Under-Secretary of department, 100
Small Businesses, Minister of State, 120
Social Development, Ministry of State, 22, 194
Social Science and Humanities Research Council, 121-122
Solicitor-General, 19, 21, 145; Deputy Solicitor-General, 100
Status of Women, Advisory Council on, 121, 123
Supply and Services, Department of, 22, 57; Deputy Minister of, 100; Minister of, 19
Supreme Court of Canada, 182

Tariff Board, 127

Task Force, Internal, 142; on Decentralization, 142; on Direct Job Creation, 142; on Canadian Unity, 6, 151, 174
Tax Review Board, 127, 128
Taxation, Royal Commission on, 150
Transport, Department of, 140, 142, 146; Deputy Minister of, 100; Minister of, 19
Treasury Board, 7, 24, 42-43, 51-53, 55-56, 60-63, 67-68, 75, 79, 80, 85, 95-96, 98, 111, 126, 193, 196-198; President of, 16, 19, 59, 111; Secretariat, 3, 7, 21, 43, 51-52, 54, 56-59, 62, 65, 67-68, 71, 77, 81, 82, 85-87, 96, 98, 111, 137, 139-142, 196-198
Tri-level Consultation, 171
Trudeau, Prime Minister, 6, 20, 27, 35; administration of, 3, 17, 23, 24, 26, 33, 35, 78, 99, 136, 146, 152-153, 159, 167, 193

Unemployment Insurance Commission, 23
Urban Affairs, Minister of State of, 19; Ministry of State for, 21, 22, 142, 147, 171; Secretary to, 100

Van Loon, R., 157
Veilleux, G., 169
Veterans Affairs, Deputy Minister of, 100; Minister of, 19

"Way Ahead," The, 5, 120
White Papers, 152-153, 158
Whittington, M., 157